GW00691277

West Ham United

West Ham United
An Illustrated History

John Northcutt & Roy Shoesmith

Breedon Books
Publishing Company
Derby

First published in Great Britain by
The Breedon Books Publishing Company Limited
44 Friar Gate, Derby, DE1 1DA
1994

Copyright © John Northcutt & Roy Shoesmith

All Rights Reserved. No part of this publication may be reproduced,
stored in a retrieval system, or transmitted in any form, or by any
means, electronic, mechanical, photocopying, recording or otherwise
without the prior permission in writing of the Copyright holders, nor
be otherwise circulated in any form or binding or cover other than in
which it is published and without a similar condition being imposed
on the subsequent publisher.

ISBN 1 873626 93 2

Photographic Acknowledgements
The illustrations in this book have been supplied by the EMPICs agency of
Nottingham and the Hulton-Deutsch Picture Library of London.

Printed and bound by Butler & Tanner, Frome and London.
Covers printed by BDC Printing Services Limited of Derby

Contents

This book is dedicated to the memory of
Bobby Moore, OBE

Introduction

BOTH of us are pleased to have been given an opportunity to write this history of our favourite football club. It has been a labour of love and many long hours have been spent in compiling the story. Although we have not been able to cover everything, we feel that we have included the main events since the days of Thames Ironworks 100 years ago. Described are the highlights in the club's history including the first FA Cup Final at Wembley, the glory of winning the European Cup-winners' Cup and the winning of the Second Division championship in 1958 and 1981. Recalled are the great names such as Vic Watson, Jimmy Ruffell, Bobby Moore, Geoff Hurst and, more recently, Trevor Brooking and Billy Bonds.

Our earlier book *West Ham United A Complete Record*, first published in 1987 and updated 1993, contains a wealth of statistical information whereas this book portrays in words and pictures the story as described by Roy up to 1945 and is continued by John to the present day. Finally we hope that this book brings back memories for the older fans and also gives pleasure to all who follow the team in Claret and Blue.

John Northcutt
Roy Shoesmith
July 1994

Early Days

FORMED in 1895 to help fill the leisure hours of a shipyard's work force, Thames Ironworks Football Club was an instant success. Taking advantage of the plight of another popular local club which eventually folded, the Irons, as they quickly became known, recruited a number of its players and officials and set about establishing themselves as the premier club in the district.

It cost 2s 6d (almost 13p in modern currency) to be a member for a year but the club was also heavily subsidised by funds from the parent company's enthusiastic managing director, Arnold Hills.

It was probably Hills, with his Old Harrovian background, who managed to obtain entry into the FA Cup. The new club's first Cup game was a preliminary-round tie at Southern Leaguers Chatham which was, not unexpectedly, lost. Hills helped in other ways: virtually all the Thames Ironworks matches in that first season were 'friendlies' and some of these were played under artificial light. Thames Ironworkers lighting engineers, with Hills' blessing, installed the equipment which, although unreliable in the beginning, improved with every game.

Another individual who was instrumental in getting the Thames Ironworks FC under way was Dave Taylor. Taylor was a foreman in the shipyard and in his spare time, such as it was, he refereed local soccer matches. He initiated proceedings by placing an appeal for members in the columns of the *Thames Ironworks Gazette*. It was his hope that four teams could be fielded but this did not work out despite an encouraging response. After getting the club up and running Taylor handed control to Ted Harsent and returned to refereeing.

The Thames Ironworks FC team pictured in 1895, during the club's first season and before they assumed the title of West Ham United. Alas, the names of these earliest of the club's players have long been lost.

At the end of its first season the new club was in possession of the West Ham Charity Cup, a splendid achievement that ended with a gruelling three- match Final against Barking. The other end of the season had kicked-off with a friendly fixture at home to Royal Ordnance, who were considered a sort of nursery side of the Woolwich Arsenal FC. This ended all square at 1-1 but more interestingly, a witness at the game, the *Kentish Mercury* correspondent, observed that a number of the Irons had been prominent with other East London clubs the previous season.

Taking an upward step, the Thames Ironworks FC joined the newly-formed London League for 1896-97. Arnold Hills was the first president of this competition and Francis Payne, an official of the Ironworks Sports Association, was recruited to a group drafting the new League's rules.

Strengthened by the arrival of four Reading discards, Davey, Hatton, Rossitter and Holmes, Irons went into their first-ever League encounter against Vampires at Hermit Road on 19 September 1896. A comfortable victory over Vampires was followed, 17 days later, by another against 1st Scots Guards. The reason for the extended period between games was simply that the London League's First Division comprised only eight teams at this time.

Within days a double blow struck. First, the Irons were crushed 8-0 in a FA Cup qualifying-round tie at Sheppey United and on arrival back at Canning Town they learned they were to be evicted from their ground.

According to the ground agent, the club had violated its tenancy by erecting a pavilion and a perimeter fence and charging admission to matches.

Until fresh facilities could be found the Irons were forced to play a series of matches on opponents' grounds. Two London Senior Cup-ties proved successful but League points were lost on a visit to eventual champions, 3rd Grenadier Guards.

A little over five weeks after the eviction from the Hermit Road ground, Arnold Hills found a piece of land in Browning Road, East Ham. It was expected that the Irons would make a permanent home here but it was not to be, for something even better turned up.

An Essex Senior Cup-tie opened the new ground at Browning Road but it was not a happy beginning as visitors Leyton eliminated the Irons by the odd goal in five. Irons, however, had an extended interest in the London Senior Cup. A third-round tie started late due to Wandsworth's late arrival. With Irons leading 7-0 and ten minutes to go, the referee abandoned the game because of bad light. Irons appealed to the London FA, asking to be awarded the tie due to Wandsworth's late arrival. Wandsworth's counter was that the fog that stopped the tie was the same fog that delayed them. The London FA ordered the tie to be replayed and Irons came out on top again but only by 3-1.

The fifth-round tie occupied the next four Saturdays. The opponents on each occasion was Bromley FC. The first match was postponed, the second was abandoned in extra-time, the third undecided after extra-time and the fourth went to Second Division Bromley by 2-0.

In March, the Irons surrendered the West Ham Charity Cup to West Ham Garfield, who won a bad-tempered match at the Spotted Dog, Clapton, by a goal to nil.

In the London League, the Ironworkers found the 3rd Grenadier Guards far too good for them. A 5-0 win virtually assured the military men of the League title.

For their second assault on the London League

championship, in 1897-98, the Ironworkers reinforced their ranks with local goalkeeper George Furnell, who was once associated with the Old Castle Swifts, Simon (Peter) Chisholm, an Inverness Scot, and Jimmy Reid, once of Hibernian but more recently of Reading.

At this time the club regularly included only two players who had been first-team performers back in the early days at Hermit Road, George Gresham and Charlie Dove.

New playing kit was issued and this comprised of 'Royal Cambridge Blue' shirts; white knickers, red cap, belt and stockings.

The new kit went with the new stadium, for the Memorial Grounds, opened the previous June, was now the new home of the Thames Ironworks FC.

Fourteen weeks prior to the opening day, the land occupied by the splendid new stadium had been a wilderness. Now it was the equal of any in the country. Not only was it a football arena, it had also had a cycle track with banking at the turns, plus facilities for many other sports. One area of the ground contained an outdoor swimming pool over 100 yards in length.

Unfortunately, by the time the football season was due, a little of the new ground's novelty had worn off. On the day of the first match, a friendly against Northfleet, less than 200 fans paid admission and rain threatened. When the rain did come, Francis Payne, then the secretary of the Thames Ironworks Federated Club, sent word that every spectator should be accommodated under cover of the grandstand.

When the League matches began, Irons were in fine form, winning their first six games and avoiding defeat until the penultimate game which was at Brentford. This defeat, on the ground of their nearest rivals, almost cost them the title. Had Barking Woodville failed to deprive the Bees of the two points in the final match, the championship would have gone to West London.

Redhill provided the opposition in the first FA Cup-tie to be played at the Memorial Grounds when they were defeated 3-0 in a preliminary round. Ironworkers progressed to the second qualifying round at the expense of the Royal Engineers Training Battalion but came unstuck at St Albans, who won 2-0. It was the third successive season that Thames Ironworks had been knocked out of the FA Cup by a Southern League side.

A championship in only their third season was a remarkable accomplishment but the 'arrival' of the Thames Ironworks was marked in another small way when both the club's full-backs, Walter Tranter and George Neil, were selected to play for the London League against the London FA at Kilburn in December. Jimmy Reid was also picked as a reserve. These appear to be the first players of the Ironworks to receive any kind of representative recognition.

Successful applications were made for entries into both the Southern League (Division Two) and the Thames & Medway Combination for 1898-99, but a more significant change happened when the club took the decision to take its place among the paid ranks. There was a good deal of internal discussion on the subject and it is known that Mr Hills with his university education was most certainly against paying footballers.

When the Thames Ironworks took the field at Sheerness to play Sheppey United in the Thames & Medway Combination on 1 September 1898, it was a professional unit. But the change of status did not seem to open the doors to success, for the Irons were beaten in their first five outings in that same competition. The tide turned in the last days of October and from then until the end of the season, only two League matches were lost. This period included a sequence of 17 consecutive wins. Despite this marvellous run and the winning of the Southern League (Division Two) championship, Irons were still forced to do battle in the Test Matches.

As it happened, the Test matches proved needless for the senior section of the Southern League was extended by the addition of two new clubs for 1899-1900.

Convinced that the side required some strengthening for its campaign in the higher sphere, Arnold Hills took the uncharacteristic step of providing funds for that purpose. During the summer of 1899 he is alleged to have given the club, through Francis Payne (the football club secretary at the time), £1,000. This was to be used to induce an unattached Midlands player to join the Thames Ironworks FC. An agent was employed for this exercise who was himself a professional footballer named Charles Bunyan. Bunyan's claim to unwanted fame was that he had kept goal for Hyde FC in an FA Cup-tie against Preston North End and had conceded 26 goals.

Anyhow, Bunyan bungled his day out in Birmingham. He missed his appointment with the target player and in an effort to redeem himself approached another. He was caught in the act and deemed to be poaching, was brought before the Football Association.

After due consideration the FA decided that

Bunyan had been in the employ of the Thames Ironworks FC at the time of his misdemeanour and promptly suspended him for two years. For their part, Irons were fined £25 and suspended for the first two weeks of the new season. Francis Payne, absent from the hearing, was suspended just the same.

Before his departure, Payne, busy in the transfer market, had already brought Bill Joyce, Harry Bradshaw and Kenny McKay from Tottenham Hotspur plus Syd King and Alec Gentle from New Brompton. Bradshaw possessed an England cap, whilst Syd King was so highly regarded that Thames received a request for his transfer from Derby County before he had even kicked a ball for the club.

Armed with this new firepower, the Ironworkers began their campaign with an excursion to Reading but came back empty handed. The *Reading Standard* acknowledged that the visitors were a capable side but that anybody could get up a good team with limitless 'readies'.

Results improved after the Reading game and progress was made up the League and in the Cup until, in a mud bath at Tottenham, Irons went down 7-0 to the Spurs. Thereafter, the season disintegrated and in the final weeks following the withdrawals of Cowes and Brighton United. Irons found themselves fighting for survival in the Test Matches. There was, however, a moment of great rejoicing in April when Irons defeated FA Cup Finalists Southampton by a convincing 4-1.

The saddest event of the season occurred on Christmas Day when it was learned that the club's skipper, Harry Bradshaw, had died. Although he had made some recent appearances, his death was attributed to an injury received in a match against Bedminster the previous October.

In July 1900, activity in the financial affairs of the Thames Ironworks Shipbuilding Company led to a 'divorce' between the football club and the parent company. The football club was relaunched under the new title of West Ham United and there was an issue of 2,000 shares at 10s (50p) each. Continuing his philanthropic behaviour, Arnold Hills not only promised to purchase one share for every one sold but also to allow the new club rent free use of the Memorial Grounds for the next three years.

A 'Penny Handbook' was issued for season 1900-01 and it contained the outcome for the annual close season transfer merry-go-round. West Ham's staff seemed to have acquired a distinct Scottish flavour about it, Hugh Monteith, Charlie Craig, Len Raisbeck, Roddy

MacEachrane, Jimmy Reid and Billy Grassam were known to be Scots and there may have been others. All these were in the side that trounced a weak Gravesend United 7-0 in the opening match. In scoring four times on his debut, Billy Grassam set a record not equalled until February 1946 by Don Travis.

Alas, Hammers were never able to touch these heights again. In fact, their next best score was four (once) against New Brompton in a Cup replay. This 4-1 Cup win set up a tie with local amateurs Clapton, who already had 60 goals to their credit in all matches. There was great interest in the district and 12,000 fans gathered at the Memorial Grounds to witness this tie, the third largest assembly in the stadium's short history. The outcome was a draw. Clapton doubled admission prices for the replay at the Spotted Dog but 5,000 still turned up. Another stirring battle took place and it required three goals from Billy Grassam to finally put down the amateurs. A worthy prize awaited the victors . . .a home tie with Liverpool, the Football League champions that year. Hammers copied the example of Clapton and doubled their admission charges but the scheme backfired . . .only 6,000 turned up.

This stage of the FA Cup competition was called the intermediate round, it took place after the qualifying rounds and before the competition proper. Liverpool were concerned only because their secretary had overlooked to submit the club's claim for exemption from the qualifying competition. The Merseysiders were successful at the Memorial Grounds by a single goal, but went out at Notts County in the next round.

The death of Queen Victoria in late January 1901 caused not only great sadness throughout the realm but a measure of confusion and discord in the soccer world, The Football Association called for a stoppage to all soccer on the Saturday following the monarch's death. The professional organisations like the Football League and the Southern League objected to this decision on the grounds that a stoppage was an infringement of a professional footballers' right to earn a living.

A circular sent to all clubs in those competitions found that most of their members supported the Football Association's decision. So it was left to each club to make its own choice. West Ham's game at Watford was one of four Southern League fixtures that went ahead. On the day of the funeral, Saturday, 2 February, every club in the land respected the Football Association's call.

West Ham United in 1901-02, when they finished fourth in the Southern League. Fred Corbett, the man in the centre of the front row, scored a hat-trick when the Hammers beat Wellingborough Town 4-2 at the end of September that season.

Luton Town's visit on 9 February 1901 marked the opening of the London Tilbury & Southend's Railway's new station at West Ham (Manor Road). It was hoped that the new station, which was almost adjacent to the stadium, would solve the Memorial Grounds' accessibility problem. It probably did but the crowd figures showed no significant increase.

For the second year in succession, the Millwall fixture was abandoned because of fog. This normally well-attended event was re-run on a bitterly cold Thursday afternoon in March and, not surprisingly, only 2,500 paid to get in.

In comparison with seasons past, 1901-02 was a huge success. A rip-roaring start of six wins and two draws in the opening eight fixtures set the tone. A mid-season hiccup of seven defeats in 11 games was followed by a concluding 11 without defeat. The side had quality performers in all departments, from Hugh Monteith in goal, Charlie Craig and Syd King in defence, Roddy MacEachrane and James Bigden at half-back, and Billy Grassam and Fred Corbett up front. Occasional appearances were made by two improving young local players, Bill Yenson and Dick Pudan. Unfortunately West Ham's relatively successful season served only to arouse the curiosity of wealthier clubs and it was not long before a number of these young men were on the move.

There was a curious start to this campaign when Midlands club Wellingborough Town failed to arrive on time and the kick-off was delayed by some 20 minutes. The 20 minutes proved crucial, for the light failed rapidly near the end and the referee was forced to abandon the match. The score was 1-1 at the time but when replayed a month later, Hammers triumphed by 4-2.

On 2 November, another unusual event took

Action at the Memorial Grounds during the Southern League match between West Ham United and Plymouth Argyle in January 1904, shortly before the Hammers moved to the Boleyn Ground.

Plymouth Argyle goalkeeper Pinnell thumps the ball away from a West Ham attack. The game ended in a 1-1 draw before a crowd of 8,000. At the end of the season, the Hammers were 12th in the Southern League.

place when the Ironworkers were forced to field two first XI's on the same day. An administrative error overlooked the need to rearrange a Southern League fixture against Spurs in order to accommodate an FA Cup-tie against Leyton. The reserve XI was upgraded and sent to do battle with Leyton (and won) whilst the senior team was defeated 1-0 at Canning Town by the

North Londoners. This match against Tottenham Hotspur attracted the largest turn out for any football match played at the Memorial Grounds. . .17,000 spectators.

Before the season's end Bill Jones who had joined Hammers mid-term from Kettering Town became the first player to be capped whilst serving with the club when he appeared for Wales against England at Wrexham.

Having served a sort of probationary period, Syd King was appointed secretary during 1901. His career had taken this course due to an ankle injury received against Spurs a couple of years before, but he still played occasionally.

The side that had finished fourth the previous year had been plundered, Monteith had joined Bury, Craig had gone to Nottingham Forest, MacEachrane to Woolwich Arsenal and Ratcliffe to Doncaster Rovers. On paper the intake looked just as impressive. McAteer came from Bolton Wanderers, Joe Blythe from Everton and Farrell from Northampton Town, but the three most interesting newcomers were Barnes, Campbell and Eccles.

William Barnes was a local man, having appeared with South West Ham and Leyton before travelling north to join Sheffield United for whom he had scored the winning goal in the previous April's FA Cup Final. John Campbell, from Glasgow Rangers, was said to be part of a 'sale' of players to help pay for the damage following the Ibrox Disaster of 1901.

George Eccles' big games was still in the future . . .he was to train three Bolton Wanderers sides to win the FA Cup, one of them against the Hammers in 1923.

Of the side that took the field for the first match of 1902-03, only Linward, Bigden and Grassam had played in the final match of the previous campaign. Grassam scored regularly throughout the season but Hammers failed to match the previous term's achievements. On travels they were defeated 6-0 at both Southampton and Reading, the eventual champions and runners-up respectively, and 5-1 at Wellingborough Town. In the FA Cup, Hammers put up a spirited fight at Lincoln but, handicapped by an injury to Kelly, they went out to the Leaguers. The Imps would be Hammers' first opponents when they eventually made it into the Football League.

In the meantime, the East Londoners were about to start a period of mediocrity that they have seldom matched. Not once in the years between 1902 and 1915 did the Boleyn men threaten to win promotion and not once was the club menaced by relegation.

Good players and one or two outstanding players served the club, notably Danny Shea and Syd Puddefoot. Others, like Harry Stapley and George Webb, won England caps, although Stapley's was at amateur level. There were a number of excellent performances in the FA Cup. Manchester United were knocked out at the Boleyn in 1911 and Newcastle United only just earned a replay a year or two earlier. The Manchester team contained one of the few great players to escape Hammers local scouting network – Harold Halse, who had a spell as an amateur with Wanstead. There were others but, by and large, Syd King managed to maintain a fair mixture of local and imported talent in the side.

Increasing discord between Arnold Hills and the Hammers committee hastened the club's departure from the Memorial Grounds in 1904. A chance meeting with a member of a religious brotherhood solved the club's ground problems, for 1904-05, when they were offered a home at Upton Park. On a reconnoitre one Sunday morning, a committee group found 2,000 spectators watching a 'pub match' which answered their doubts regarding accessibility to the new ground. Some hurried construction work was undertaken but the stadium was ready for the new season. Millwall opened the new term and the new ground but in their haste, Hammers had hopelessly mistimed this event. It would have been far wiser to have awaited the first Saturday for Millwall's visit. Only 10,000 witnessed the Thursday evening fixture, a game that would surely have attracted double that figure on a Saturday.

On paper West Ham's team for 1903-04 was as good a side as they had ever had. In Charlie Satterthwaite they had one of the hardest strikers of a ball in the country and he was backed up by William Barnes, 'Sunny Jim' Kirby, James Bigden and, late in the season, by Bill Bridgeman. Two other players of note were Tommy Allison, who would become the first Hammer to earn a benefit with the club, and Jack Hilsdon, older brother of George Hilsdon, who began and ended his career at Upton Park but spent his best years at Stamford Bridge.

Hammers averaged a little over a goal a game in finishing 12th of 18 teams, and in the Cup a single goal by Fulham's Fletcher was sufficient to knock them out. All the bright moments of this final season at the Memorial Grounds were contributed by Charlie Satterthwaite. His fierce

West Ham in 1905-06. Back row (left to right): Hammond, McCartney, Kitchen, Cotton, Gardner. Middle row: W.White, E.S.King (secretary), Allison, Hindle, Piercy, Jarvis, T.Robinson (trainer). Front row: Ford, H.Winterhalder, McAllister, Mackie, Hilsdon, Bridgeman, Wilkinson, Watson, Blackburn, A.Winterhalder. Hammers finished 11th in the Southern League this season.

West Ham's Boleyn Ground pictured in 1905. The ground was named after the nearby mansion.

shooting claimed six goals against Brighton in two League games and an FA Cup-tie.

The final match at the Memorial Ground was turned into farce when the referee allowed both teams, West Ham and Swindon Town, to play until half-time wearing colours that were almost identical.

Only six members of the playing staff survived the clear out of summer 1904. Kirby, Barnes Lyon, Griffiths and Satterthwaite all went and the trainer Bill Johnson too. The new trainer was Tom Robinson, who was trainer to the early

Thames Ironworks team . . .and Robinson's assistant was 26-year-old Charlie Paynter.

Provincial teams provided most of Hammers new staff for 1904-05. Matt Kingsley and Harold Bamlett were signed from Newcastle United, whilst Jack Flynn and Joe Fletcher came from Reading. Manchester United supplied William McCartney, who two years earlier had won his only Scottish cap whilst with Hibernian. Perhaps the most impressive capture was 'Chippy' Simmons, who had been the mainstay of the West Bromwich Albion attack for the previous

West Ham in action at White Hart Lane in September 1906 when the start of the football season was greeted by a heatwave with temperatures into the 90s. A crowd of 17,000 saw the Hammers win 2-1 and at the end of the season they were fifth in the Southern League.

six seasons. Simmons had taken part in an England trial and was thrice an England reserve during 1902-03.

Syd King chose Dave Gardner, who had seen service with Third Lanark, Newcastle United and Grimsby Town, to skipper the side. There were mixed results, a great start and a fine finish but in the middle a spell of nine consecutive defeats that included six with a 1-0 scoreline. One of those was a Cup-tie at home to Brighton, who won both the League encounters as well. Hammers were certainly repaid for the Satterthwaite blitz of 1903-04.

Goalscoring, a lost art in the first part of 1904-05, returned with a bang after Chris Carrick, a former outside-left with Middlesbrough, established himself in the first team at the end of January. A dramatic improvement in the output resulted, and hoisted the club to a safe 11th position.

Another interesting debutante that season was former Plashett Lane schoolboy George Hilsdon. Although he scored regularly for the reserves, and on his first senior outing, he could never hold down a place for long. At the end of the following season he called it a day at Upton Park and was taken on by John Tait Robertson at Chelsea, with startling results.

In a Southern League match at Brighton in March, Matt Kingsley the West Ham goalkeeper, became involved in a fracas with the home side's Herbert Lyon. Lyon, a former Hammer, escaped censure but Kingsley was not so lucky. He subsequently served a suspension and was not retained for the following season.

New arrivals for 1905-06 included Kingsley's replacement, George Kitchen. Formerly with Stockport County and Everton, Kitchen had won a First Division runners-up medal with the Goodison club in 1902. In his time at the Boleyn,

Kitchen was considered the best goalkeeper in the Southern League. Among the rest of the new intake were Herbert and Arthur Winterhalder, who were, unbelievably, not related. Herbert had been around a bit with Plymouth Argyle and Sheffield United, whilst Arthur had been plucked from local amateur soccer. Fred Blackburn, an English international, arrived from Ewood Park and he was to make more than 220 appearances. Halfway through the season Harry Stapley, a well-known local amateur, joined the club, and at the same time Billy Grassam returned to East London after an absence of two and a half years.

Exempt until the competition proper in the FA Cup for the first time in the club's short history, Hammers lost a splendid opportunity of further progress when, after holding Woolwich Arsenal 1-1 at Plumstead, they went down 3-2 in the Upton Park replay. In the League, Hammers gained doubles over Swindon Town and Queen's Park Rangers, whilst Tottenham Hotspur and Reading each won four points off the Boleyn men. West Ham's defeat at Reading was their seventh on consecutive visits.

Syd King's men put paid to the Elm Park 'bogey' in their very next trip but by far the most outstanding results of 1906-07 were the two victories over League champions Fulham. Both matches ended 4-1 in Hammers' favour.

The Southern League championship hung on the outcome of the second meeting. It was the last day of the season and if Portsmouth had won well at Leyton, at the same time as Fulham were being overrun at Upton Park, the title would have gone to the south coast side.

A debutante in that vital end-of-season clash with Fulham was Tom Randall, who became Hammers' skipper in the years leading up to World War One.

In September 1906, Upton Park witnessed a

West Ham goalkeeper George Kitchen, who made 205 Southern League and FA Cup appearances for the club – and scored six goals from the penalty spot. Kitchen joined the Hammers from Everton in 1905 and recovered from a bad injury at Newcastle in 1908 to carry on serving the club until being transferred to Southampton three seasons later.

fierce and bad tempered Western League match between Hammers and Millwall.

The *East Ham Echo* reported: 'From the very first kick it was seen that there was likely to be some trouble. All attempts at football were ignored'.

Matters came to a head when West Ham's Jarvis smashed Deans of Millwall hard against a metal advertising board. Deans retired to the dressing-room badly hurt and took no further part. Jarvis received only a caution from referee Case but the incident and the background to it came to the notice of the Football Association. They decided that Jarvis' behaviour warranted 14 days' suspension and that the Hammers should post warning notices, seeing as fist fights on the 'banks' had accompanied much of the action on the field. And referee Case did not escape the FA's wrath, being suspended for the remainder of the season.

In the Southern League's Second Division, Hammers reserves finished runners-up but understandably the League rules would not allow two teams from the same club to compete in the same division.

Everton, who finished third in the Football League that season and were also runners-up in the FA Cup, were West Ham's conquerors in a second-round tie at Upton Park. Making a note of the trouble given them by West Ham's talented young Arthur Winterhalder, the Merseysiders signed him at the end of the season. In one super performance, against the Spurs, Winterhalder scored a hat-trick in a 4-2 win at the Boleyn. Teammate Lionel Watson bettered this by notching two hat-tricks, one against Luton Town and another over Fulham. Yet another three-timer was recorded by Billy Grassam, but in that instance Hammers were beaten 4-3 at Portsmouth. Despite these goalscoring efforts,

West Ham's leading marksman was Harry Stapley who finished the season on 20.

Because of his school-teaching duties, Stapley was unable to play for Hammers in midweek games at places like Bristol and Plymouth, but again he was the most regular goalscorer in 1907-08. His title, however, was now under threat from 20-year-old Danny Shea. Recruited from Manor Park Albion, for whom he was a prolific scorer, Shea made his first appearance for Hammers at Norwich City at the beginning of December, the *Athletic News* describing it as 'a promising debut'.

Trouble erupted in the opening game against Swindon when Frank Piercy came into conflict with Bannister, his opposite number in the visitors' team. Following a bout of fisticuffs, referee Rowbotham thought it sufficient just to caution both men but the Football Association deemed otherwise. Piercy received a four-week suspension and Bannister was banned for six weeks. As in the Millwall incident of a year earlier, the referee was punished as well 'for failing to keep order'. Mr Rowbotham was reduced to the role of linesman for the rest of the season.

In the second game, against Tottenham Hotspur, there was trouble of a different kind. Both Hammers full-backs Bill Wildman and Archie Taylor were badly injured in the first half and unable to take the field for the second but the home side's nine men performed wonders to salvage a point from the game.

A trip north beyond Kettering for a Southern League match was unheard of until Bradford joined the competition for this one season. Hammers' turn for the long trek to Park Avenue came in February and it gave Syd King a chance to renew an acquaintance with Charlie Craig, his former full-back partner in the old Thames Ironworks team. The friendship ended at the touch-line, however, for King's men took both points back to London.

Friendship seemed to be at a premium in the very next fixture against Millwall, when a bad tackle by Frank Piercy on Comrie, 'who left the field in an unconscious state', earned him his marching orders. It would be Piercy's second appearance before the Football Association that season.

Tenth place had to suffice for 1907-08, but third could have been achieved had not the side lost seven points to the bottom clubs, Leyton and New Brompton.

Midland Leaguers Rotherham County provided the first-round Cup opposition and 'were unlucky to lose' according to the *Morning Leader*. The narrowest of victories earned West Ham the doubtful honour of a trip to St James' Park to face current Football League champions Newcastle United. At full-back in the Magpies side was Dick Pudan, an East Londoner who had made half a dozen appearances for the Hammers in their days at the Memorial Grounds.

The match was marred by a serious leg injury to George Kitchen, the West Ham goalkeeper. Forced to leave the field, his place was taken by Frank Piercy, who had to survive nearly 40 minutes against a now rampant set of Newcastle forwards. In the end the Magpies could not be denied and two goals from Bill Appleyard settled the issue.

David Clarke deputised for the injured Kitchen for the rest of the season but the senior man's safe hands were badly missed as Brentford, Northampton Town and then Queen's Park Rangers pumped four goals past him and the Hammers slumped from fourth to finish tenth.

A large attendance of 3,000 greeted the players at the first public trial match of 1908-09. The customers were pleased to see George Kitchen back between the posts after his long absence. There were several new faces, notably Jack Foster from Sunderland, Millwall's Fred Shreeve, who had earlier seen service with Burton United in the Football League, and Herbert Ashton, who would shortly pair up with Danny Shea to form one of the most impressive wing pairings in the country. An equally important capture was Bill Yenson from Queen's Park Rangers. Yenson had skippered the West London club to the Southern League championship the previous season. He had been a Hammer before joining Bolton Wanderers, with whom he gained a FA Cup Final runners-up medal in 1904.

When the new season got under way, Yenson found himself facing his old Rangers pals in his first match. Shea was not included in the side which beat the Rangers 2-0, but he was chosen for the game against Crystal Palace. The first game in which Shea partnered Herbert Ashton was against Luton Town on 26 September. West Ham won 4-0 and although Shea failed to score, Ashton got his one and only goal of the season.

Included in the *East Ham Echo's* report of the match against Luton Town was the disclosure that the West Ham United sides were no longer being selected by the club's directors. This task has now been undertaken by Mr Syd King, who should know better than anybody the capabilities of his players. Referring to the directors' selections the

Echo added: '. . .frequently there were suspicions of favouritism in their choice'.

One of King's selections, Jack Foster, scored a hat-trick against Portsmouth in October, and another, Danny Shea, went one better with four against Plymouth Argyle in the last days of December.

On Christmas Day, 15,000 assembled to see Southampton beaten yet again on a visit to East London. Poor Saints, who last won at the Memorial Grounds in 1902-03, had to wait until December 1938 before their next successful trip to West Ham and one can add a couple of FA Cup-ties as well as wartime encounters that also went against them.

Hammers reached the third round in the FA Cup of 1908-09 and each tie went to a replay. After a goalless draw at Queen's Park Rangers, a goal from Danny Shea settled the Upton Park replay. A second-round tie at Elland Road, Leeds, attracted 31,000, more than 30 per cent up on Leeds City's next best for 1908-09, but Hammers brought the tie back to Upton Park by holding the home side 1-1.

To avoid clashing with the Millwall-Woolwich Arsenal replay, Hammers chose Thursday rather than Wednesday for the second meeting. And they were rewarded when 13,000 fans turned up. Leeds scored early and hung on until Danny Shea found his range and equalised in the last few minutes of normal time, then scored the decider in the last minute of extra-time.

Admission charges were increased but failed to deter 17,000 cramming themselves onto the unterraced banking to witness the third-round tie against Newcastle United. A measure of the interest this tie aroused can be gauged by the fact that the *Athletic News* gave it 20 column inches of match report.

The account of the game was full of praise for both defences with West Ham's Archie Taylor being the outstanding performer. The match, however, needed another performance for neither side could manage a goal at Upton Park.

After the great Colin Veitch had missed a penalty, Albert Shepherd scored one for the Magpies to hold an interval lead in the replay at St James' Park. Gallant Hammers came back when Danny Shea equalised and a ding-dong battle was only resolved by Anderson's goal for Newcastle eight minutes from the end. The Geordies were knocked out in the semi-finals that season but won the championship of the Football League.

There was a reaction to this Cup-tie defeat, for

West Ham United in 1909-10. Back row (left to right): Hammond, Shreeve, Dawson, Kitchen, Fairman, Bourne. Middle row: C.Paynter (assistant trainer), Whiteman, Stanley, Lavery, Woodards, E.S.King (secretary-manager), Wagstaff, Piercy, Randall, Rist, T.Robinson (trainer). Front row: Armstrong, Ashton, Shea, Cannon, Webb, W.F.White (chairman), Haynes, Carvossa, Waggott, Blackburn, Caldwell, Silor.

Hammers lost the next two League games without scoring. At League leaders Northampton Town they were beaten 6-0, but the *Athletic News* sympathised: 'Strenuous Cup-tie efforts have left there mark on West Ham, for it was a tired and depleted team that did duty at Northampton.'

That season went down as the only one in Hammer's history in which they failed to win a match on their travels. The closest they came was at Norwich City in December when, after leading 3-1 at the break, they were defeated 6-3.

Normal pre-season optimism was in evidence in August 1909 . . .and was proved justified when Hammers opened with three wins. The second of these at Norwich City, was particularly satisfying in view of the previous season's result.

There was a change of some significance in the boardroom when chairman Joseph Grisdale was elevated to president and William White was installed as his replacement. Mr White would be chairman through some of the club's most momentous years.

New players for West Ham's 11th attempt at a senior Southern League title included Fred Cannon from Queen's Park Rangers, Bob Whiteman of Norwich City and Bob Fairman, who arrived from Birmingham.

In December 1910 the *Athletic News* carried a front page item on Finchley-born Fairman. Part of it read: 'When Brighton opposed West Ham the other week at Upton Park, a wag pointed out that on one side there was a back named Blackman who was a fair man and on the other there was a back named Fairman who was a black man. The latter was R.Fairman, the long, lithe dark featured player, who, by his good and

consistently improving game, has made himself an immense favourite with the West Ham crowd'.

Another newcomer for 1909–10 was George Butcher, an 18-year-old well-sinker from St Albans. He was still at Upton Park two seasons after the end of World War One but then moved to Luton Town with whom he finished his career in 1925.

For West Ham, finishing ninth was an improvement of eight places over the previous term and there were no heavy defeats until runners-up Swindon Town won 5-0 at the County Ground in the final match of the season. Danny Shea once again headed the goalscoring and for a spell was the leading marksman in the whole country. But nobody else at Upton Park reached double figures, although left winger Thomas Caldwell's eight included a hat-trick against Bristol Rovers.

The midweek return fixture at Eastville provided a nice little touch when, shortly before kick-off, the West Ham party made it known that they would have liked an earlier start in order to make train connections.

On hearing this the Bristol side hurried their preparations and the game kicked-off ten minutes early. In the Rovers side that afternoon was Fred Corbett, another migrant from East London who had spent time in West Ham's colours at the Memorial Grounds.

Drawn at home in the FA Cup, to Lancashire Combination side Carlisle United, Hammers led for a long time until ten minutes from time when Randall brought down a visiting forward and Carter levelled the scores from the penalty spot. The northerners were induced to replay the tie at

Upton Park and it was fixed for the following Thursday.

West Ham made no mistake this time, winning 5-0, although the second half produced some violent behaviour from both sides.

Only Derby County had succeeded in scoring more than two goals against the Wolves at Molineux before the visit of Hammers for the second-round FA Cup-tie on 5 February. Beaten just twice at home, the midlanders crashed 5-1 in front of a 17,000 attendance, their second-highest of the season. Shea was in dazzling form and scored three goals, but the whole team played brilliantly. The *Sportsmans'* correspondent wrote: 'At every point of the game West Ham United were superior to the Wanderers.'

The *Athletic News,* too, had complimentary things to say, opening its report thus: 'To say that West Ham sprung a surprise at Wolverhampton would be to put it mildly. The fact is that most of those who assembled at the Molineux Grounds were inwardly convinced that their favourites would, in racing phraseology, "romp home". But right from the kick-off they were disillusioned.'

For the second season in succession, Hammers faced Queen's Park Rangers in the FA Cup. The West Londoners had already beaten the Hammers at Upton Park so they were confident of doing likewise on their own patch. But the Boleyn Boys survived this one after being in front through George Webb and might even have won, had a linesman been alert to an offside transgression that led to W.H.O.Steer levelling the score.

Some 18,000 assembled for the following Thursday afternoon replay and another epic ensued. Play was halted for a few minutes when a wall collapsed due to the crush, but nobody was hurt. With no score at the end of 90 minutes, the tie went into extra-time and even the extra period was almost up when Rangers' amateur centre-forward Steer burst through the home defence and grabbed the winner.

The sides faced each other once more before the season was over and that match produced six goals. Half an hour remained and West Ham, with goals from Shea, Waggott and Curtis led 3-0, but in a desperate finish third-placed Rangers levelled the scores, one of the goals being credited to Bill Barnes, a former Hammer from the Memorial Ground days.

Within 12 minutes of the start of the 1910-11 season, West Ham United had scored three times. Visiting Southend United did not know what hit them as Ashton, Webb and Fred Blackburn all

got the ball past former Hammers goalkeeper David Clarke. United, however, had something in reserve for they came back strongly with three goals of their own to snatch a point.

There were few new faces in the Hammers' line-up for the start of this campaign but there were some changes as the season progressed. Bill Kennedy, a schoolteacher from Grays, joined the club and James Rothwell, a full-back, came from Crosby on Merseyside. Later in the season, Fred Harrison, the former Southampton hot-shot, was transferred from Fulham, and George Butcher established himself in the first team at the expense of Fred Blackburn. Danny Shea added 24 more League goals to the 48 he had already notched for the Hammers, and Frank Piercy became the first West Ham player to reach 200 appearances for the club.

During the next couple of seasons, Fred Blackburn and Herbert Ashton would become the only other West Ham players to achieve this figure before the start of World War One.

A final Southern League placing of fifth was the best since 1906-07 and the single home defeat, by Northampton Town, the best since 1898-99 when the club was still known as the Thames Ironworks. Another high was set when Hammers won 6-0 at Southend United, their record away win in the Southern League. Danny Shea scored four times in this match.

For all this, it was the FA Cup performances that brought West Ham United to the notice of the nation. When they kicked-off their fourth-round tie against Blackburn Rovers on 11 March, the club was only 90 minutes away from a semi-final place.

All Hammers' Cup opponents this season were members of the Football League First Division and all four of them were previous winners of the trophy.

A first-round tie against Nottingham Forest was played in fog so thick that the *East Ham Echo's* reporter found it impossible to record some spells of the game: '. . .evidently there were no very close attempts to score as the crowd behind the goal were comparatively undemonstrative . . .the game was nothing more or less than a pure farce under the conditions and description is out of the question'.

In an interview with Frank Carruthers for the *All Sports* magazine in February 1923, Danny Shea confessed to punching both goals into the Forest net in full view of several opponents.

Doubling admission prices for the second-round tie against Preston North End showed the

Hammers board had learned nothing from similar acts in the past. Whereas 20,000 could have been expected to attend this game, the 'shilling gate' reduced it to 13,000. The Lancashire side included Arthur Winterhalder, a former Hammer, at outside-left, but he made no impression as three goals by George Webb sent Joe McCall and his men home empty handed.

The third-round draw gave West Ham a plum home match with the Football League's leading side, Manchester United. Again, admission charges were doubled, but this time the attraction was too great, for everybody wanted to see this game . . .whatever the cost.

On the big day, the crowds began to gather hours before the start and such was the number inside at 3pm, half an hour prior to kick-off, that it was thought wise to close the gates.

The *East Ham Echo* correspondent 'Rambler' described the scene: 'Every vantage point was seized upon by the spectators. Some climbed up the telegraph pole, others sat on the top of advertisement hoardings and looked every minute as if they would topple over, while others seated themselves on top of the covered stand. Round the banks there was one huge mass of humanity, packed like sardines in a box but all as happy as could be.'

The contest proved a lot more even than anybody had anticipated. The Lancastrians supplied the subtlety and craft, whilst Hammers provided the enthusiasm.

And it was the enthusiasm that won on the day for this splendid encounter ended with an astonishing result: West Ham United 2, Manchester United 1.

Danny Shea and Tommy Caldwell scored West Ham's goals, Caldwell's coming in the 88th minute. When the referee sounded the final whistle, the crowd invaded the field and chaired the left winger to the dressing-room.

The *Morning Leader's* football reporter said: 'The height of human happiness appeared to have been reached at Upton Park on Saturday when West Ham United in the last two minutes of a match of thrills provided the crowning sensation of a winning goal in the Cup-tie with Manchester United. It was in every way a great achievement which will best be remembered by the ecstasy of the East End crowd that gave itself over to headlong joy it was a privilege to share.'

Hopes of further Cup progress were high when Hammers were paired with Blackburn Rovers in the fourth round. At the time, Rovers were without a win in 18 League excursions but

they did have two away Cup successes under their belt.

In the meantime, West Ham rested five men, who were 'nursing minor injuries', for their next Southern League match, and released George Webb to the England amateur side at the Crystal Palace. The much weakened Hammers side went down to Northampton Town 2-1, their only home League defeat of the season.

George Webb, who appeared for both the full England side and the amateurs, was not the only Hammer to receive representative recognition. Danny Shea, George Kitchen and Webb himself also represented the Southern League in the inter-League games that were popular at this time.

There was an attendance of 20,000 for the Blackburn Rovers FA Cup-tie, a large gathering by Upton Park standards, but a figure that paled when put alongside the assemblies at the other three ties that afternoon. The Bradford City-Burnley game attracted 39,000, the Newcastle United-Derby County game some 59,000, and the clash between Chelsea and Swindon Town was watched by over 77,000.

The *Athletic News* deemed the Hammers tie worthy of its senior reporter being in attendance and the redoubtable J.H.Catton ('Tityrus' to his readers) was among the 20,000 to witness the match. Rovers, skippered by the England captain Bob Crompton, had been twice ahead in the match but goals from George Butcher had recovered the situation both times. As the tie entered its final minutes, Fairman missed his tackle on Welsh international Davies. As a result, Kitchen was required to make a double save but could not hold the ball on either occasion and it was Davies again who managed to prod home the winner.

In his 30 column inches account of the match, Catton was sympathetic to the East Londoners: 'West Ham have had a splendid run of success, and have no need to feel the least discredited by this overthrow.'

Earlier, he had enthused over the Hammers attack: 'I must confess to being charmed by the Southern forwards. As a body more talented more thrustful more tricky and swifter in their enveloping movements than the Rovers. The rest of the 11 did not attain the same standard. The half-backs were honest plodders, the full-backs hardly up to a first-class club standard, and the goalkeeper, Kitchen, not so faultless as I have seen him'

He went on: 'I should doubt that there has

been a finer Cup-tie this season. I cannot recall having seen a more entertaining match'.

Before the season came to an end, Hammers' ranks were reinforced by the arrival of Fulham's centre-forward Fred Harrison. He made a scoring debut in a 4-1 victory over his old employers, Southampton, and doubled the Saints' agony by notching the only goal of the return game a couple of days later.

Preparations for season 1911-12 went ahead without popular goalkeeper George Kitchen, who after six years and 184 games had decided it was time to move on. His passion for golf influenced his choice when he was offered a part-time job of coach at a Bournemouth Golf Club. He joined nearby Southampton.

Syd King's only major signing that summer was Vic Glover, the Southampton skipper for the previous two seasons. New local talent came in the form of Joe Hughes, a goalkeeper from South Weald, and Frank Burrill, a Manor Park youth who later appeared for Wolverhampton Wanderers in the 1921 FA Cup Final.

Failing to find the net in four of their opening six fixtures, Hammers languished in the lower regions. Results picked up a little after a 7-4 score over Brentford. Rippon of the Bees recorded a hat-trick, but two Hammers, Shea and Kennedy, did likewise.

In addition to their normal fixtures, Hammers had to fit in two games against Fulham 'as a consideration for the transfer arrangements involving Fred Harrison and George Redward' at the back end of the previous season. About the same time the clubs clashed in the London Challenge Cup. The tie went to a replay, which the Craven Cottage side won 5-2, and cost Bob Fairman a broken thumb. Thus, it could be accepted that Fulham FC were not 'flavour of the month' that September.

Old rivals Millwall, enjoying a sequence of rewarding visits to Upton Park, ran out of luck in November when two goals by Fred Harrison ended their recent dominance. It was Tom Randall's first game as skipper of the side and Joe Hughes' debut in goal. Two spectators were seriously injured and taken to hospital during the crush on the terraces, and George Webb and Millwall's Jim Jeffrey together assisted one of the injured to the pavilion. There was some explosive scoring by the Hammers. At Northampton Town they were two up in ten minutes but went down 3-2. At Stoke the home side recovered from two down in 15 minutes to win 4-3 with a hat-trick from a centre-forward making his first appearance

in that position. But at home to eventual champions Queen's Park Rangers in March, Hammers snatched three goals in the final 15 minutes. On Christmas morning, against Leyton, Herbert Ashton scored in the opening minute and missed another glorious chance only seconds later.

A young Charlie Buchan played in this game and in the next day's return fixture which had to be abandoned due to the atrociously muddy conditions. Many years later, Buchan, in his autobiography *A Lifetime in Football* related how he almost became a Hammer when West Ham's Charlie Paynter was sent to watch him playing Sunday morning soccer for a North Woolwich team. Sunday football was banned by the Football Association but Paynter did as he was told. He reported back to his superiors that the kid was so small and frail that it would be wise to wait a couple of years then take another look. By then it was too late, of course.

At centre-forward for the Hammers in the abandoned fixture at Leyton was Bill Kennedy, a teammate of Buchan's in their days at Northfleet. Kennedy found a temporary place in the West Ham team because of the departure of George Webb to Manchester City. Still an amateur, Webb agreed to join City provided no money changed hands. But when the Hyde Road club later visited the Boleyn for a 'friendly in consideration' Webb claimed that his proviso had been violated and refused to play for City again. George Webb, allegedly a Freemason, died of consumption in 1915 at the age of 28.

The future was equally tragic for Bill Kennedy, who damaged a knee in the replayed FA Cup-tie against Middlesbrough and did not play again. This young man was, however, fit enough for military service and made the ultimate sacrifice whilst serving with the London Scottish Regiment during World War One.

Another casualty of this season was Frank Piercy, who played the last of his 214 games against Plymouth Argyle at Upton Park on 20 January. A number of players were tried at centre-half but without success. Poor George Redwood, on his first attempt, came up against Crystal Palace's new signing Edwin Smith, who notched three of the visitors' six goals in a record Hammers home defeat which stood for many years.

Millwall had hoped West Ham United would be the first visitors to their new ground at New Cross. Southern League fixtures were arranged to this end but, regrettably, work was delayed and the date had to be put back. In the event it was on 9 March 1912 that Hammers made their first appearance at The Den, an occasion they marked by going down 5-1.

In the FA Cup, West Ham put out Football League side Gainsborough Trinity before being paired with Middlesbrough at Ayresome Park. That season 'Boro finished a healthy seventh place in the Football League's First Division so it was no mean achievement when Hammers managed to force a replay against a side unbeaten at home that season. On the following Thursday the teams faced each other for the replay. 'Boro included Elliott and Cail, their leading marksmen, and although Elliott did score it wasn't enough as goals from Herbert Ashton and Fred Harrison saw Hammers through.

Third-round opponents Swindon Town had already won a Southern League match at the Boleyn in November and were confident of repeating their triumph in the Cup. As the highest scoring side in the Southern League for the previous four seasons, Swindon's visit aroused a good deal of attention in the East End. On the day some 20,000 witnessed the tie which went to a replay, George Butcher's tenth minute goal for Hammers being cancelled out by one from Albert Fleming before the break.

By the time the replay took place it was known that the winners' prize would be a lucrative home tie against First Division Everton.

Beaten only once and averaging three goals a game on their own ground, Swindon presented something of a major obstacle to Hammers' further progress. The problem was magnified somewhat by an injury to centre-forward Fred Harrison, who was forced to miss the following Wednesday's replay. Weakened by his absence, the visitors were comfortably beaten by four goals to nil. Some newspaper reports attribute two of Swindon's goals to Hammers full-back Vic Glover. But the *Sportsman* gives him credit for only half that number. To underline their superiority, the Wiltshire club again defeated Hammers, this time 3-1, in an end-of-season League match.

If Swindon Town could have continued their successes over Hammers into 1912-13 they would have captured the Southern League championship, for the three points they surrendered to the Boleyn men were the three required for the title. Indeed, Hammers had done remarkably well against the two top teams, Plymouth Argyle and Swindon Town, in winning seven out of eight points off them.

Supporters had to wait 51 years for a near-repeat when six points were won off Liverpool and Manchester United in 1963-64.

Points won at the expense of Argyle and Swindon in 1912-13 enabled Hammers to occupy third place at the season's end . . .their highest finishing position for any year between 1899 and 1915. The reason for this upturn in fortune could have been the return of centre-forward George Hilsdon from Stamford Bridge. Or maybe the introduction of the Ilford youth Albert Denyer, who played for England in the first-ever Schoolboy international in 1907. Between them the pair scored 24 times, but leading scorer Danny Shea topped them both with 15 . . .and he played for only half the season. Shea's transfer to Blackburn Rovers in the early days of 1913 realised over £2,000, of which Daniel's share was something like £550.

That kind of money was considered a fortune in those days, but it was part compensation for a benefit due the following season. Playing his last match in West Ham's colours against Watford at the Boleyn on 4 January Shea thus ensured he was not Cup-tied when he joined Blackburn.

More than three inches of snow prevented the start of Hammers' Cup adventures for 1912-13. The tie, at The Hawthorns, against the previous seasons losing Finalists, never stood a chance of being played on the original date, but it did get under way two days later and a goal from Fred Harrison, to one by Harry Wright, earned the Londoners another chance.

On Thursday afternoon of the same week, the sides met again but couldn't be separated although 30 minutes extra-time was played. At no time in the three and a half hours so far played had the Hammers been in front. But all that changed at Stamford Bridge, the venue for the second replay. Performing on familiar territory, Hilsdon scored a goal of dubious legality after only seven minutes. This set the Boleyn men on their way and further goals five minutes either side of half-time, by Hilsdon and Denyer, decided the issue.

The *Morning Leader* correspondent wrote: 'A good many people all over the country will rub their eyes when they read that West Ham beat West Bromwich Albion in the first round of the Cup by three goals to nil. It was of course quite on the cards that West Ham would win, but a victory by three clear goals was undreamt of . . .the Midlanders have done enough this season to show that they are one of the best teams in England.'

West Ham attack the Chesterfield goal at Upton Park during the 8-1 win over the Derbyshire club in the first round of the 1913-14 FA Cup. Puddefoot scored five times, including a hat-trick in only seven minutes. In the third round, West Ham were themselves beaten heavily, losing a replay to Liverpool at Anfield 5-1.

Hammers' reward for ending Albion's Cup hopes was an away tie at Aston Villa. The clubs had met only once previously, in a friendly. Villa's current side included goalkeeper Sam Hardy, Clem Stephenson and Harold Halse, who had already tasted defeat at the hands of West Ham when he was with Manchester United. Halse was not ready to suffer again. Villa were far too good for Syd King's men and won easily by 5-0. The Birmingham men went on to win the Cup that year. From the Cup defeat at Villa until the end of the season, Syd King's men were undefeated, winning six and drawing seven of their last 13 matches.

Several new men were introduced in the early weeks of 1913-14 including Thomas Lonsdale, a goalkeeper from Grimsby Town. Tom Brandon, son of a Scottish international, joined from Blackburn, and Alf Leafe, a goalscoring inside-forward, came from Sheffield United. Later in the season Syd Puddefoot, who played a few times the previous season and was scoring regularly for the Reserves, would get an extended run. A

couple of other interesting newcomers were Arthur Stallard, who was to lose his life in World War One, and Jack Tresadern, a Leytonstone-born Barking amateur whose service with Hammers would extend beyond the heady days of 1922-23. Fred Harrison, the only notable departure, had moved to Bristol City.

By scoring in his first four matches, Leafe made a good first impression. And it got even better when he recorded a hat-trick at Coventry City in November. But then 19-year-old Syd Puddefoot arrived and he found the net on 13 occasions in his first 11 games. Five of these came in a first-round FA Cup-tie against Chesterfield, but he proved he could find the net when opposed by a quality defence, scoring in both games of a replayed Cup-tie against Liverpool.

Young Puddefoot had netted 15 times when he sustained a serious ankle injury in an abandoned game at Watford. Hammers were leading when torrential rain caused a halt to the match. Alas, when it was re-run two weeks later, Watford produced a deluge of goals and won 6-0.

Another casualty of 1913-14 was skipper Tom Randall, who injured a knee playing against Cardiff City on Easter Monday. The injury not only curtailed his season but seriously restricted his appearances in 1914-15.

In the home game against Norwich City on 21 March, Herbert Ashton became the third West Ham player, behind Frank Piercy and Fred Blackburn, to reach 200 appearances for the club.

During the summer, as football prepared for the new season, the opening battles of the World War One were fought in Belgium and France. By the time the start of the soccer season arrived, hostilities had been in progress for about four weeks. Nevertheless, football's administrators decided to make a start, despite massive criticism. The 'anti' lobby pointed out that while some fit young men were getting paid for playing football, others were paying with their lives in the carnage across the Channel. It was soon realised, however, that football had a part to play in helping to maintain the morale of the nation, not only at home, but in the trenches too.

Gillingham opened the 1914-15 season with their usual unsuccessful visit to Upton Park. Only twice (in 1907-08 and 1908-09) had the Kent side recorded victories at the Boleyn in 15 attempts.

With 18 goals, Puddefoot was Hammers' leading marksman for the last pre-war season, but only two of these were scored on opponents' grounds. For the last 11 matches, Arthur Stallard was recalled and his seven goals included three on opponents' grounds plus the last one scored in peacetime competition by a West Ham player for the next four years.

For the third time in eight seasons, West Ham were paired with Newcastle United in the FA Cup. Bill McCracken, at full-back for the visitors, was the only player from ether side to have played in the earlier meetings of 1908 and 1909. After holding a two-goal lead following errors by the home goalkeeper Joe Hughes, Newcastle employed desperate tactics to save the game after two goals from Alf Leafe brought Hammers level.

Because of the war effort, FA Cup replays were prohibited in midweek so this tie had its second performance at St James' Park on the following Saturday. It was to prove yet another disappointing trip to the North-East, for despite goals from Casey and Leafe, the Magpies went one better and progressed into the second round. Their downfall came in a quarter-final replay against Chelsea. Hammers' misfortunes at St James' Park continued until May 1947, when they were successful for the first time.

Although the decision to continue with soccer throughout the war was still considered to be the correct one, it was thought that a different set-up would be more appropriate in view of the fact that attendances had fallen dramatically during the latter half of the first wartime season and that travelling difficulties could be responsible for this.

The soccer administrators decided that regionalisation was the answer and the system was installed for the second season. As expected Hammers were grouped with the other Metropolitan clubs in what became known as the London Combination. For 1916-17, some other non-Metropolitan clubs were included which involved journeys to places like Portsmouth and Southampton, in what were to be Hammers' longest scheduled trips. The following season saw some pruning with the two Hampshire clubs being left out. Hammers' longest trips were now only as far as Brentford and Fulham.

West Ham were extremely successful in the new surroundings, bearing in mind that five of the other competitors were Football League clubs, and two of them, Spurs and Chelsea, were recently of First Division standard. Throughout the conflict, Hammers won more matches and scored more goals than any other side in this London-based competition. In capturing the championship for 1916-17, Syd King's men recorded 110 goals in 40 games.

There were complaints that Hammers had won the title with a large number of 'northern imports'. King never denied this and the *Athletic News* backed him, stating that the achievement was all the more commendable considering the club had used 49 players due to constantly enforced team changes.

From the outset King was recruiting from wherever he could. Danny Shea came back to help out when his club Blackburn Rovers decided to wait (in vain) for the early end to hostilities. First of the big names to appear was Walter Masterman, a goalscorer for Sheffield United in the 1915 FA Cup Final. In March, Andy Cunningham of Glasgow Rangers turned out for the Boleyn side at Stamford Bridge. He had been expected at Fulham but chose the Hammers instead. Part of his debut was at centre-half following the dismissal of Bill Askew for violent play.

Cunningham gained a commission during his military service, a distinction that also came the way of Jack Tresadern. Of professional footballers who did military service a large proportion went into the Army. Hammers had a couple, A.Appleby and Herbert Ashton, who served as ground crews with the Royal Flying Corps, but Alf Leafe appeared to be the only West Ham player with any kind of wartime service when he enlisted with the Royal Naval Air Service.

Thirty-eight players were used in 1915-16, when Hammers gained a final League placing of fourth. Football League clubs Chelsea and Arsenal occupied first and third, whilst Millwall finished runners-up. Even more players were used in the subsequent wartime seasons, 49 in 1916-17 and 55 in 1917-18. The last figure was exceeded by seven when 62 players wore the West Ham shirt during 1918-19.

Countless players made only one appearance, possibly plucked from the crowd to make up the team. But the majority were established pre-war professionals looking to supplement their meagre service pay. One individual who appeared for Hammers in March 1917 is listed as 'J.Day'. It was his wish that he remained anonymous, but he was known to at least one man present. It just so happened that J.H.Catton ('Tityrus') was reporting the match (against Spurs) for the *Athletic News* . . .and Catton knew everybody in football. To his credit, the *Athletic News* man respected the player's wishes.

He wrote: ' . . .on the other hand, a famous back of international calibre was able to appear as the right-back for West Ham. He wished to pose as 'J Day'. I am sorry, for that must prevent me from tendering a well-deserved tribute to one of the best full-backs of the day and one who is usually seen on the left. At the opening of the game, 'Day' beat three opponents and cleared his lines. Soon folks were asking "Who is the left-back?" They had reason to do so for his cool, calm and collected game, his exact calculation where he could get the ball, his neat and clever play stood out boldly. He was beyond compare the most artistic and, at the same time, the surest defender on view. He had a perfect day for he never made a mistake. His power of recovery was not seen, for he had no occasion to prove it.'

The player's style indicates the mystery man could have been Jesse Pennington, the West Bromwich Albion and England full-back.

From a soccer point of view, West Ham United had a splendid war and the club's consistently good performances must have, at least temporarily, raised the spirits of many a Cockney youth serving his country in France. There were, however, moments of sadness at the Boleyn when news of felled former colleagues filtered home. Many supporters must have recalled the exploits of former players like Bill Kennedy, Fred Cannon and Frank Costello, who never returned from the battlefields, but when the news of the death of Arthur Stallard was received there was great shock. Hackney-born Stallard was with Chatham before coming to Upton Park in 1913-14. In 13 games prior to the outbreak of war he had netted eight times. In the following two seasons he made only spasmodic appearances but still produced 17 goals from 24 games – and these figures do not include the five he scored against Millwall in a friendly in April 1916. Stallard must have been an important part of West Ham's plans for when peace was restored.

Occasionally the press tried to balance the endless bad news coming from the Continent with something a bit more cheerful. A little item that appeared on the front pages of both the *Sportsman* and the *Athletic News* in September 1916 concerned a Private Tolcher of the Royal Irish Fusiliers.

The unfortunate Tolcher had been at Guinchy in France during the heavy German shelling of the town. He not only received physical injuries but was also struck dumb in the bombardment and was subsequently shipped back to the United Kingdom.

Whilst convalescing at home he was taken to see a match between Millwall and West Ham at The Den. The usual partisan passions marked this event but Hammers were soon in control. Ashton put West Ham in front and they were pressing for another when McDougall, the Liverpool man, found himself an opening and doubled Hammers' score. The small East End contingent together with the hitherto dumbstruck Tolcher erupted into great rejoicing. Leading 3-0 at the break, West Ham went on to inflict one of only two home defeats on the Lions that season.

At the conclusion of the campaign the clubs occupied the two top places in the Combination, to the chagrin of the Football League contenders. What became of Private Tolcher remains a mystery.

Before the battles were over and peace was restored, the Football League declared its intention to enlarge its own set-up from 40 clubs, the pre-war number, to 44 when normal soccer was resumed.

In its edition of 3 March 1919, the *Athletic News* devoted its entire leader column to West Ham United's case for admission to the Football League. But even with the support of the nation's most popular sporting newspaper, Hammers failed to top the poll. That distinction went to Coventry City. The voting resulted:

Coventry City 35
West Ham United 32
Rotherham County . . . 28
South Shields 28

The four successful candidates would be part of the Football League's 22-club Second Division for 1919-20.

On the Monday following the voting the *Athletic News* carried this item: 'Joy at West Ham last Saturday as news was received that the club's application to join the Football League was successful. It was significant that of the many letters of congratulations' only one was from a Southern League club . . .Swindon Town. Hammers were fined £500 for not giving the required notice of resignation (which should have been submitted prior to December 31st of the previous year) according to Southern League rules. As the Southern League had not been in existence since 1915, to whom could the West Ham club have notified their intentions?'

The Football League, Wembley and Promotion

FOR THE first time in their history, West Ham United began a new season in August when on the 30th of that month in 1919, they faced Lincoln City in their first-ever Football League match. The teams on that historic occasion were:

West Ham United: Hufton; Cope, Lee, Lane, Fenwick, McCrae, D.Smith, Moyes, Puddefoot, Morris, Bradshaw

Lincoln City: Blakey; Jackson, Ward, Bryan, Ormiston, Addinall, Lamming, McCulloch, Egerton, Chesser, Ball.

The general increase in admission prices to one shilling (5p) failed to deter 20,000 from attending Hammers' entry into a new era. Trailing by a penalty goal at half-time, the Upton Park lads restored equality through Moyes in the 65th minute. In the next game, away at Barnsley, West Ham were not so lucky. Again they were one goal in arrears at the break, but in the second half ran out of steam completely as the Yorkshire side, containing the legendary pair Frank Barson and Dicky Downs, piled on six more. That 7-0 defeat at Oakwell together with similar scores at Everton (1925) and Sheffield Wednesday (1959) still stands as Hammers' record defeats.

To their credit Hammers learned lessons from Oakwell, for only South Shields (who won 3-0 on 20 March) succeeded in piercing the West Ham defence more than twice in a match for the remainder of the season.

Good fortune, never very far away, was demonstrated at St Andrew's, Birmingham in October when the home team missed two penalties and were then beaten by a last-minute goal from George Kay, his first for the club. Stoke also missed a penalty in a match at Upton Park that eventually finished 1-1. In a FA Cup replay at the Boleyn, Southampton's Arthur Andrews broke a leg and the depleted Saints were easily beaten.

West Ham themselves were not infallible from the 'spot' with Frank Burton failing at Huddersfield. The match at Leeds Road took place less than 24 hours after the crisis meeting which almost saw the Yorkshire club move to Leeds.

Hammers' disciplinary record in 1919-20 was nothing to write home about. Jack Tresadern, playing in only his tenth game for the club (including his pre-war appearances), lost his temper in the home match against Rotherham and received his marching orders. And late in the season at Bury, George Kay and the Shakers' Gregson were dismissed following a bout of fisticuffs.

Visits from promotion-seeking rivals Huddersfield Town and Tottenham Hotspur both cracked the Upton Park ground record for League matches. First it was the Yorkshiremen, on 27 December, who filled the place with 25,000; but on the second Saturday in March, Spurs' visit increased that figure to 30,000.

Three weeks earlier, West Ham's FA Cup run had been ended at White Hart Lane in a convincing 3-0 victory for the Spurs. This was the first opportunity for revenge and everybody wanted to be there. The interest created by this match recalled the FA Cup clash against Manchester United nine years earlier.

The *Daily Chronicle* described the 1920 scene: 'Nearly half an hour before the kick-off at Upton Park on Saturday, the gates of the ground were closed and between the touch-line and the barricades there was a crowd of a thousand spectators, while even on the top of the grandstand people were perched in dozens.

Outside, thousands of people thronged and a

West Ham's first manager, E.S. 'Syd' King, (right), a former Thames Ironworks player and a colourful character, who took over as manager in 1902. King always remained friends of the Press and that helped when the Hammers were looking for a place in the Football League after World War One. King was in charge during a golden era at Upton Park – into the League, promotion to Division One and the first Wembley FA Cup Final – and it was so sad he left in controversial circumstances in 1932. Charlie Paynter (left),was Syd King's right-hand man as the Hammers emerged from the war ready to take their place in the Football League and achieve almost immediate success in the higher sphere. He began as an unpaid helper at the Memorial Grounds and eventually succeeded King as manager and held the post until 1950. Thus, after first appointing King in 1902, West Ham had only two managers in the next 48 years.

large force of police was necessary to keep hundreds of intending spectators from getting into the ground by a neighbouring allotment, although in many instances these enthusiasts succeeded in eluding the police and clambering over the railings'

The match was marred by an injury to Skinner which reduced the visitors to ten men. Two goals from Syd Puddefoot, bringing his total for the season to 18, to a penalty goal from Arthur Grimsdell won the points for Syd King's men. It also brought to an end Spurs' unbeaten sequence of 14 League and Cup matches.

Of the 39 players who made at least one appearance for Hammers in 1919-20, more than half were retained for 1920-21. Two notable signings were Victor Watson and Danny Shea. The latter was, of course, the club's goalscoring hero of eight years earlier. But Watson, from Cambridgeshire, was one for the future, for he would, in due course eclipse all the goal-grabbing

achievements of Shea and Syd Puddefoot, his present team-mates. In one spell of four matches in September and October 1921 (against Cardiff City twice, Coventry City and Leicester City), the trio formed the spear-head of Hammers' attack, but this lethal threesome could manage only two goals between them. Another recruit that season was Jimmy Simmons, a scorer for Sheffield United in the 1915 'Khaki' Cup Final at Old Trafford. It was at Sheffield, against the Wednesday, that Hammers were removed from the FA Cup following a blunder by the normally reliable Ted Hufton.

Cardiff City, newly elected, to the Football League, went straight through the Second Division and into Division One at their first attempt. But Hammers deprived them of two points in drawing both engagements and Danny Shea got his only goal of the season against the Welshmen.

On Christmas Day, 21-year-old Syd Bishop

West Ham skipper George Kay, who made 259 League and Cup appearances for the Hammers and led them to Wembley in 1923.

an earlier game suggested that the referee should be on the lookout for Birmingham's robust method of play which has probably been responsible for their rise up the Second Division. A League Committee ruled that the comments were objectionable and uncalled for and West Ham were told they must refrain from making such remarks in future.

Robust play, however, was not beyond the capabilities of some of the Boleyn men. Bill Cope, for instance, was particularly gifted in this respect and in the 1-0 defeat at Bristol City in February, he was sent off for a vicious tackle on Pocock, City's leading marksman.

Another West Ham player found that his illegal antics had not escaped the notice of the press. The *Daily Chronicle* correspondent at the West Ham-Barnsley in March wrote:'Burton, besides playing badly, committed so many fouls that at length he came into conflict with the Barnsley centre-forward, and Spoors was unjustly sent off the field.'

Apparently in an effort to redeem himself 'Burton together with many of his colleagues and a large section of the crowd protested loudly, but the referee refused to be merciful'

Until Syd King signed Wilf James from Portsmouth in January 1921, the West Ham manager had a continual headache with the inside-left position. Nine different players had played there prior to the arrival of James, who cost £1,000. James, like Bishop, scored on his debut but his goal output during his stay at Upton Park was pretty minimal. On the other hand, Syd Puddefoot enjoyed his best peacetime season, netting 29 times. Twice he recorded four in a match, and on another occasion a hat-trick. In the whole of the Football League his total was exceeded only by Joe Smith (Bolton Wanderers) and Tommy Browell (Manchester City).

The Reserves had a good season too. They captured the London Combination champ-ionship with four points to spare over Queen's Park Rangers. In a Combination fixture in October, West Ham Reserves defeated Arsenal 5-1. Tom Whittaker, later to become a successful manager at Highbury, led the Gunners' attack, whilst the match was refereed by Harry Curtis, who in the years ahead would take Brentford to the heights.

An interesting statistic of this season was that Notts County were the only visitors to Upton Park to score more than one goal.

Returning from a successful summer tour of Spain, the Hammers were keen to get started on

made his League debut at home to Birmingham and scored a goal that put a stop to the Midlanders' sequence of ten consecutive wins. There were 37,000 at Upton Park that day, which was at that time a record crowd for the ground. At St Andrew's two days later, an even bigger assembly greeted the sides. Sixty thousand were present as the Blues defeated Hammers 2-1 to haul themselves into third place in the table. The attendance was 29,000 above Birmingham's average that season and 20,000 better than for the Midlands derby against Wolves.

After the match at the Boleyn, Birmingham lodged a complaint with the Football League, stating that the West Ham programme notes for

West Ham in April 1923, on the verge of their historic Wembley appearance. Back row (left to right): E.S.King (manager), Henderson, Bishop, Kay, Hufton, Young, Tresadern, C.Paynter (trainer). Front row: Richards, Brown, Watson, Moore, Ruffell.

the new campaign. So, it seems, were the clubs' supporters, for 12,000 of them attended the pre-season public trial which provided local charities with £420.

The previous season had seen the departures of George Butcher, to Luton Town, and Danny Shea, to Fulham, and during the break Frank Burton had moved to new Football Leaguers Charlton Athletic. Within six months the Hammers' greatest asset, Syd Puddefoot, would be gone as well. His destination . . .the unlikely little town of Falkirk in Scotland. In a newspaper interview Syd King is reported to have revealed that when Falkirk made their official approach regarding Puddefoot, the Hammers' attempted to deter the Scots with a prohibitive price tag of £5,000. But the Scots, defying their traditional instincts, paid up without question.

Losing a sharpshooter of Puddefoot's quality was sure to affect the promotion challenge and it did. From being within easy striking distance at the time of his leaving, the Boleyn men lost five of their last seven matches and finished fourth.

In maintaining an unbeaten home record until March, Hammers had prevented 12 visiting sides

from scoring. But Rotherham County began the rot by upsetting the Boleyn men in their 17th home match. Thereafter the promotion challenge evaporated. Vic Watson now had the responsibility for scoring goals and soon struck up an understanding with Jimmy Ruffell, who had made his debut in December. Yorkshire-born defender Jack Hebden was signed at the back end of 1920-21 from Bradford City, but in his 20th game for the Hammers he broke an ankle against Derby County and played no more League football until early in 1922-23.

Swansea Town were West Ham's conquerors in the FA Cup, but it took them three attempts, the last of which was at neutral Ashton Gate.

The 1922-23 season was the true watershed in West Ham United history. Though not entirely successful − finishing runners-up in two major competitions might be considered cause for celebration at many sporting clubs − failure at this point in the club's history could well have condemned it to a future of alternating Second and Third Division soccer.

A dip into the transfer market brought Dick Richards (Wolverhampton Wanderers), Billy

West Ham supporters arrive at Wembley for the 1923 FA Cup Final, unaware that they are about to witness -or did they? – one of the most famous games in the history of football. Note the large 'hammer'. Today it would be an inflatable.

Charlton (South Shields) and Charlie Crossley (Everton) to Upton Park. The last named was Everton's leading scorer in 1920-21, whilst Charlton had played for England at schoolboy level. Another newcomer was Billy Moore, who felt his chances of displacing Charlie Buchan in the Sunderland side were so minimal that he opted to join Hammers.

It was hoped that the side would challenge for a promotion place, but after seven defeats in the opening 13 fixtures the future looked decidedly bleak. Opening the campaign with a home defeat against recently-relegated Bradford City, Hammers quickly made amends by getting the decision in the wool town seven days later. But this was the only result to enthuse over for some little while. At the beginning of November, a Leeds United debutant, Percy Whipp, scored a hat-trick against the Hammers that sent the club plummeting down to 18th place in the table. But that was as bad as it got, for the return match at home to Leeds United a week later began a sequence of 32 League and Cup games that included only one defeat.

At the end of this splendid run, Syd King's

team were about to contest the FA Cup Final and were posed to capture the Football League Second Division title. Things went a little awry at this stage, due mainly to the team's tiredness resulting from eight matches already in April and the Cup Final still to come. Of the Hammers' team, only Dick Richards had 'been here before' but his unhappy experience with Wolves in 1921 had been only as far as the semi-final, after which he had been dropped.

Throughout April the local *East Ham, Echo Mail and Chronicle* gave extensive coverage to West Ham's activities. There were long articles (by 'Scribo') on Charlie Paynter, George Kay and Syd King as well as a description of the new stadium at which the Final tie was to be contested. The *Sportsman* reported in the week leading up to the Final that the Hammers team would be attending the Adelphi Theatre for a performance of the *Battling Butler*. But shortly before that, manager Syd King would be broadcasting to the nation on the the new radio system (2LO), on his team's prospects at Wembley. On another excursion, the team was at the Epsom Races on the day outsider 'Dry Toast'

Crowds swarm towards the Wembley turnstiles for the 1923 Cup Final. Interest in the game took the authorities by surprise, leading to some of the most remarkable scenes ever seen at a football match.

PC Storey on his white horse, Billie, attempts to push back the crowd. Ever since the game has been known as 'the White Horse Final'. Of course there were other mounted policeman doing an equally sterling job, but Billie stood out.

More mounted officers attempt to hold the Wembley crowd in check.

Nobody seems quite sure what to do next. Policeman chat to the crowd whilst two apparently unconcerned supporters take a stroll across the pitch.

Some fans took a slightly safer route into the stadium where they probably found themselves still unable to see the action.

But this fan seems absolutely intent on getting in to see the 1923 Cup Final, even if it means risking life and limb.

West Ham players look perplexed as the match is delayed while the mammoth task of clearing the pitch gets under way

David Jack scores the historic first Wembley goal for Bolton Wanderers.

Heads high in the Bolton defence as West Ham mount an attack.

won the City and Suburban Handicap. Despite their recent accomplishments on the field, Hammers were clearly the outsiders for their coming contest against Bolton Wanderers, although Corinthian of the *Daily Chronicle* fancied Hammers because of the hard pitch.

There was minor panic in the West Ham camp when it was discovered Ted Hufton would require surgery on his left knee . . .only three days before the Final. In that short space of time Hufton was restored to full fitness along with Len

Young and Jimmy Ruffell, whose readiness had also provided last minute scares.

Simon Marland's *Bolton Wanderers: A Complete Record* aptly describes this first Wembley event as 'a Final that will be remembered more for what happened off the pitch'.

The *Sportsman's* headline read 'Chaotic FA Cup Final . . .Record Crowd and Indescribable Scenes'. About the match itself Bolton won because ' . . .they were well balanced and better together'

This time Jack is beaten to the ball by the West Ham defence.

Corinthian of the *Daily Chronicle*, who had forecast a Hammers triumph, attributed Bolton's victory to the superiority of their half-backs, Nuttall, Seddon and Jennings.

The local *East Ham Echo* had a little more to say about the basic reason for Bolton's success but came to the same conclusion: 'Bolton won probably because they were more experienced and better fitted temperamentally to stand the strains of the extraordinary conditions . . .and in any case because they played better football'.

As the world now knows, the event, which began 40 minutes late, was saved by the presence of HM King George V and the hardworking Constable Scorey and his white steed. The Cup went north to Bolton for the first time following two previous attempts. A goal by David Jack inside three minutes might have been neutralised by Vic Watson soon after, had not the Hammer blazed over the bar from close range. After Bolton's second goal eight minutes into the second half, which got under way without a break, the game petered out with no further incidents of note.

The players who took part in that memorable first Wembley Cup Final were:

Bolton Wanderers: Pym; Hawarth, Finney, Nuttall, Seddon, Jennings, Butler, Jack, J.Smith, J.R.Smith, Vizard.
West Ham United: Hufton; Henderson, Young, Bishop, Kay, Tresadern, Richards, Brown, Watson, Moore, Ruffell.

The dissatisfaction felt in the East End could be read in the columns of the *East Ham Echo:* 'There is talk of a protest to the FA against regarding the game as the FA Cup Final, but disappointed and dissatisfied as they must be with it the West Ham directors and their team are too good sports to do that. The game such as it was, was played through to an end – and there is an end of it.

'One can understand how Mr Syd King feels about it when he says, "I am too disappointed to talk; I haven't got over it yet. I want to forget it"'

Perhaps the unluckiest person in the district was the Mayor of East Ham. The *Echo* told of his Wembley experience: 'The Mayor of East Ham had booked a guinea seat and went with a party of friends to see the Final. He managed to get in but found that the seats booked for his friends had been commandeered. He came out for a moment to confer with them about it . . .and lost his own! The gates were shut and he was closed out.'

Billy Moore takes a pass from Jimmy Ruffell and the Hammers press again.

For Hammers, a rapid recovery from their Wembley setback was required if the other prize, promotion to Division One, was not to elude them. The first of two matches still to play was at Sheffield Wednesday only 48 hours after the Cup Final. Without the services of Ted Hufton, Hammers won 2-0 to hoist themselves to the top Division.

	P	W	D	L	F	A	Pts
West Ham Utd	41	20	11	10	63	37	51
Leicester City	41	21	9	11	65	42	51
Notts County	41	21	7	12	45	34	51

The last fixtures of 1922-23 paired West Ham United with Notts County and Bury against Leicester City.

At Gigg Lane, the kick-off was 15 minutes prior to that at Upton Park, where, in the 38th minute, Hill, the County inside-left, scored the goal that proved to be the Nottingham side's ticket into Division One. Up in Lancashire, Bury were now in control of West Ham's immediate future but from there the news was good and with 15 minutes to go at Upton Park, Hammers learned that they would be a First Division side for 1923-24.

As well as the acclaim lavished on the club, several individuals received well-earned recognition. Vic Watson and Jack Tresadern were among four Second Division players selected for the England side at Hampden Park,, whilst Billy Moore and Ted Hufton together with Tresadern, were members of the FA party that went to Sweden at the end of May. Welsh international Dick Richards, already capped for the Principality, won further caps following Hammers' splendid season.

Into the First Division

A SHORT tour of Austria was undertaken at the end of May 1923, but the Hammers players required by England for their trip to Sweden were unable to go.

For their first season at the highest level, Hammers did not feel the need to reinforce their ranks by spending large sums on new players. None the less, there were some new faces when the staff was recalled for pre-season training. A trawl of the local amateur talent brought in Jimmy Collins (Leyton), Bill Kaine (Sterling Works) and Jim Barrett (Fairbairn House). A couple of players for whom money was paid were Tommy Yews from Hartlepool United and Norman Procter of Rotherham County. Procter's only goal the previous season had come in the Yorkshire club's home encounter with the Hammers but it failed to save them from the drop at the end of April.

The *Athletic News'* annual preview of clubs carried in the paper's August issues said of West Ham: 'Those in charge of the team are quite aware of the many pitfalls which lie ahead. Consequently there is no spirit of boastfulness at Upton Park.'

Of the 22 clubs in membership of the First Division at the start of 1923-24, only two, Sunderland and Burnley, had never faced Hammers in any kind of match before. In Sunderland's case this was put right immediately when Hammers kicked-off the new season at the Roker Park ground and collected a point off Charlie Buchan's team. In the Sunderland side that afternoon was a young man called Ernie England, who, seven years hence, would be serving the Hammers.

Two days later, a goal by Albert Fletcher was enough to gain the points off Arsenal in the Hammers' initial First Division home match. But in the return, watched by 40,000 at Highbury, Hammers were crushed 4-1, thanks to a double strike by the Stanley Earle, his only goals for Arsenal that season. Arsenal's four could be regarded as a bonanza at a time when goals were generally hard to come by. The sophisticated interpretation of the offside law as it then stood meant that goals were a more precious commodity than they had ever been. How valuable they had now become is illustrated by Hammers' playing record at this stage of 1923-24.

P	W	D	L	F	A	Pts
11	3	5	3	5	7	11

Five goals scored, 11 points won . . .never had so little produced so much!

Within a couple of weeks Hammers themselves touched the gold standard by scoring four times against Birmingham, but at the end of a season that had seen them involved in eight goalless draws, only 40 goals had been registered.

Former Hammer Dan Burgess was a member of the Aberdare Athletic side drawn to play at Upton Park in the FA Cup first round. The Welsh club were at that time in the Football League's Third Division South and were no match for the home team, who won 5-0. The next round brought Second Division leaders Leeds United to Upton Park. George Kay netted his fourth of the season but it only prolonged the agony into a second match which the Yorkshiremen won 1-0.

Bill Brown was one of only two Hammers to receive any international recognition when he was capped for England against Belgium in November, but by February 1925 he had gone to Chelsea in a vain bid to help them avoid relegation.

Eight months after the 1923 FA Cup Final, West Ham and Bolton met twice in eight days in Division One. The game at Burnden Park ended in a 1-1 draw and the Trotters won 1-0 at Upton Park. This photograph shows West Ham on the attack in the second game. At the end of the season the Hammers finished 13th in their first season back in the top division.

In the 1923-24 FA Cup, West Ham, Finalists the previous season, got no further than the second round, losing a replay at Elland Road. Here, George Kay has just scored the Hammers' goal in the 1-1 draw at Upton Park.

A West Ham player tumbles but still keeps possession during the game against Manchester United at Upton Park on the opening day of the 1925-26 season, the first campaign under the new offside law. Stan Earle gave the Hammers a 1-0 win, but despite the good start they finished 18th.

Before the new season got under way his example had been followed by Norman Proctor, who went to Leicester City, and Frank Richardson, who joined Swindon Town. Of the new intake only Stanley Earle and Sam Jennings were known to the locals and both were on show in the first home match which was won 1-0 against Preston North End. Jennings scored the only goal for the game and Earle did likewise at Blackburn seven days later. Despite this promising start, Hammers found it difficult to score and it was not until 25 October, the 12th fixture, that they managed two goals in a single match. Ted Hufton was missing until the home encounter with Leeds United in March, but even so he was back for only two games before being out for another four-match spell.

His absences were adequately covered by Tommy Hampson and Bill Kaine. Two of the 1923 stalwarts, Syd Bishop and Jack Tresadern, struggled to retain a place in this West Ham side, In the end Tresadern gave up and moved to Burnley. Bishop hung on a bit longer before joining Chelsea in 1926.

Due to poor results on their travels, Hammers were forced to settle for 13th place at the season's end. They did surprise Huddersfield Town 2-1 at Leeds Road in January, but this one sparked the Yorkshiremen to greater effort and they collected the championship by avoiding defeat for the remainder of the campaign. One of Hammers' goals at Huddersfield was scored by Vic Watson and was one of his sequence of 11 scored in ten consecutive matches.

Other important goals were netted by George Kay at Stamford Bridge to eliminate Arsenal in the thrice played first-round tie, and by Tommy Yews and Jimmy Ruffell to record West Ham's first-ever success on a visit to Nottingham. The occasion was also a Cup-tie.

For the third time since the war, West Ham's interest in the FA Cup was ended by a side from a lower division. This season it was Blackpool who convincingly won a third-round replay by 3-0, thereby avenging their KO at the hands of the Hammers in 1907.

After much discussion and limited experimentation there was a change in the offside law for 1925-26. Instead of three, now only two opponents were required to be between an attacker and the opposition goal-line when the ball was played forward.

This law had been the subject of controversy for many seasons past and some clubs, notably Notts County and Newcastle United, had reached a high level of efficiency in its application. One match between the two allegedly had 20 of its participants trapped in an area ten yards either side of the halfway line for long periods.

Headwork at Upton Park against Newcastle United in September 1925. Vic Watson scored the only goal of the game.

Hammers were not untouched in the debate. From Ivan Sharpe's 1952 book *40 Years in Football*: 'Along with John Sharp of Everton, the loveable soccer and cricket international, I counted the number of offside stoppages in Everton's home match with West Ham United in December 1924. They totalled 41! Which really calls for 41 exclamation marks.'

On the Monday morning following the first Saturday's fixtures under the altered law, West Ham's skipper Billy Moore is quoted by the *Daily Chronicle:*'I am not in favour with the change in the offside law. It has turned the game round and the team which can play the kick and rush game the best will nearly always win. This is putting a premium on those players who stud the game from a scientific point of view. In fact it robs the game of most of its science.'

For West Ham the season opened with a visit from newly-promoted Manchester United, which gave the patrons an early demonstration of the changed law. At Upton Park they only saw one goal, but at Villa Park ten goals were scored by the home side against Burnley.

The Manchester United match also marked the opening of the new East Stand, a splendid double-decker edifice which represented the club's remarkable progress over the previous few years. Ground capacity was now claimed to be 45,000, but this figure was rarely approached.

There were no fresh signings but A.T.Earl was now a professional and the gifted amateur Vivian Gibbins had promised to appear more often. In the event Gibbins played only once, in what proved to be Hammers' best performance of the season. In the 6-0 thrashing of Bolton Wanderers in February, two goals from Gibbins were supplemented by two from Vic Watson and a further couple from Jimmy Ruffell. Bolton's side that afternoon contained eight men who had taken part in the 1923 Cup Final and the three missing – Finney, Jennings and Butler – were still first-team regulars. West Ham, on the other hand, fielded only five survivors from that epic day nearly three years before.

Finishing the season in 18th place, Hammers escaped the drop by only two points. Only one game was won on an opponents ground (at Cardiff in September) and the side failed to survive a third-round trip to Spurs in the FA Cup's revised format.

For the third time in four seasons Vic Watson was West Ham's sharpest shooter. But he could not manage a hat-trick like Jimmy Barrett or Stanley Earle, whose threesome came in the Christmas Day home fixture against Aston Villa. The 20-year-old Barrett appeared in all 42 League games and played in five different positions in doing so. His three games at centre-forward netted him five goals.

Barrett was one of four Boleyn men to achieve maximum appearances in 1926-27, but his 34 games at centre-half were courtesy of a nose injury sustained by George Kay in the Hammers' close season tour of Spain which kept him side-lined for much of the season.

West Ham improved 12 places on their final 1925-26 position and won ten games on their travels. Their most emphatic win was 7-0 against Arsenal on the first Monday in March. This date also marked the death of Arnold Hills, the club's benefactor and co-founder back in Victorian times.

Improved marksmanship in the final 17 games could be attributed to the inclusion of Joe Johnson at inside-left. The former Crystal Palace and Barnsley man could not find a place in the side until February, but scored on his debut against Huddersfield Town and set off a sequence of 27 matches in which the Hammers netted at least once in each. Failing to win any of the last five games deprived Syd King's men of a higher place and a tendency to become complacent when facing inferior opponents cost them in the Cup. After Vic Watson's hat-trick had ousted

Spurs in front of a new record attendance at the Boleyn, Hammers fell in a fourth-round replay at Brentford, who finished 11th in the Third Division South.

Two West Ham men, Ted Hufton and Stanley Earle, won England caps in the same international against Ireland in Belfast.

West Ham began the 1927-28 season with 23 goals in the opening eight matches, which raised a few eyebrows, but a resounding 7-0 crash at Goodison Park in October brought everybody down to earth. This was a very unusual season because Everton, who won the championship, finished only 16 points better off than the teams which were relegated. West Ham's tally was only two points superior to the clubs in 21st and 22nd places and only five points inferior to Derby County, who finished fourth.

All five of Hammers' regular forwards scored into double figures: Jimmy Ruffell led the way with 18, followed by Vic Watson (16), Vivian Gibbins (14) and Tommy Yews and Stanley Earle on 11 each. Joe Loughlin, an import from Newcastle United, was the only significant newcomer and he was on the mark three times in his first two outings. He lost his place in the side and did not reappear until the last two games of the season, which were his final outings before being transferred to Coventry City in January 1929.

At Bramall Lane on Boxing Day, West Ham ran into in-form Harry Johnson. The Yorkshireman netted five times that day to establish a record individual score for goals against the Upton Park club.

On 14 January, West Ham won a third-round FA Cup-tie at Fratton Park by 2-0. A week later they went back with exactly the same side for a League match and were defeated 2-1. Huddersfield Town, First Division runners-up that year, put an end to any hopes Hammers had in the competition by winning 2-1 at Leeds Road. The Town went on to the Final as the hottest favourites in years but came unstuck against a plucky Blackburn Rovers side containing a former Hammers hero, Syd Puddefoot.

Pre-season public trials were never reliable indicators of how a club might perform when the real thing begins. But Hammers' patrons must have been expecting something special after 20 goals were scored in the two preview games prior to the start of 1928-29. Hammers blasted off with four against Sheffield United and in the next four games, three of which were away from home,

Hammers' goalkeeper Ted Hufton rushes out to clear with his feet against Aston Villa at Upton Park in September 1928. Capewell is the Villa forward. West Ham won 4-1 but again finished in a lowly position in Division One.

they hoisted their total to 16. Leicester City then burst the balloon with a 5-0 win at Filbert Street.

Thereafter West Ham edged their way down the table but on the way became the only side to defeat Sheffield Wednesday, the eventual champions, during that club's successful 16-match run in November and December. The Wednesday avenged this setback by winning the return 6-0. Another 6-0 defeat was sustained at Derby County where Ted Hufton made a first-minute blunder. That let in Harry Bedford, who for the rest of the match completely dominated Hammers' centre-half Charlie Cox and ended the game with four goals.

At the season's end none of the top three in the First Division had won a point at Upton Park. Aston Villa, third that year, lost 4-1 in a match in which a shot from Vic Watson was struck so hard that the ball burst. It was Vic Watson who grabbed the headlines in February with a six-goal demolition of Leeds United in a magnificent 8-2 victory. Watson would be a thorn in the side of Leeds United for the next few seasons, saving his best scoring performances for them.

Sunderland, who clawed their way back to 3-3 after being 3-0 in arrears in a December League match returned in January for a third-round Cup-tie. Again, the Roker men were desperately unlucky, for after outplaying West Ham for much of the match, they were beaten by a last-minute goal from Stanley Earle.

Earle was again on the mark in the next round. The opposition, the famous amateurs, Corinthians, attracted a crowd of 42,000, the season's largest at Upton Park. Press reports stated Hammers wore their unpaid opponents down with a fast pace which was sustained throughout the 90 minutes. The legendary Howard-Baker kept goal for the visitors on this occasion.

The *Daily Chronicle* commented on his only error: 'Just one slip by Howard-Baker in an otherwise splendid display cost them the first goal of the game. Yews ran through, then in towards goal. He shoots with tremendous power and although he did so on this occasion, Baker got down to the ball cleanly and well. The amateur goalkeeper had the ball in his arms but as he tried to get up on his feet, he slipped in the mud and lost hold of the ball which rolled just over the line. Spectators sighed rather than cheered.'

Further goals by Stanley Earle and Vic Watson ensured Hammers a place in round five. The opposition here would be Bournemouth and Boscombe Athletic, who had come first out of the bag. They were currently placed eighth in the old Third Division South and only Walsall had been able to put a blot on a splendid home record. On the day, Bournemouth were heavily handicapped by the absence of Ronnie Eye, their leading marksman, who was nursing a shoulder injury. Snow threatened to delay the tie but willing helpers managed to make conditions playable.

The *AFC Bournemouth Official Championship Souvenir* (1987) makes this reference to the tie: 'The icy conditions may have led to a fatal lapse by Isherwood which allowed Yews to open the scoring for the visitors, but after that gift goal, West Ham allowed Boscombe to dominate.'

The match ended all-square at 1-1 and four days later the sides met again at Upton Park. This time Hammers won 3-1 without moving into second gear but poor Isherwood was again a contributor to West Ham's good fortune. Frank Poxan of the *Daily News* was at Upton Park that day: 'West Ham's first goal came at the end of 12 minutes play and it was an exceedingly lucky one. Ruffell got the ball on the left and ran close in before shooting at an acute angle. A poor shot it was, too, and no danger was threatened from any other West Ham forward as the ball flashed straight across the goalmouth. Isherwood, the Boscombe left-back, was facing his own goal and he had the mortification of seeing the ball cannon off his leg past McSevich. Isherwood's chagrin must have been the greater because it was as a result of a blunder by him in Saturday's match that West Ham got their goal.'

After seeing off Bournemouth, Hammers were South-coast bound again when drawn to meet old Southern League rivals Portsmouth at Fratton Park. Pompey occupied 22nd place in Division

One at the time of this encounter but, inspired by Welsh international left-winger Freddie Cook, they left the field at half-time with a three-goal lead. Fifteen minutes into the second half Hammers received their 'shot' of inspiration when skipper Stanley Earle switched Vic Watson and Jim Barrett. The reaction was immediate as two goals in 15 minutes by the 22-years-old brought Hammers back into the contest and only a desperate last-ditch clearance by Portsmouth full-back Mackie prevented the tie going to a replay. Portsmouth went on to reach Wembley and avoid relegation that year.

Of the five West Ham forwards who had scored double figures in 1927-28, four of them, Watson, Ruffell, Yews and Gibbins, repeated the performance in 1928-29.

At the start of 1929-30, Ted Hufton was the only player serving the Hammers who had been on the staff when West Ham joined the Football League in 1919. Now approaching his 36th birthday, his position was under threat from three other 'keepers – Dan Bailie, George Watson and Bob Dixon.

In fact it was the last name, Dixon, a recruit from Stoke, who would share the goalkeeping duties with Hufton over the next two campaigns. Two newcomers each from different ends of the country and both named Wade would contend the full-back positions with Reg Goodacre, another new boy, and the established Alf Earl.

It was Earl who began the season on the wrong foot by scoring against his own side in the opening fixture at Ewood Park. Luckily, Jones the Blackburn right-back, returned the favour before the break but careless defending cost the Londoners two goals in the final 15 minutes and they had to settle for a draw. On four occasions Hammers scored five against visiting sides and ended the term with 86 goals.

In the FA Cup, the Boleyn men reached the sixth round for the second season running, getting rid of Notts County, Leeds United and Millwall before Arsenal got in the way. Arsenal like Huddersfield Town and Portsmouth, Hammers' conquerors in the two previous tournaments, went on to Wembley.

An early appearance at Wembley was Millwall's aim when they found they were drawn to play Hammers in the fifth round. Claiming that thousands would be denied a chance to see the match if it were played at Upton Park, the South London club suggested Wembley be made available to satisfy the expected demand for tickets. The appeal fell on deaf ears. In the event

Ted Hufton manages to push an Arsenal shot around the post during the FA Cup sixth-round tie at Highbury in March 1930, but West Ham lost 3-0.

Hammers increased admission to 2s (10p) and that reduced the attendance to 25,000.

West Ham's success in 1929-30 lay in the performances of Vic Watson, whose 42 goals placed him at the top of the Football League's First Division marksmen. The only player in the whole of the League to exceed Watson's total was Jimmy Hampson whose 45 ensured First Division soccer at Blackpool for 1930-31. Watson scored in 30 of the 40 League matches in which he took part. His contribution to the Cup run was eight, of which Leeds United were on the receiving end of four, and at Wembley in his first international for seven years he notched two against Scotland.

There was an interesting diversion from football in September when Hammers met Fulham in a swimming contest at West Ham Baths. West Ham were represented by three current players (Walter Pollard, Charlie Cox and George Watson) plus back-room boy Alf Leafe, whose own playing career had been divided into two parts by World War One. Jack Hebden was allowed to compete in this particular event, although he was not now connected with either club. In fact it was he who had initiated the annual contests a few years earlier.

In the New Year, the Boleyn management announced that the club was planning a tour of South America. Matches had already been arranged in Valperaiso and Lima and it was expected that further games would be staged in Buenos Aires. But it fell through and the club substituted a trip to Sweden, Denmark and Germany.

Hammers got off to a blistering start for the new campaign of 1930-31. Nine goals were scored in the defeats of Huddersfield Town and Liverpool. The Merseysiders crashed 7-0 to a rampant West Ham led by Vic Watson in sparkling form. He was responsible for both goals against the Yorkshiremen and four of those that got past Arthur Riley, Liverpool's South African goalkeeper. The promise of a rewarding season was shattered in the very next game, however, when Aston Villa's Pongo Waring claimed four goals in his sides 6-1 victory. Middlesbrough emphasised the deficiencies in West Ham's rearguard by piercing it three times at Upton Park only 48 hours later.

When the dust had settled on 1930-31 Hammers had conceded 44 goals at Upton Park (which is still a record) but they had scored 56. Thus the Boleyn regulars had witnessed 100 First Division goals . . .an average of 4.76 per game when the average for the division was 3.94 per

Ambulancemen dish out buckets of barley water during the game against Huddersfield Town at Upton Park on the opening day of the 1930-31 season which got under way in soaring temperatures. The Hammers overcame the heat to win 2-1.

game. In one amazing spell in the New Year, Syd King's men scored 15 times in five games but could show only three points for their efforts.

Long absences by Hufton and Watson handicapped the side, but new recruit, Wilf James from Notts County, played well, a fact recognised by the Welsh selectors who capped him before the season was over.

Watson's absence allowed Viv Gibbins an extended run in the first team and his 21 outings produced 18 goals. The amateur notched West Ham's only Cup goal that season as his team went out 3-1 at home to Chelsea. A week later at Stamford Bridge he was once more on target against Chelsea but the Blues finished a goal superior.

A first-ever victory at Burnden Park got Hammers off to a splendid start for 1931-132. Tom Simms, the *News Chronicle* reporter, wrote: 'West Ham are going to be a force to be reckoned with this season . . .they completely overplayed Bolton Wanderers . . .Though they won by only one goal, the Londoners were never in danger of

Three months later, in December 1930, temperatures were very different when Manchester City visited Upton Park. Here City's Bobby Marshall slips as he attempts a shot as West Ham goalkeeper Bob Dixon and defenders Jimmy Collins and Alf Earl look on.

defeat. It was a case of West Ham first Bolton Wanderers nowhere.

Syd King's men followed this up with 3-1 win over Chelsea but then the season turned sour. The next seven games included six defeats . . .and a win against Newcastle United that cost the side the services of Tommy Yews for the next 15 games. Jack Wood filled in for Yews, and a few games later a deputy had to be found for Ted Hufton who was missing for the next 18 matches. Being well-blessed with goalkeepers, West Ham did not feel Hufton's absence overmuch. Tommy Dixon took on the 'keepers duties and a comparison of figures show that Hammers performed significantly better during his tenure.

The close season signing of Tony Weldon from Hull City had been expected to add punch to the forward line but Hammers management was soon wishing the cash had been spent reinforcing the back-line. After ten minutes of the match with Cup-holders West Bromwich Albion on 7 November, the visitors were four goals ahead . . .and all scored by one man, W.G.Richardson.

Within the week David Jack of Arsenal all but emulated Richardson's performance, in netting

three in the Gunners' 4-1 triumph over the Hammers at Highbury.

Staging a mini-revival, Hammers went eight games with only two setbacks . . .their best spell of the season. Among the four victories in this period was a 4-2 success against the eventual League champions, Everton, in which Jimmy Ruffell turned on some first-half magic to produce a hat-trick.

In December, a discontented Vivian Gibbins played his last game for West Ham. This very capable amateur, who first appeared for Hammers back in 1923, took his services across London to Brentford.

Two goals by Vic Watson prolonged Hammers involvement in the FA Cup and ended the hopes of injury-hit Charlton Athletic who played an hour of this tie with only ten men. For the second year in succession Chelsea applied the KO to West Ham. The 3-1 score was the same on both occasions but there was a change of scenery for the second match which was played at Stamford Bridge.

On a Wednesday afternoon in March 1932, Alf Chalkley, a full-back in his first season with the

Right: West Ham's Viv Gibbins watches his shot go wide against Aston Villa at Upton Park in January 1931. But Gibbins scored twice in a remarkable 5-5 draw. Below: This time Gibbins beats the Villa 'keeper to slam the ball home. Still the Hammers wallowed in the lower reaches of the First Division.

Hammers, earned himself a place in the record books. Playing for West Ham against Manchester City in a re-arranged First Division match at Upton Park, he scored his only goal of the season.

The *News Chronicle* reported it thus: 'The most remarkable incident associated with this match at Upton Park was the goal from which West Ham equalised 15 minutes from the end. It was scored by Chalkley, the left full-back, who when taking the kick was a few yards behind the half-way line. Chalkley was no less surprised than his colleague at the sequel and another astonished player was the Manchester City goalkeeper. . . .the ball that Chalkley kicked went straight through the air on its way into the net and Langford just had time to make a gesture at stopping it.'

City's goal in this drawn fixture was credited to young Matt Busby, also his only score of the season. The game also marked the return of Syd Puddefoot to the East Londoners, his ten years' absence having been spent at Falkirk and Blackburn Rovers.

Despite a string of poor playing performances, Hammers did not feel threatened by relegation. In mid-March they stood 15th in the table with nine games remaining and seven points between them and the nearest relegation spot. The club seemed totally unprepared for the disasters that lay ahead. Three shocking errors by Dixon led to a 3-1 defeat at The Hawthorns and got Hufton reinstated to the first team. But even his heroics couldn't keep the scores down, defeats at Sheffield Wednesday (6-1), bottom-of-table Blackpool (7-2) and at top-of-the-table Everton (6-1) sent the Londoners plummeting down the table. The only relief from this monotonous sequence of adverse results was Arsenal's surrender of one point when forced to survive 88 minutes at Upton Park without injured Scottish star Alex James.

After seemingly heading for certain relegation, Hammers arrived at their final fixture with a better than even chance of extending their stay in the top flight.

Bottom places in the First Division before the last games on Saturday, 7 May 1932 were:

		Home			Away					
Pos		P	W	D	L	W	D	L	F	A	Pts
20 Blackpool	41	9	3	8	2	6	13	62	101	31
21 West Ham	41	9	5	7	3	2	15	60	104	31
22 Grimsby	41	10	4	5	2	2	18	64	97	30

End of season fixtures for the relegation candidates were:
Chelsea (12th) v West Ham United (21st)
Grimsby Town (22nd) v Sheffield Wed. (3rd)
Sheffield United (7th) v Blackpool (20th)

There were a number of permutations to the outcome of this vital contest. Basically Hammers needed a point more than Blackpool and for Grimsby not to win.

Manager Syd King made drastic changes in the West Ham line-up. Versatile Jim Barrett was moved up to inside-left to support Watson and Tommy Yews given the inside-right position as partner to Jack Wood. The half-back line for such an important occasion was a little short on experience, namely Fred Norris, Wally St Pier and Joe Musgrave . . .only 24 appearances that season between them.

In the event they were easily beaten at Stamford Bridge and the other two results went against them as well. Charlie Buchan an old adversary with Leyton, Sunderland and Arsenal and now a football correspondent with the *News Chronicle* commented: 'West Ham United went out of the First Division of the Football League in an inglorious manner at Stamford Bridge. They made a poor effort to succeed against Chelsea, and it was hard to realise from their exhibition that this was one of the most vital matches in the history of the club . . .true they led by a goal at the interval but that was simply because the Chelsea forwards tried to reveal how clever they were with the ball . . .Proceedings developed into comedy when the news came through that Blackpool had won at Sheffield.'

Early in the second half Ferguson put Chelsea on terms and then ' . . .West Ham threw away the chance of a lifetime of regaining the lead. Allowed to go on when the Chelsea defence appealed for off-side, Watson and Russell had only Millington to beat. Watson passed to Ruffell but the outside-left misjudged the pass and Millington saved his final effort . . .Judged by this display West Ham will need to strengthen the team in practically every department in order to figure prominently in the Second Division next season.'

Pre-war Claret and Blues

BUCHAN'S warnings went unheeded and Hammers began the next campaign, 1932-33, with six men from the side that had failed so miserably at Stamford Bridge still in their line-up. The team at Swansea for the opening match also contained Jimmy Collins and Bob Dixon, who had each made contributions to the previous season's fall, plus an ageing Syd Puddefoot whose net-busting days were surely past.

Two fresh faces were those of Arthur Wilson and Hugh Mills. Newcastle-born Wilson joined Hammers from Southampton for whom he had scored 12 times in 62 League outings since August 1927. Mills was an unknown quantity, his career so far being confined to Glasgow junior soccer. The Scot's three years at Upton Park was spent mainly in the 'stiffs' but if figures are any guide to a player's ability, then his 16 goals in 23 first-team appearances was certainly recommendation for more senior duty.

Hammers began where they had left off in May. Four defeats and a draw in the first five matches preceded the initial Football League meeting with old rivals Millwall. A fine 3-0 victory over the Dockers (or Lions as they now preferred to be called) was followed by a lapse and three defeats in successive matches. One of them, a 6-0 thrashing, at Lincoln City, was the Imps' best-ever performance against West Ham.

During this poor spell, Hammers had brief glimpses of several opponents who would figure as team-mates in future years. Tudor Martin scored for Swansea at Vetch Field but Charlie Bicknell (Bradford City) Bill Adams (Southampton) and Tommy Tippett (Port Vale) did not match that distinction in their games against the Hammers. Yet another opponent, Plymouth's Jack Leslie, would, 40 years hence, find himself employed in the West Ham United boot-room.

As West Ham's situation deteriorated, so did the relationship between Syd King and the club's board. After many years of happy co-existence the club's perilous position in the autumn of 1932 was giving King an uneasy state of mind. This was reflected in his attitude at a board meeting where he verbally abused several directors who quizzed him about his dedication to his task. To compound his insubordinate behaviour, he was in an allegedly intoxicated condition.

Charles Korr's book *West Ham United*, published in 1986, describes the Boards reaction: 'The Directors met to discuss King's future and decide how to clear up the problems he had created for them. The formal resolution of the board stated that "owing to his insubordination and drunkenness (the discussion showed that the phrase was not limited to the events of the previous night), Mr E.C.King be suspended for three calendar months from the 9 November 1932 without salary and further stipulate that he shall not visit the ground during this period" The resolution of the board left open the possibility that King might be reinstated at the end of that period if the directors were satisfied with his conduct. However, his salary would be reduced to £8 per week and his position would be that of secretary. The resolution was precise in its wording and left no question that King's role in directing the players at West Ham was over. Members of the board might have anticipated that King would not return to the club in any capacity but had no way of knowing that he would commit suicide barely two months after his suspension.'

Syd King's demise had been swift but Hammers were most fortunate in having to hand a ready-made replacement in 53-year-old Charlie Paynter. Until now trainer and coach, Paynter was thrown in at the deep end in more ways than

West Brom goalkeeper
Pearson takes the ball off the
feet of the Hammers' Arthur
Wilson in the FA Cup
fourth-round game at Upton
Park in January 1933
when West Ham went
through 2-0.

Brighton defenders turn
away in despair as Jackie
Morton's winner hits the
back of their net at Upton
Park in February 1933, in
the FA Cup fifth round
replay.

one. With his side propping up the entire table, his task appeared awesome but he was encouraged by a few early results. A 5-2 home win over Grimsby Town was followed by the side's first away point in a goalless draw at top-of-the-table Stoke City. In a 7-3 victory against Charlton Athletic, five different Hammers contributed but none got as many as Cyril Pearce, the visitors' centre-forward, who scored all his side's goals.

A point was pinched at White Hart Lane where Spurs, third in the table, had already scored 35 goals against visiting opposition. Charlie Buchan, proven so accurate in his assessment of Hammers back in the previous May, reported the match for the News Chronicle: 'When the final whistle sounded at White Hart Lane, the West Ham players ran off the field shaking hands with one another and feeling very pleased with themselves. They had every right to, as they fully deserved the valuable point they took from Tottenham Hotspur, a point that will help them considerably in their struggle to leave the lower rungs of the Second Division ladder.'

Maintaining this fine form, Hammers suffered only one setback to the end of the year. Good progress was made in the FA Cup as Corinthians and West Bromwich Albion became the Boleyn men's victims in the third and fourth rounds respectively. The tie against the amateurs took place at The Crystal Palace, home of the FA Cup Final in the years preceding World War One.

For their fourth-round tie at Upton Park, West Bromwich Albion fielded eight of the side that made the devastating opening to the League encounter of 14 months before. There was no repetition of that display, however, as Albion, seventh in the First Division at the time of this match, missed a second-half penalty and went out of the Cup 2-0.

Hammers prepared for their next Cup match, a fifth round tie at Brighton, with a 6–1 defeat at Bury. In this match centre-half Jim Barrett scored a goal for each side to assist in third-placed Bury's double over the Londoners.

Brighton had battled their way to round five after beginning their Cup quest way back in October with a first qualifying round match against Shoreham. Since the serious part of the competition had been in progress they had seen off Crystal Palace, Wrexham, First Division Chelsea and Bradford (Park Avenue). Their FA Cup-ties of 1932-33 had realised 41 goals so far.

By half-time in the match against the Hammers that figure had risen to 43 but West

Ham had been credited with a goal, too, scored by Vic Watson. Ten years earlier, Vic Watson scored a vital equaliser on the same ground to maintain Hammers' FA Cup interest in that historic season of 1922-23. Now, In front of a new Goldstone attendance record of 32,310, Joe Musgrave levelled the scores in this 1932-33 clash and the replay went back to Upton Park.

Gallant Brighton were beaten at the Boleyn by a Jack Morton goal four minutes into extra-time. In his report for the News Chronicle, Frank Thorogood confessed to a little emotion over the result: 'A long experience of the hectic atmosphere of Cup-ties should have left me critically cold over the result of this replay, but when Morton scored what proved to be the winning goal four minutes after the beginning of extra-time I was almost persuaded to become a partisan and shed pious tears for the losers for although West Ham deserved to win during the last half an hours play, I thought it a bitter blow for a team which on the general run of the game had played the better and more scientific football'.

With the awkward lower division opposition out of the way, Hammers could now concentrate their attention on Birmingham, the next hurdle on the road to Wembley.

The Upton Park senior team had undergone a number of changes since the loss of First Division status but the influence of new manager Charlie Paynter was gradually being felt. At full-back, Albert Walker, previously with Bolton Wanderers and Barrow, was now partner to Alf Chalkley. Up front Ted Fenton had been given an early season try-out and Jack Morton was now firmly established in the team. Near the end of the season, Joe Cockroft would join the club from non-League Gainsborough Trinity, whilst Len Goulden would change his allegiance from Leyton/Chelmsford City to the Hammers. Clearly, moves were afoot to recover the club's lost position.

A scheduled Second Division match at Oldham Athletic was postponed on 25 February, but the day was marked by an event that could have had much more serious consequences.

The incident received minimal attention in the columns of the News Chronicle three days later: 'As a result of a motor accident last Saturday, George Watson, West Ham's goalkeeper, is ruled out of the sixth round Cup-tie against Birmingham at Upton Park. Because of Watson's mishap, Patrick McMahon, who is only 20, will make his senior debut. McMahon was secured

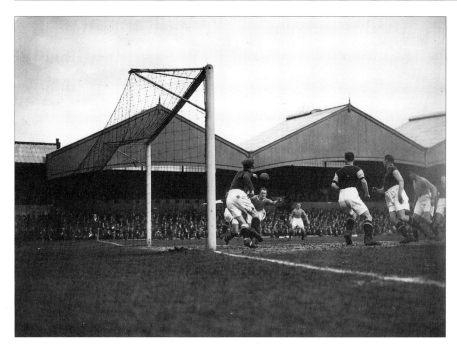

West Ham goalkeeper George Watson fails to stop a header from Everton's Dunn in the 1933 FA Cup semi-final tie at Molineux.

last September from St Anthony a Glasgow junior club. Watson had 20 stitches in head wounds and several in the throat. He is making good progress in St Barts Hospital. Jim Barrett was also involved in the same accident but escaped unscathed.'

Birmingham's path to the quarter-finals had been via Preston North End, Blackburn Rovers and Middlesbrough, all from the First Division. West Ham, London's last survivor in the current competition, could claim only one First Division scalp so far.

On the day of the match, 44,232 were admitted to the ground, but for many years this figure was quoted as 44,810 due to some ground official including the transfer turnstiles where fans could move from the terrace to the stand on payment of an additional sum.

Hammers delayed team selection until an hour before kick-off, then picked Walter Pollard at inside-right in preference to Syd Puddefoot. It was a smart move by Charlie Paynter, for Pollard not only created an open goal for Wilson to put Hammers 3-0 ahead, but snatched a goal for himself as well. However, these two incidents were but garnish on a triumphant occasion.

The tie had been won a little earlier as related in the next issue of the *Ilford Recorder.* 'Two miracles in two minutes – that was how West Ham passed into the semi-finals of the English Cup by beating Birmingham at Upton Park by four clear goals. No one who saw the match can deny that West Ham deserved to win, but without the smiles that fortune bestowed upon them I wonder where they would have been. At the end of half an hour's play they were struggling

rather adversely against the Midlanders, who were always the cleverest side and always the most dangerous. The first blow came when Barkas, the best full-back on the field, put past Hibbs, and then barely two minutes later Morton scored direct from a corner kick.'

Now, Hammers were not only the last surviving London team but the only non-First Division side remaining in the tournament. Their rivals at this stage were Manchester City, Everton and Derby County. The Rams had required a replay to get past Sunderland but were nevertheless favourites to lift the trophy mainly by virtue of their higher placing and slightly better results against the others in the League competition.

Had Hammers been able to choose their semi-final opponents, Manchester City (because of their fickle League form) might have been their choice, but each of the First Division trio presented an awesome prospect when viewed from West Ham's precarious position in Division Two. The draw, however, decreed that Hammers should meet Everton at Wolverhampton.

Molineux was an excellent choice of venue for both clubs. West Ham, in fact, had never been beaten there and many supporters could recall the epic second round tie of 1910 when Hammers, led by George Webb and Danny Shea, crushed the Wolves 5-1. Everton, too, had a liking for the ground, having won on more than half their visits.

Nearly 38,000 gathered for the 'Goliath v David' Cup semi-final where Everton were clearly the favourites. Hammers adopted spoiling tactics to bring the Merseymen down to their level, but George Watson, back in goal following his motor mishap, was much the busier 'keeper. After six minutes Everton went in front from a Jimmy Dunn header and held the lead until three minutes before the break when Vic Watson copied Dunn's example and levelled the scores with a header. Jim Barrett kept a tight rein on Everton's menace Dixie Dean, but Warney Cresswell, the Toffees' English international right-back, did a similar job on Hammers Jack Wood.

With seven minutes to go, Ted Critchley manoeuvred himself into a shooting position and got the ball past a lunging Jim Barrett and unsighted George Watson for the decider.

Everton went on to an emphatic 3-0 victory over Manchester City in the Wembley Final a few weeks later.

Cup success caused Charlie Paynter's team to get behind with their Second Division fixtures and in consequence they were forced to fulfil eight League and Cup engagements during a 23-day period in March. On the first day of April, League leaders Stoke City included 19-year-old Stanley Matthews and the Second Division's leading goalscorer Jimmy Palethorpe in their line-up and plundered two goals (and the points) that sent Hammers back into the crisis area.

		Home			Away					
		P	W	D	L	W	D	L	F	A	Pts
16	Grimsby T	35	5	9	3	4	2	12	60	78	29
17	Lincoln C	34	8	5	4	1	5	11	59	71	28
18	Oldham A	35	7	3	7	4	3	11	47	71	28
19	Burnley	34	5	7	4	3	4	11	56	69	27
20	WEST HAM	35	9	6	3	0	3	14	63	80	27
21	Chesterfield	35	8	5	5	1	4	12	48	73	27
22	Charlton A	34	6	3	7	3	4	11	53	74	25

Defeat at fellow strugglers Charlton Athletic plunged the Hammers even deeper into the relegation mire. On Good Friday rock-bottom was reached following a 1-0 defeat at Chesterfield, the previous occupants of the 22nd spot. In the latest two games, at Charlton and Chesterfield, Len Goulden then Joe Cockroft were drafted into the side and, as if by magic, the team started to click.

Four consecutive matches were won, three of them against teams in the top six places in the division. Such was the recovery that the final fixture at Plymouth Argyle didn't need to be won . . .and it wasn't.

Continuing the spectacular late form that preserved their Second Division status, Hammers began 1933-34 with an impressive victory over recently relegated Bolton Wanderers.

No significant new signings were made by Charlie Paynter but some experienced back-up was recruited in the form of Tommy Tippett (Port Vale) and Jack Landells (Millwall), who were both forwards. Landells had ended a eight-year association with Millwall in which he'd scored 69 times in 176 League outings.

Installed in the first team from day one, England Schoolboy international Len Goulden missed only two League games to the end of the season. He netted a hat-trick in the 4-4 draw at Plymouth Argyle and although he scored only four more times, he received rave notices for virtually every performance.

The most explosive start to any match at Upton Park occurred against Second Division leaders Preston North End on 23 September when Hammers scored three times in the first 12 minutes. Five goals ahead at the break Paynter's men declared at 6-0. The *News Chronicle* headed its report: 'THREE UP IN 12 MINUTES – WEST HAM WALK OVER PRESTON'.

The paper told its readers 'This was not a match it was a walk over. In the changed conditions underfoot, Preston were hopeless. Lowe slid and fell during the final minute to give Watson the opportunity, which he missed to put on what should have been West Ham's tenth goal. But it was not the altered conditions alone that were to blame for the Second Division leaders downfall. West Ham were streets ahead of them in all departments, forward and at wing half-back. The backs could not be compared as the home pair had so little to do, while Rutherford, the new goalkeeper from Watford, was not once really tested.'

Charlie Paynter had signed Jack Rutherford on the advice of Ted Hufton. The former Hammer, side-lined by injury for much of the time since joining the Hornets, thought Rutherford worthy of a place at Upton Park. Following a brief three-match return by George Watson, the former Watford man took over for all but three of the remaining matches.

On 25 November the visit of Southampton allowed three senior Hammers, Jim Barrett Vic Watson and Jimmy Ruffell, to renew acquaintance with George Kay, their former skipper. Barrett had superseded Kay, now manager of the Saints, as the Hammers centre-half. Kay had parted company with West Ham over six years before, yet these three men plus Jimmy Collins, who also played under Kay, were

Vic Watson leaps up in front of the Bradford City goalkeeper during the FA Cup third-round tie at Upton Park in January 1934. Watson scored twice as the Hammers won 3-2.

still first-team performers at Upton Park. Between them they amassed over 1,200 appearances for West Ham and there was still a little way to go.

If anybody thought there was limited mileage left in any of them it wasn't George Kay, for in the close season of 1935 he signed Vic Watson for the Hampshire club and squeezed another 36 games out of him.

A fine run carried the Hammers through 18 matches in which they suffered only four defeats. For a couple of weeks they occupied third place but too many drawn games prevented a sustained assault on the top spot. This was held by Grimsby Town for all the period between October and May and earned them the title and promotion. The Mariners' visit to the Boleyn proved unproductive and their experienced full-back, Hughie Jacobson, been made a donation to West Ham's score repeating his generosity of 11 months before.

By mid-February Charlie Paynter's boys had slumped to below halfway in the table and had crashed out of the FA Cup before 52,000 at Tottenham. It was the fourth time that Spurs and Hammers had clashed in the FA Cup since World War One, and 1939 would add yet another meeting.

There were smiles of satisfaction among Hammers officials in March as 20-year-old Ted Fenton scored his first goals for the club . . .a hat-trick against Bury. A couple of weeks later the young man snatched the winner in the odd goal defeat of Manchester United at Old Trafford that set his side on the way to a maximum six-point Easter.

Vic Watson's 26 goals ensured he was the club's leading scorer for the ninth of his 14 seasons at

Upton Park. The following season, however, would be his last before moving to the South Coast to join Southampton.

Because the Hull City ground was closed under an FA suspension, Hammers opening fixture of 1934-35 was postponed for three weeks. The Boleyn men started their season at home to Burnley on the following Monday evening and were beaten 2-1. After a comfortable 3-1 home win against Nottingham Forest, two resounding defeats set the alarm bells ringing. The first, a 5-2 reverse in the return Burnley fixture, gave the Lancashire club's supporters a chance to see their former goalkeeper Herman Conway in action with his new employers.

Within a week, another four goals were shot past Conway as Brentford repeated their 4-1 victory of a year earlier. Refusing to be panicked, Paynter made only minimal changes. Dick Walker, a recruit from the West London club Park Royal, was rested after two games and veteran Jimmy Collins was recalled to first-team duty. The full-back pairing of Albert Walker and Alf Chalkley was left undisturbed, as they were all season, but Paynter must have had another look at the pair following a 4-0 beating in the re-arranged Hull City match. A host of missed chances at Anlaby Road caused the Hammers manager to make alterations elsewhere and it was Vic Watson and Jimmy Ruffell who were missing for the trip to Bradford (Park Avenue) in late September.

There was much sadness around Upton Park in October, when the club announced the death of William F.White, the club chairman for the past 25 years. In his playing days Mr White had appeared for a rival team, St Luke's, but changed sides in 1903 when he secured a place on the Hammers board. He worked hard for the club and on occasion loaned it money. He was also a great supporter of the club's overseas trips and in 1931, at the age of 65, undertook the arduous motor coach trip to Switzerland.

The loss of the chairman came hard on the death of G.F.Davis, who had passed on just prior to the commencement of the season and J.W.Y.Cearns, the club's senior director, whose death in April had severed another link with the Thames Ironworks days. Both the latter men had been connected with the West Ham United club since its inception. This was certainly a sad period for the Hammers and Charlie Paynter in particular, for he had a long association with all three of those mentioned but none more so than his former mentor Tom Robinson, whose death in September 1934 at 83 must have caused him special upset.

Without the services of Watson and Ruffell, West Ham stopped unbeaten Bradford Park Avenue and at the same time registered their own first away win of 1934-35. A fortnight later Hammers inflicted a first home defeat on Norwich City and went on to record five consecutive wins. Hugh Mills, recalled to the side for the visit to Bradford, had scored in each of these. Hammers' run of success was halted at Old Trafford but Mills continued his agreeable habit until his failure to score in the away fixture at Bradford City cost him his first-team place. His ten appearances in 1934-35 had produced 11 goals, yet he never again appeared in West Ham's League side.

A revitalised Vic Watson returned to the West Ham team with a three-goal burst in the 4-0 home win against Notts County and triggered off a remarkable spell in which both he and Jimmy Ruffell scored in each of the next six League games. Of the 20 goals scored in this sequence, Watson claimed nine, Ruffell ten and Jack Wood one.

Defensively, Hammers were much meaner than a year ago. The ball was still getting past Conway but not in such quantity. At the season's end the figure was 63 conceded, a dramatic drop and the lowest number recorded by Hammers since the change in the offside law nine years before.

Charlie Paynter had now installed Ted Fenton at right-half alongside Jim Barrett and Joe Cockroft and these three, apart from a two-match absence by Fenton in January, saw out the season as the club's half-back line.

A splendid Christmas double over Bury hoisted West Ham to second place in the table behind Brentford. Both clubs had 32 points but the Bees possessed a superior goal-average. An opportunity to go top went begging as Hammers surrendered maximum points to two lower-placed rivals, Hull City and Nottingham Forest. The latter setback was all the more frustrating because Forest's success was their only win in a string of nine matches. Continuing their sudden reversal of form in the FA Cup the Boleyn men let Third Division North Stockport County off the hook when big Jim Barrett gifted them an own-goal equaliser three minutes from the end of the tie at Upton Park. The replay at Edgeley Park was barely three minutes old when the winner was struck.

The *News Chronicle* had 'Vulcan' at the match:

. . .on the play spectators will agree that Bradford City by virtue of defence alone were a trifle unlucky not to share the points. Backs and halves, noticeably Bicknell, Peachey and Mitchell, behaved well after a shaky start and the goalkeeping of Swindin reached a high standard. About 15 minutes from the end when the scoresheet still remained blank, Swindin in the course of his gallant work, received a nasty injury to his knee and thus handicapped he was beaten by Mangnall who scored the only goal of the match. The City goalkeeper had to be assisted off directly afterwards and Birkin made two very good saves in his absence. Swindin with great courage now returned, but the match had then been lost and won.'

The goalkeeper mentioned here is George Swindin who would later enhance his reputation with Arsenal in the years following World War Two.

Attired in an unusual white shirts and shorts, Hammers faced bottom-of the-League Notts County at Meadow Lane in what was a benefit for long- serving Magpie Mills. Poor Percy played a part in the defeat of his side by putting past his own goalkeeper Knox for West Ham's second goal. Some reports credit Jack Morton with the goal as it was his centre that Mills diverted.

The next three fixtures brought two wins and a defeat (at Blackpool) and on Saturday, 27 April, Hammers went to Burnden Park for their most important match of the season. A win would put them out of reach of Bolton Wanderers, and possibly Blackpool, and back into the First Division. A draw or a defeat would prolong the agony for another week.

The top of the Second Division on 27 April 1935 looked like this.

		Home			Away					
	P	W	D	L	W	D	L	F	A	Pts
1 Brentford	39	18	2	0	7	6	6	87	42	58
2 West Ham	40	17	1	2	8	3	9	77	60	54
3 Blackpool	40	16	3	1	5	7	7	78	54	52
4 Bolton W	39	15	1	3	9	2	9	90	46	51

Reporting the match for the *News Chronicle*, S.W.Bayley said that:'West Ham played football worthy of their position as contenders for First Division status at Burnden Park but Bolton played better. Wanderers reached an extremely high standard and Bill Cook was in his trickiest mood. West Ham were by no means easy victims. Their long accurate passes frequently spelled danger – Ruffell being the chief source of trouble – but they lacked just the requisite finishing touch near the penalty area. Goulden was another star in the West Ham attack, but Mangnall did not have too good a day.

Bolton secured the lead at the end of 23 minutes when Walton successfully headed past Conway following a corner. It was a surprise shot that put West Ham on terms. Four minutes later Goulden seized the ball some 25 yards out and let go with a great and unexpected drive which went into the Bolton net with home goalkeeper Jones quite unprepared. West Ham's fate was sealed in the first six minutes of the second half when inspired forward work brought the Wanderers two splendid goals from Westwood whose fierce drives left Conway helpless.'

The game drew a gate of 34,375, the highest League attendance at Burnden Park thus far in 1934-35. A midweek visit from Second Division leaders Brentford upped that figure to over 46,000 and the two points captured by the Wanderers in that game hoisted them into second place, a point better off than West Ham.

With a promotion place still unclaimed, the struggle for Second Division honours went to the last matches of the season. West Ham finished their campaign at Upton Park against already-relegated Oldham Athletic whilst Bolton had what appeared a more difficult trip to Blackpool. The Seasiders however had never had a success over Bolton in the eight matches played at Bloomfield Road. The top of the Second Division on Saturday, 4 May 1935 . . .the final day of the season.

		Home			Away					
	P	W	D	L	W	D	L	F	A	Pts
1 Brentford	41	18	2	0	7	7	7	89	47	58
4 Bolton W	41	17	1	3	9	2	9	95	47	55
2 West Ham	41	17	1	2	8	3	10	78	63	54
3 Blackpool	41	16	3	1	5	7	9	78	56	52

Charlie Paynter's men easily defeated Oldham Athletic but the effort was all in vain as Bolton bagged the point they needed at Blackpool.

Charles Buchan was at Upton Park for the *News Chronicle*: 'Against Oldham, West Ham, without over exerting themselves played well enough to gain a deserved victory over a poor side. It seemed to me that they were more concerned with the result at Blackpool rather than their own game. Yet they were never in danger of conceding a point. Having taken an early lead West Ham allowed their thoughts to stray Northwards. When the half-time news arrived that Bolton were on level terms the crowd spurred them on to greater efforts but

once it became known that Bolton were in front shortly after the interval all the interest in the game evaporated. It became a dull exhibition affair. In common with the crowd I must confess that I found the waiting period the more exciting. As time wore on it became apparent that Bolton must get the vital point. Even when the crowd learned that Blackpool had equalised the news came too late to rouse any great enthusiasm.'

Thus it was Bolton, as it had been in 1923, who denied Hammers a major football prize. Fourteen players plus Charlie Paynter and five directors made a 14-day tour of Sweden in May, a reciprocal visit for that made by AIK of Stockholm to Upton Park the previous winter. Four games were played and all ended in victory for the Hammers.

There was off the field drama in the Swedish capital when Hammers director Frank Pratt was taken ill. He was initially attended by West Ham's inside-forward Dr James Marshall, who diagnosed appendicitis. Mr Pratt was rushed to a local hospital where he underwent surgery.

Two fresh faces were in the opening match line-up at Norwich City's new ground at Carrow Road. Keeping goal was Vincent Blore, previously of Derby County and Aston Villa, while up front Peter Simpson was at centre-forward. On paper Simpson, a Scot, was a real capture for in six seasons with his former club Crystal Palace he'd found the net no less than 165 times in 195 League and Cup games. Hammers had obtained him pretty cheap too, having used Jack Wood in a part-exchange deal.

Regrettably Simpson's output didn't quite match what was expected of him. His 36 first-team appearances in two seasons saw him register 12 times before he moved on to Reading.

Blore, who was on the losing side five times in his first eight games, lost his place at that stage and appeared in an isolated game a few weeks later. In the meantime, Herman Conway's return seemed to inspire the team to more effort and it wasn't long before the Hammers were climbing the table. Between 6 October and 22 February only Fulham claimed maximum points in a League match. There was of course the unfortunate FA Cup episode when Luton Town, then in the Third Division South, won a replay at Kenilworth Road by 4-0. But that was just a hiccup.

In November, Charlie Paynter's men had won at Manchester United and a couple of weeks later, in a match of three scored penalties in seven minutes, took a point off Charlton Athletic at The Valley. These two clubs won promotion in May.

The death of King George V in the last week of January put the nation in sombre mood, but West Ham were on a high. A 2-0 win at Doncaster Rovers at the end of January put them into third place behind Charlton Athletic and Sheffield United. Marksmen in this match were Peter Simpson and Harry Lewis. The latter, a 24-year-old former Welsh schoolboy international, had seen Football League experience at Southend United and Notts County. His claim to fame at Upton Park was that he achieved a scoring rate of a goal-a-game in his Hammers career which lasted four matches. A number of former Hammers can equal the strike rate but not for as many as four matches. Lewis' figures, though, were boosted by a hat-trick against Bury on 1 February, a day that witnessed Joe Cockroft's first goal for the club. The day had another significance, for the goals by Cockroft and Lewis, mentioned here, were but four of the massive total of 209 scored by the Football League's (then 88) member clubs, equalling the record number scored on a single day set in 1932.

During the latter half of 1935-36, Paynter made a couple of notable signings. First, in January, he obtained the transfer of Fred Dell, Dartford's much sought after forward. Sunderland's manager Johnny Cochrane had offered the Kent non-Leaguers £3,000 for the youngster but the youth didn't want to go too far from home. With Arsenal, Derby County and Millwall all making soundings, Paynter got him for a bargain £1,250.

But it wasn't without cost, Charlie Buchan's column in the *News Chronicle* told of Paynter's adventures when obtaining the lad's signature:'West Ham United have beaten such clubs as Arsenal, Aston Villa, Derby County, Millwall and Sunderland in the race for the services of Fred Dell the Dartford inside-right. Their successful overtures can no doubt be attributed to Charlie Paynter the successor to Syd King as West Ham's team manager. The story of the efforts made by Paynter make interesting reading. last Friday he spent such a long time arranging matters to his own satisfaction between Dell and the Hammers that on his own homeward journey he missed the last ferry at Woolwich. This meant a circuitous route via the swing bridges with no conveyance available. On the way Charlie caught a severe chill and in consequence could not attend his club's match

last Saturday. It was the first match he had missed in his 30 years association with the club.'

Just prior to the March transfer deadline, Paynter made another important purchase when he brought Charlie Bicknell to Upton Park. Captain of Bradford City for the last two seasons, Bicknell's first appearance at the Boleyn had been back in August of 1932. Since then he'd brought his total of Football League appearances to 319. His figure included two seasons as a Chesterfield player in the late 1920s.

One of Bicknell's first appearances in the claret and blue was at Valley Parade against his old colleagues. Despite it being April, snow had fallen in the city on the morning of the match and was succeeded by a bitterly cold gale-force wind. An attendance of 12,000 had come mainly to see their old warrior, but City were also on a sequence of seven consecutive home wins and another today would set a new club record.

Jim Barrett lost the toss which forced his side to face the fierce wind. At the end of 45 minutes Hammers trailed by a goal but were undismayed for the wind was about to become their tool. But disaster struck within two minutes of the restart when Jeffries evaded a challenge from Albert Walker and slipped the ball to Bruce, who coolly slotted in Bradford's second goal. Paynter's men fought back in spirited fashion but were unable to recover the deficit. Each side scored a further goal, thereby giving the home side their new 'record home-win sequence' but creating for Hammers a steeper hill to climb for promotion.

Three of Hammers remaining four fixtures were away from home. At Filbert Street a last-minute goal by Leicester City's Dewis robbed Hammers of a crucial point and made the final home match of 1935-36 a real four-point cruncher against South London rivals Charlton Athletic. The leading places in Division Two on the morning of the Charlton match were as follows:

		Home			Away					
	P	W	D	L	W	D	L	F	A	Pts
1 Manchester U	38	15	3	2	5	7	65	78	38	50
2 Charlton Ath	39	14	5	0	6	5	9	84	55	50
3 West Ham	39	13	5	2	8	3	8	84	59	50
4 Sheffield U	39	13	4	2	5	7	8	70	46	49

Not surprisingly, the clash received quite a bit of attention which was reflected at the gate. The *Sunday People* reported 43,328 inside the ground when the gates were shut 40 minutes prior to kick-off but the general consensus from literature published since is nearer 42,000. In any event the figure exceeded that at all other matches in the

UK except the Scottish Cup Final at Hampden Park (89,000) and the Arsenal-Aston Villa game at Highbury (58,000).

The *Daily Mail's* correspondent W.W.Bouchier opened his Monday morning account for the match with: 'The victory on West Ham's ground that put Charlton well within sight of promotion was well earned. On the day they were beyond dispute the better team. In circumstances calculated to create an attack of nerves, Charlton largely escaped, and because they definitely proved themselves a team for the big occasion few begrudged them what was their finest victory of the season. Individually, save for Hobbis, they were not superior to the home men. In tactics however they gave West Ham a lesson.'

The main tactic was Don Welsh's shadowing of Jim Marshall which completely nullified the Scot's effectiveness. Prior gave Charlton the lead but the scores were levelled by Peter Simpson before half-time. Hesitancy on the part of West Ham defenders allowed George Robinson to plough his way through the Hammers' rear to restore the South Londoners advantage and Hobbis, with a long-range swerver, deceived Conway to gain Charlton Athletic two priceless points.

Hammers now required a couple of heavy winning margins to catch Charlton and the other promotion hopefuls, Manchester United, whilst Sheffield Untied, although still mathematically in contention, could be excused for not paying more attention to their League engagements with a Wembley encounter with Arsenal due on the last Saturday in April.

Two points were gained from the final couple of League matches, a 3-2 win at Port Vale and a 4-2 defeat at Bramall Lane but the real promotion battle had been lost in that tactical defeat by Jimmy Seed's Charlton Athletic.

There was, however, one distinction that Hammers earned in 1935-36, and it was the Football League's highest scorers away from home. The 39 scored on opponents' grounds couldn't be matched by any of the other 87 clubs.

Mangnall, missing for long spells, was the Hammers' chief marksman with 23, whilst Goulden (15) and Jimmy Ruffell (ten) each got into double figures.

Determined not to fail a third time, Paynter prepared for a fresh assault on promotion in 1936-37. Virtually all the players who had taken the club to the brink in 1936 were still available, except Dave Mangnall who had thrown in his lot with Millwall. And although Hammers still

retained Pete Simpson, Tudor Martin the experienced Swansea man was recruited as back-up.

'Will they be lucky the third time?' asked Charlie Buchan in his *News Chronicle* preview of the coming season: 'They say that only a poor start has prevented them achieving their ambition in each of the last two seasons. Given a flying start they are confident that the reverse will be the case this time.'

Beginning their pursuit of promotion with a home win over Tottenham Hotspur on the opening day Hammers quickly returned to previous patterns by losing the next three games. One of these unhappy events saw the remarkable debut of Tudor Martin at Newcastle where he scored three times in a 5-3 defeat.

By match number seven Charlie Paynter's boys were languishing in 19th place and he was forced to take action. The purchase of Arthur Weare, the Welsh goalkeeper of Wolverhampton Wanderers, enabled Conway to be rested and on the same day that Weare made his debut – in the 4-1 win over Leicester City – Charlie Walker took over from his namesake, Albert, at left-back.

Gradually the team was strengthened, first by the return of Charlie Bicknell following an appendicitis operation, and then by the replacement of Jim Barrett by Dick Walker. Barrett's overthrow was probably hastened by the previous week's fixture against Burnley when 17-year-old Tommy Lawton netted both his side's goal in a 2-0 win. This match also witnessed the, then, rare occurrence of a spectator on the pitch. The *News Chronicle* reported: 'The intruder was heading for the referee until Charlie Bicknell halted his progress.'

Former Southampton skipper, William Adams, made his first appearance, for Hammers, against the Saints at The Dell. A second-half goal from Adams added to the one by Foxall inflicted the Hampshire club's first home defeat and produced West Ham's first away win. Adams' first-team career at Upton Park lasted only two more matches but Tommy Green, a £3,000 buy from West Bromwich Albion, proved a bit more durable. Twenty-three-year-old Droitwich-born Green formed a right-wing partnership with Stan Foxall which saw out most of the rest of the season.

Another Midlander to arrive about this time was Birmingham centre-forward Sam Small. He made his first senior appearance in the 5-1 win at home to Bury and scored twice.

West Ham's forays into the transfer market and

the attempts by Paynter to turn Hammers' season around made little impact on the press. The newspapers, and indeed the whole nation, had only one subject on their minds during recent weeks . . .the plight of King Edward and his probable Abdication.

On Boxing Day the Hammers slammed Spurs by 3-2 at White Hart Lane to make it a double over the North Londoners, It was one of five they achieved during the season. On the other side of the coin, only Newcastle United and Burnley managed to take four points from the Hammers. Burnley's double extended the astonishing dominance the Turf Moor club had achieved over West Ham in recent times. The last ten League matches between the clubs had produced eight wins and two draws for the Lancastrians.

Another Lancashire side who were becoming a little tiresome was Bolton Wanderers. In this 1936-37 season they again blocked Hammers' path to FA Cup glory by winning a third-round replay by the narrowest of margins at Burnden Park.

Boxing Day's triumph at Tottenham had another significance – it set in motion a run of 22 League matches from which the Hammers collected 33 points. But the effort came far too late to cause any anxiety to the leading clubs, Blackpool and Leicester City. Hammers eventually finished in sixth place a far higher position than at one time looked likely.

In May, Len Goulden became the first Hammer for seven years to be capped for England. He scored on his international debut against Norway in Oslo.

Paynter made the capture of the 1937 close season when he signed Archie Macaulay from Glasgow Rangers for £5,000. The 22-year-old auburn-haired inside-left became an instant favourite at Upton Park when he scored twice in the Hammers' second public trial. Macaulay had missed the earlier trial in which Sam Small had also collected a few admirers by scoring the winning sides four goals on an inclement afternoon.

Charlie Bicknell was made skipper when the serious business got started which was at Villa Park. From the size of the crowd, some 45,000, it was apparent that hopes were high that the Midlanders would 'bring something home' this year.

Unable to repeat last season's success at Villa Park, Hammers went down by two clear goals. But it was another seven matches before the Londoners again tasted defeat.

For the first home match, against Swansea Town, a new boys' enclosure with its own sixpenny turnstile entrance was opened. It was situated at the West corner of the North Bank. Not long after its opening, however, some boys found it provided a way into the shilling enclosure by scaling the high railing partition. Management soon put a stop to this by placing a deterrent in the vicinity . . .in the shape of a policeman.

Victories in the first four home matches coupled with a share of the points on three excursions put Hammers up among the leaders but the side still hadn't managed a win on an opponent's ground. There was, however, wide appreciation of their play.

After the match at Southampton, the local *Football Echo and Sports Gazette* reported: 'Rarely has such brilliant play in attack been seen at The Dell as that which came from West Ham this afternoon. Macaulay, who was a mastermind, and Morton who showed amazing speed an ball control on the left wing were two stars and their work should have meant an easy victory for West Ham.'

If the West Ham defence had been as good as their attack they could be marked down even thus early in the season as hot favourites for promotion.

And a fortnight later, following an odd goal defeat at Hillsborough, the *Sheffield Green Un'* said: 'Though the first half at Hillsborough was goalless there was much to enthuse about, notably West Ham's combination and understanding.

'It was lucky for Wednesday that the shooting was not so formidable as the leading up work. The Hammers set Wednesday an example in combination and keeping the ball on the floor.'

At home the teamwork was equally as impressive but the maximum reward just as elusive. Against Fulham at Upton Park, Joe Cockroft almost presented the bottom-of-the-table visitors with two unearned points. After being in complete control of the game, Hammers' concentration lapsed and Fulham managed an isolated raid. Thinking the ball had crossed, the West Ham goal-line Cockroft picked it up but the referee thought otherwise and awarded Fulham a penalty. Jack Weare in the Hammers' goal saved Cockroft's blushes as well as Woodward's fierce shot.

A failure to score in five of the opening ten fixtures caused Paynter to enquire about Blackpool's goal machine Bob Finan, but he got

A Bradford defender gets in a tackle on West Ham's Jackie Morton at Upton Park in September 1937. The Park Avenue club were beaten 3-1.

had progressed beyond the third round.

Herman Conway was now back between the posts and his tenure would last until the penultimate game of the season. His second game back was at Bradford (Park Avenue) where local centre-forward George Henson had scored four FA Cup goals against Newport County a week ago. Henson managed to get the ball past Conway once and the goalkeeper was probably thankful to have caught him on an off day, for the Bradford man hit the back of the Blackburn Rovers' net six times in his next match.

Still unhappy with the output of the men he selected at centre-forward, Paynter, after deciding that Williams wasn't sufficiently effective, chose young Benny Fenton as a replacement but after two matches Fenton was dropped in favour of Sam Small. The former Birmingham man lasted five matches, then Williams was recalled for one match, then Stan Foxall wore the shirt for two games. At this point Archie Macaulay came into the reckoning after scoring six times in a London Combination match against Queen's Park Rangers. Immediately installed as the first-team centre-forward, Macaulay made a sound start with two against Nottingham Forest, one of which was a last-minute winner. But he soon became afflicted with the 'anti-scoring complaint' and added only one more whilst at centre-forward.

Altogether six men – Small, Williams, Benny Fenton, Foxall, Macaulay and Goulden – were tried at centre-forward but none gave satisfaction. The problem lingered right up to the outbreak of World War Two and grew worse in 1938-39 when, at different times, seven men were given the opportunity of making a name for themselves.

Of 42 Second Division matches played in 1937-38, Charlie Paynter's men had failed to score on 14 occasions, easily the club's worst performance since the change in the offside law. There had been worse before the change. In 1908-09 and 1919-20, for instance, 15 matches

a negative response from manager Joe Smith, an adversary in the 1923 FA Cup Final.

In the end, Paynter enticed Rod Williams, of Reading, to Upton Park. The 28-year-old Welshman had been around a bit, having served Norwich City, Exeter City, Reading, plus a number of non-League clubs. In every instance he appears to have given value for money and he gave no less at West Ham where his nine outings produced five goals . . .the best goals per game strike rate at Upton Park in 1937-38.

Three of Williams' goals came in the Christmas games against Norwich City, but in the next match, against League leaders Aston Villa, he squandered a splendid scoring opportunity when pout clean through. Villa's equaliser in this encounter came after Weare had the ball knocked from his grasp by one of his own defenders and in attempting to retrieve it had pushed it over the line. It was a just outcome for Hammers' goal had been donated earlier by George Cumming, the visitor's Scottish international full-back.

The draw for the third round of the FA Cup paired West Ham and Preston North End at Deepdale. North End were placed fifth in the First Division at the time of this tie and only Charlton Athletic had been successful on the Preston ground since the start of the season. Facing Hammers on this bright winter afternoon was Bill Shankly, but the man who ended the Londoners' interest was George Mutch, Preston's 5ft 6in centre-forward who scored a second-half hat-trick. It was now four years since West Ham had seen West Ham goalless. Curiously, Hammers' best year in this respect was 1931-32 when, despite getting relegated, the side managed to score in all but four matches.

Three consecutive defeats at the beginning of April 1938 put paid to the slight hopes Hammers still held of promotion. During the match at Burnley a fire broke out in a wooden structure behind the main embankment, sending clouds of smoke across the pitch. Neither side was able to take advantage of the situation but Jack Morton did miss a penalty . . .after the danger had been averted. Interestingly the *Blackburn Sports Telegraph's* account of the game contains no suggestion of crowd evacuation.

Finishing the season on a high note, the Boleyn men had a splendid victory over Manchester United which forced the Old Trafford club to delay promotion celebrations for another week. Then with their last chance, Hammers recorded their first away win of the season by beating Chesterfield 1-0 at Saltergate.

Only one public trial was staged at Upton Park prior to the start of 1938-39. This was due to the Football League's decision to keep Saturday, 20 August free for a one-off programme of matches up and down the country to raise money for what the League called its Jubilee Fund. Hammers opponents on this day were Fulham, who were beaten 4-2.

The *Stratford Express* reported: 'Except for an occasional brief period this match at Upton Park on Saturday on behalf of the Football League's Jubilee Fund was a "go easy" affair and perhaps one could not blame the players for not risking injury with the League campaign opening on Saturday. As it was, Walker, the Hammers centre-half, received a nasty rap on the foot and did not come out after the interval.'

Hammers began with a couple of rapid raids that produced goals in the first and fourth minutes. The rest was very dull and only enlivened by two spectacular dashes through the Hammers defence by Ronnie Rooke to plunder Fulham's two goals. Most of the 14,000 onlookers would probably have preferred to be at The Oval where Len Hutton was just setting off on the way to a massive 364 against the Australians.

By coincidence, The Cottagers had an early opportunity for vengeance when the clubs faced each other the very next Saturday in the first match of the League season. The East Londoners were minus Dick Walker, injured in the last meeting. Hammers scored twice through Archie

Macaulay but it was not enough to prevent Fulham taking the points 3-2.

Maximum points were surrendered in the following two games as well before Charlie Paynter's men surprisingly brought two points back from Maine Road in a Wednesday evening encounter. This match saw the last senior appearance of Jim Barrett. After more than 460 outings, his only first-team games from here on would be wartime fixtures. Big Jim, as he was affectionately known, weighed in excess of 14st and had a shot like a cannon. He scored over 50 goals in his 15-season first-class career and played in virtually all positions in the side.

Strengthened by the return of Dick Walker, side-lined through the injury received in the Jubilee Fund match, the 'goals against' column began to look a little more respectable. With Macaulay still wearing the number-nine shirt, Benny Fenton and Sam Small shared the appearances at inside-right.

Coventry City came to Upton Park in mid-September with a commendable record of only three goals conceded in their opening five fixtures. They left with that figure more than doubled as Benny Fenton and Archie Macaulay each scored twice. The Scot was on the mark again a fortnight later, this time with three against Tranmere Rovers who were experiencing their first season of Second Division soccer.

Further representative honours came the way of two of Charlie Paynter's men when Len Goulden and Jack Morton were selected to form the Football League left wing against the Irish League in Belfast. The pair had been England partners against Czechoslovakia at Tottenham the previous December.

At this time the whole country was experiencing a spasm of mild euphoria following Prime Minister Neville Chamberlain's return from Munich with his famous piece of white paper.

On the day following Chamberlain's paper waving return, Hammers were visiting bottom-of-the-table Chesterfield. The political good news, however, only served to lift the home side who won by a single goal. By the middle of December, Hammers' League position had improved considerably. Jack Morton's goal against Burnley not only gave West Ham a rare victory over the Turf Moor side but also hoisted the club to within five points of leaders Fulham.

An interesting milestone was reached at West Bromwich on 10 December. When Archie Macaulay scored Hammers first goal, it was the

500th away goal the Londoners had scored in Football League matches since admission to the competition in 1919.

A double derby clash with newly-promoted Millwall was the Christmas fare for 1938. A heavy snowfall prevented the first match, at The Den, from taking place. And when the return fixture was played at Upton Park the following day, a thaw had reduced the pitch to a sea of mud. With a 42,000 mix of Hammers and Lions fans inside the ground, it was probably thought unwise to call it off at such a late stage. In the event both sides contributed to one of the most exciting games ever seen on the ground.

The *Stratford Express'* correspondent opened his report: 'There were no goals but plenty of thrills at Upton Park on Tuesday in this match which was the return of the one which could not be played at New Cross the previous day and more than 42,000 spectators saw play packed with incident throughout. West Ham were lucky to get a point, yet probably they would have won the match in the closing stages but for Foxall slipping up on the treacherous turf when he had the Millwall goal at his mercy. It looked a certain goal as he ran forward towards the goal, but at the moment he was about to shoot he slipped and fell and the chance was gone. It was the easiest of the match but had Millwall been beaten as a result of it they would have been very unfortunate.'

In goal for West Ham was 22-year-old Harry Medhurst, playing in only his second game. The *Stratford Express* commented 'I watched with interest the displays of Medhurst in goal in his first two League matches and was impressed with the clean way in which he fielded the ball. He had not much to do against Fulham but he was fairly well tested against Millwall, and the test was all the harder because of the slippery state of the ball.'

Medhurst, formerly with Isthmian Leaguers Woking, played more than 100 games for Hammers during the war. In the season of readjustment, 1945-46, he was the only Hammer with a 100 per cent attendance record. But in 1946-47 he was transferred to Chelsea, in a deal that brought Joe Payne to Upton Park.

But back in 1938, Medhurst managed to retain his first-team place in all but one of the remaining games. He took part in the splendid victory at Hillsborough where West Ham won for the first time since 1923, although only seven encounters had taken place in the meantime. The 4-1 triumph must have been particularly galling for Wednesday, for it was their only setback in a nine-match sequence, the other eight of which had been wins.

There is little doubt that the high spot of West Ham's 1938-39 season was the FA Cup competition. For the last four seasons their challenge had been ended, in sequence, by Stockport County, Luton Town, Bolton Wanderers and Preston North End, and in each case in the third round. This season they were a bit more determined and their increased resolution carried them as far as the fifth round. The Cup run included a thrice-played fourth-round epic against North London rivals Tottenham Hotspur.

A narrow 2-1 verdict at muddy Loftus Road set Hammers off on their FA Cup crusade of 1938-39. Facing Hammers in the Queen's Park Rangers goal was a young Reg Allen, who had been between the posts on the afternoon Archie Macaulay scored his double hat-trick in a Combination game the previous March. After the war, Allen was transferred to Manchester United for £11,000, a record for a goalkeeper at that time. Rangers had been defeated only once at home up to the time of this tie, but goals from Foxall and Morton ensured it was Hammers who progressed to round four.

For the fifth time since 1919, Hammers were paired with North London rivals Tottenham Hotspur. All the previous clashes had gone the way of the home side, which gave West Ham their only win in the series, in 1926-27.

As might have been expected, the 1939 event provoked quite a lot of interest despite counter attractions at Chelsea (who were playing Fulham), Millwall (against First Division Grimsby Town) and Arsenal (against Charlton Athletic in a First Division derby clash). With all this high-class soccer action about, Clapton Orient, not unexpectedly, had one of their lowest turnouts of the season for the visit of Aldershot.

Reserved and numbered seats for the Spurs tie were priced at 5s (25p) and 3s (15p) whilst standing on the terraces would cost 1s (5p).

The *Tottenham Herald* announced that, in preparation for the match, West Ham went to the seaside (to an unnamed destination) whilst Tottenham Hotspur went to Southend. Spurs filled some of their time there watching the Shrimpers overcome Chesterfield in an FA Cup replay. The local newspaper also revealed that Spurs would be wearing numbered shirts and that Hammers wouldn't.

A special LNER train service was provided from Enfield Town to Canning Town, to transport North London fans to East London. On the day, 42,716 crowded into Upton Park and they witnessed a thriller.

It was reported for the *West Ham Mail* by the 'Skipper', who headed his account: 'Flashing Foxall Goals Save Harassed Hammers After Spurs Thrusts.'

His report began: "A typical Cup-tie," I heard many of the great crowd of over 42,000 at Upton Park saying as they streamed away after Hammers' tussle with Spurs on Saturday. If they meant that the game had been a battle to the last ditch they were right, but to my mind that was about the only typical thing about this tie.

'So often does the excitement of the Cup bring the standard of play down with a bump, and so often do natural matches like this meeting of London rivals fail to live up to the high expectations of the rival supporters. "An ideal Cup-tie" is the description I would give this stirring game, for not for years have I felt so excited at a football match as I did at a match which more than realised every hope.

'All the elements of ideal entertainment for football fans were present. The players overcame shocking ground conditions in grand style and displayed remarkable speed, skill and stamina. Six goals were shared, and in an order that gave Hammers supporters alternate heart failures and raptures of delight. Then there was the schoolboy's hero worship tale come true, when Foxall was drafted into the middle in his side's hour of need and promptly scored two wonderful individual goals. The crowds intense relief at this dramatic escape of the home team was shown when they mobbed Foxall at the end.'

Hammers dominated the play and carved more openings but there was no doubting that Spurs had the greater fire power.

The report continued: 'From the home supporter's point of view, the switching of Small and Foxall when with less than half an hour to go – Spurs had established a 3-1 lead – was the feature of a match that will long be remembered. Within a couple of minutes Foxall outstripped for speed Hitchins, who had been too tenacious for Small. With his left foot – perhaps surprisingly for a man who usually plays on the right wing – he crashed in an unstoppable shot. Then with ten minutes left for play, Foxall repeated the trick with an even finer goal. He tore down the middle and appeared to have a chance to shoot with his right foot but he could not see enough of the goal to make sure, so he calmly dribbled to the left past Whatley and Hitchins drew Hooper over and

then – again with the left foot – crashed home an almost identical shot. No wonder the crowd went mad.'

West Ham's first goal had come from an Archie Macaulay penalty after Ward, the Spurs right-back, had blocked a cross from Morton with his hand.

In the last minute a mighty roar went up from the Spurs fans present as Duncan headed into the West Ham goal . . .and a sigh of relief could be heard from the home supporters as the referee ruled offside.

The teams on this important occasion were: **West Ham United:** Medhurst; Bicknell, C.Walker, Fenton, R.Walker, N.Corbett, Foxall, Macaulay, Small, Goulden, Morton. **Tottenham Hotspur:** Hooper; Ward, Whatley, Spelman, Hitchins, Buckingham, Sargent, W.G.Hall, Morrison, Duncan, Miller.

A heavy fall of snow made the White Hart Lane pitch unplayable for the following Wednesday's replay and it was rescheduled for Monday, 30 January.

Fifty-one thousand spectators were present at the Monday afternoon replay, including the *News Chronicle's* Charlie Buchan, who reported: 'After two hours of really hard work, Tottenham Hotspur and West Ham failed to settle their FA Cup difference. Nor do I think they will do so until one of them realises that football really can be played in a Cup-tie and settles down to its true League form. That was the trouble in this hectic replay. Both teams played vigour and pace before skill. Hard, first-time tackling safety methods and solo efforts were the order of the day. They provided many thrills, but they robbed the game of much of its sparkle.'

Both goals came in a three-minute spell just after the half-hour mark. Spurs went ahead when Morrison provided Sargent with an easy chance and Foxall levelled from a Charlie Walker free-kick.

In the 14th minute, Macaulay missed a penalty and near the end Small also missed an easy chance from six yards when he shot tamely at goalkeeper Hooper. During the extra half an hour Ted Fenton received an injury to his jaw. A fracture was suspected and he was taken to hospital for an X-ray.

A date for the second replay could not be agreed upon, Tottenham preferring Monday, 6 February and Hammers the Thursday of the current week. The FA was asked to intervene and decided on West Ham's choice.

Highbury was chosen as the next meeting

After Stan Foxall had equalised for West Ham in their fourth-round FA Cup-tie against Tottenham Hotspur at Upton Park in January 1939, this spectator ran on to the pitch and booted the ball back upfield. The game ended 3-3 and the Hammers eventually went through after a 1-1 draw at White Hart Lane and a 2-1 second replay victory a Highbury.

place before another 50,000-plus gate. The *Tottenham Herald* headed its account of the game: 'Spurs Go Down Fighting After Extra Time.'

'The cheering when the teams took the field indicated that Spurs had the greater measure of vocal support. Spurs kicked-off facing the sun and wind and Morton, who had caused so much trouble on Monday, was soon prominent and from one of his centres Small missed the proverbial 'chance of a lifetime' for when almost under the bar, he shot wide.'

Following a period of constant West Ham attacking, Spurs broke away and gained the lead through Morrison. For an hour the North Londoners held on to their advantage but then West Ham equalised.

The *Tottenham Herald* described it thus: 'With 15 minutes remaining, West Ham got on terms with a peculiar goal. The ball was punted forward and Foxall, now at centre-forward, raced for it as did three Tottenham defenders. But Foxall got there first and with a grand shot beat Hooper as he advanced. This was splendid opportunism on Foxall's part as it looked hopeless for one man to try to get the ball from three defenders.'

An injury to Morrison reduced Spurs to ten effective men as extra-time began. Play was even at this stage, although West Ham came closest to scoring when Hitchins cleared off his own goal-line. As the last spell of extra-time ticked away, Sam Small gave chase to a ball that was almost certain to end up out of play.

'Small surprised everyone when he retrieved a ball that looked as though it was going out of play. His centre was taken by Macaulay, who, having

an open goal, gave West Ham the victory.' Only one Football League game (against Chesterfield at home) separated the Highbury victory from the next-round opponents, Portsmouth. The Hampshire club had progressed this far by defeating Lincoln City 4-0 and West Bromwich Albion 2-0, both at home. In the League they occupied 20th place in the First Division.

It was the third time West Ham had been entertained by Portsmouth in FA Cup-ties since 1927-28, when the Hammers won a third-round tie 2-0. In 1928-29, Pompey had won 3-2 in the quarter-finals.

For this important occasion the LMS Railway ran an excursion from local stations to Portsmouth for 7s (35p) which started from Barking at 10.26am.

For those who couldn't make the trip, the Boleyn ground was hosting the English Schools FA Shield fifth-round replay between West Ham Boys and Swansea Boys.

A new attendance record was set at Fratton Park when 47,614 paid for admission. The figure included a large contingent that had travelled from East London.

Hammers were weakened even before they got on to the field when Jack Morton went down with 'flu. Benny Fenton was called in to take his place. After the event the *Stratford Express* harped on Morton's absence at regular intervals throughout its 20-column inches of match report: 'If matches were won by footballing merit and not by the number of goals scored, West Ham would have been successful in the FA Cup-tie at Portsmouth. For three parts of the game they gave the home team a lesson in football culture, but failed in the all-important factor of getting the ball into the net.'

Goals by Parke and Worrall in a ten-minute spell in the second half won the tie for Portsmouth and the newspaper commented: 'Thus they succeeded in doing twice in that short space what West Ham had failed to accomplish in an hour while they dominated the attack.'

Opportunities came and went: Fenton was robbed when well placed to shoot; Macaulay cleverly worked himself a good position but narrowly missed; Goulden tested Pompey goalkeeper Walker with a 20-yard 'stinger' which he stopped on the goal-line; and a well placed effort by Tommy Green from the edge of the penalty area beat the home goalie but was headed off the line by Rookes. The best chance fell to Foxall who, put through by Macaulay, delayed his shot too long and lost possession. With Hammers trailing by a goal, Foxall created a chance all on his own but, after weaving his way through a maze of Portsmouth defenders to within ten yards of goal, he chose to pass instead of having a go and the opportunity was lost.

Then in the 80th minute: '. . .any doubt that might have remained regarding the result was wiped away when Portsmouth scored again. The goal resulted from a free-kick just inside the Hammers half and Guthrie planted the ball well into the goalmouth. Medhurst jumped to punch it away but Worrall beat him to it and headed the ball into the net. It was the end and the better side had gone down because they had not taken their chances.'

The *News Chronicles'* Frank Thorogood agreed that the tie had been there for West Ham's taking: 'Scoring twice in the second half, Portsmouth passed into the next round of the Cup at the expense of a team who commanded so large a share of the game before the interval that victory seemed only a question of time. At half-time, indeed, home supporters were just hoping for the best and preparing secretly for the worst but eventually they had the joy of shouting Pompey to victory. On the brilliant scheming form of Macaulay in the first half together with the raiding qualities of Len Goulden and Ben Fenton, only a confirmed optimist would have predicted the defeat of West Ham.'

Hammers had little time to dwell on their FA Cup misfortunes for they were back in League action at Swansea Town on Thursday of the following week. If a reaction was expected it failed to show, but the Londoners still lost, by the odd goal of five. This match was the last senior appearance of Tommy Green, for a couple of weeks later he became a Coventry City player.

Two days after the defeat at Swansea, Nottingham Forest were beaten 5-0 at the Boleyn but there followed a sequence of nine games, in seven of which Hammers failed to score. The second of these was against a revenge-seeking Tottenham Hotspur who got what they came for and departed Upton Park with both League points. Benny Fenton, who played his last game for Hammers in this fixture, was sold to Millwall for £5,000, on the last day for unrestricted transfers.

At Norwich on 6 March, Hammers scored six. By half-time they had established a 3-0 lead, but the City cut this to 3-2 before a blistering six-minute spell increased the difference to 6-2. The *Eastern Football News* described the last West Ham goal, scored by Foxall: 'A few minutes later Foxall scored a brilliant goal. Beating man after man he still had the ball at his feet when he passed Hall, the Norwich City goalkeeper, and walked the ball into the net.'

As the season drew to a close it began to look as though Hammers had missed the promotion boat once again. The despondency following home defeats at the hands of Luton Town and Bradford (Park Avenue) was only temporarily lifted by a satisfying victory at The Den. In this match, newcomers George Foreman, playing his second game, and George Proudlock, making his debut, scored a goal apiece. Stan Foxall could have made the score even more emphatic but missed a 75th-minute penalty.

Twenty-five-year-old Foreman (no relation to an earlier Hammer of the same name) was an amateur with Athenian League club Walthamstow Avenue before turning professional for the Hammers. Although not a regular in Avenue's Athenian League championship side of 1937-38, he did gain a permanent place in 1938-39 and had netted 22 Athenian League goals in 14 appearances prior to his departure to Upton Park.

Northumberland-born George Proudlock was approaching his 20th birthday when he scored the goal at Millwall that placed him on the list of West Ham's debutant scorers, a list that did not include such names as Shea, Puddefoot, Watson or Ruffell.

Meanwhile, on the same afternoon that Proudlock was making his mark, back at Upton Park somebody even younger was doing likewise. In a London Midweek League game against Brentford, 15-year-old Eddie Chapman headed West Ham into an 18th-minute lead from a pass provided by Terry Woodgate, himself a teenager.

Young Chapman who had just completed his schooling was getting a lot of coverage in the local *Ilford Recorder* in the late 1930s. One issue highlighted his goalscoring achievements for Loxford School and others in 1936-37: 76 goals for Loxford School; 15 in seven matches for Ilford Boys; 1 in a South v Midlands Schools Trial; Total 92. In one game he is reported to have scored 12 times. At cricket too he was no slouch, his summer exploits also being well documented by the same paper.

Shortly after the London Midweek League encounter against Brentford, Woodgate was drafted into the first team for the home fixture with Bradford (Park Avenue) but it was another nine years before Chapman got his chance. By the time Chapman lined up alongside Woodgate in a Football League match, the older man had made 86 appearances.

With five matches of the season remaining, West Ham struck their richest vein of form. Only Coventry City, who had an outside chance of promotion, took a point off Hammers during this spell. Beatings were handed out to Bradford (Park Avenue) and Southampton on visits, while West Bromwich Albion and Manchester City each surrendered both points at the Boleyn. The last victory completed Hammers' second double for the season. The first had been at the expense of Norwich City.

A number of new faces had been seen in the West Ham colours in the last few matches. The most notable being that of Stan ('Dizzy') Burton, who only seven days earlier had been displaying his talents for Wolves against Portsmouth in the FA Cup Final at Wembley. Cliff Hubbard, who also made his West Ham debut in that last fixture against Manchester City, had been recruited from Hull City. Reg Gore, an outside-left from Frickley Colliery, scored on his debut against Bradford (Park Avenue) and retained his place for the last five matches. And 21-year-old Doncaster-born Arthur Banner made his only pre-war Football League appearance in the 2-0 win at Southampton.

The referee's whistle at the end of the Manchester City match signalled the conclusion of another soccer season for everybody on the field except Len Goulden. He would shortly rendezvous with the rest of the England team for a three-match tour of Italy, Yugoslavia and Romania.

By the time the playing staff returned for pre-season training in the summer of 1939, the political situation in Europe had worsened considerably. Everywhere people discussed the prospects of war, dreading a repeat of the events of 1914-18. With shrewd foresight the West Ham United chairman saw the possibility of the club's players and staff being scattered to all corner of the globe in the event of hostilities. In an effort to, at least, delay this eventuality, Mr Will Cearns recommended that the first team should enlist with the Reserve Police and the reserves with the Territorials.

The uncertain future made planning speculative and this was indicated at Upton Park, in August 1939, by the absence of any new playing staff who cost money.

As a result of the chairman's recommendations, Charlie Paynter was 14 players short at the first session of pre-season training. The absentees were at Huntingdon undergoing training with the 64th Searchlight Regiment. They were, however, back in time for the public trials which preceded yet another early start to the season to aid the Football League's Jubilee Fund.

On the hottest day of the summer, West Ham faced Fulham, the opposition in the previous year's Jubilee encounter. Watched by a 10,000 plus crowd who raised £521 for the Football League's Fund, the players and officials toiled through the sweltering 90 minutes for a 3-3 result. Within a week the new season was under way, but it reached only the second Saturday before hostilities brought things to a halt. West Ham had taken part in three matches at the time the season was abandoned.

26 August, Plymouth Argyle 1 West Ham United 3
28 August, West Ham United 2 Fulham 1
2 September, West Ham United 0 Leicester City 2

With the prospect of imminent aerial bombing, the Government issued a number of proclamations banning large gatherings of people such as at soccer matches, race meetings and cinemas. After a couple of weeks the restrictions were relaxed a little and limited assemblies were permitted in safe areas. Such an area was Bournemouth where Hammers played their first friendly of 1939-40. At soccer matches notices were posted at strategic places instructing spectators what to do in the event of an air-raid and the same directives were repeated in the programme.

Had the 1939-40 season been a peacetime competition, Hammers would have been delighted with it. There were goals galore with hefty defeats inflicted on old and traditional rivals. Tottenham Hotspur, for instance, lost all their five encounters with the Hammers and Chelsea lost all their four. Millwall did best by claiming two wins in five matches. Charlton Athletic were beaten 9-2 in one of the friendlies before the Regional League system began. In two consecutive matches in the spring, Chelsea were defeated 10-3 at Stamford Bridge and Tottenham Hotspur 6-2 at White Hart Lane. West Ham took part in only one goalless draw in all matches played after the Football League programme was aborted, and failed to score in only two others.

Few guest players were used in this first wartime season until the Hammers' Cup success caused a fixture jam which highlighted their shortage of manpower. Two fixtures were scheduled for the week leading up to the Football League War Cup Final at Wembley, and

Action in the West Ham goalmouth during the 1940 Wartime Cup Final at Wembley against Blackburn Rovers.

Hammers were forced to borrow players from elsewhere. In the event only Big Jim Barrett was a bona-fide Hammer in the match against Charlton Athletic on 5 June.

West Ham's path to the Football League War Cup Final had been via Chelsea, Leicester City, Huddersfield Town, Birmingham, and Fulham. The semi-final against Fulham at Stamford Bridge kicked off at 6.40pm in order that war workers would not be tempted to take the afternoon off. The Final itself began at 6.30pm for the same reason.

Having been released at the end of 1938–39, goalkeeper Herman Conway was unattached at the time of the Final, so in effect he was a guest. The side that took the field to oppose Blackburn Rovers in the Wembley Final of 8 June 1940 could easily be accepted as a genuine West Ham XI. Every one of them had done long stints of recent first-team duty and that qualification applied to Conway as well. It was originally intended to play an extra half an hour in the event of a draw at 90 minutes, but this was altered to 20 minutes. If there was still a stalemate at that stage, then the match would continue until one team did score and thereby end the match. The

arrangement proved unnecessary because Sam Small's 34th-minute goal was the only one scored at the end of normal time.

The *West Ham Mail's* report of the match began: A solitary goal scored after 34 minutes gave West Ham United a victory which they just deserved in the Football League War Cup at Wembley Stadium on Saturday evening. Summed up briefly: The Hammers had the better of Blackburn in the first period and scored once while the Rovers dominated the second period without success. It was neither a poor game or a great match. It was purely and simply a battle between two grand defences – probably the best in the country.

First Lord of the Admiralty, M.V.Alexander, presented the trophy and medals. Then, according to Ted Fenton in *At Home with the Hammers*: . . .'we players quietly split up and went straight back to our Service units'.

For the second wartime season the Football League introduced some new ideas, the most important of which was that points would be abolished and goal-average would decide League placings. Clubs would be segregated into north and south regions and could select their opponents. First and Second Division sides would be expected to play at least two Third Division clubs.

Hammers played eight matches against lower division clubs and were beaten twice. It was, in fact, a side that Charlie Paynter's boys didn't play that finished in top place . . .Crystal Palace. But the object of the exercise was not about winning but more about keeping the club 'ticking'. It was more profitable to lose at home to Millwall or Arsenal in front of 10,000 than to wallop Reading or Southend 10-0 before 500. Hence the League insistence that the big clubs spread themselves around a bit.

Cup-ties provided the soccer with the bite in it and the numbers that attended these competitions confirmed that this was what the soccer public much preferred. At Chelmsford in November, the Regional League South encounter between Southend United and West Ham attracted 1,000 customers, but a Football League War Cup clash, with the same sides, in March had 3,500 onlookers. There were dozens of other similar instances. Incidentally, Southend United, who were forced to vacate their ground in 1940, had sought a ground sharing arrangement with West Ham before accepting the Chelmsford City offer to use their New Writtle Street ground.

With the war now intensifying and the daily bombing a constant menace, the availability of players became more and more unreliable. The *West Ham Mail* reported events at Fulham in December 1940 when Hammers arrived a man short: 'Fate played a scurvy trick on Fulham on Saturday. J.Osborne, the Romford centre-forward, was due to celebrate his debut for them, but West Ham arrived one short, it was decided at the last moment that he should fill the gap. He partnered Chapman on the right wing, acquitted himself well and, to complete the chagrin of his team, scored the visitors' winning goal.'

A couple of weeks later both Millwall and Hammers were a man short for their group match in the London War Cup. Bill Voisey, the 50-year-old trainer of the home team, filled their vacant spot but Hammers waited until half-time for Ted Fenton to turn up.

Surprise winners in the London War Cup were Reading, who had a convincing 4-I victory over Charlie Paynter's boys at Elm Park and then snatched a point in the return at Upton Park. Arsenal were Hammers' stumbling block in both Cup tournaments. The Highbury club (although using Tottenham's ground at this time) were

victors in both legs of the Football League War Cup and performed the double against the Boleyn men in the group matches of the London War Cup. Despite their dominance of Hammers in the Cups, the Gunners were unable to get their hands on any silverware in 1940-41.

Forced to call on outside help in these competitions, Hammers used George Green and Harold Hobbis of Charlton Athletic, and Berry Nieuwenhuys, Liverpool's South African forward. The three made a number of appearances in the Regional League games as well, along with Benny Yorston of Middlesbrough and Bernard Joy, Arsenal's accomplished amateur centre-half who became a soccer correspondent with the *London Evening Star* after the war.

Failing to score in only two games ensured Hammers a high placing in the Regional League South. Their 1.794 goal-average was good enough for second position behind Crystal Palace's 1.954.

For the following season, 1941-42, the orthodox points system was restored but a crisis developed when the London clubs, supported by one or two others from the home counties, rejected the Football League's regional fixtures on the grounds of unnecessary travel and set up their own competition.

Until April of the following year, all 11 of London's senior clubs were under the threat of expulsion from the Football League, but they went ahead with their 16-club tournament which included clubs as far away as Portsmouth, Brighton and Reading after falling out with the League over travelling to Southampton, Luton, and Norwich.

Although not scoring as heavily as some of their rivals, Hammers were in third place when the season came to an end. Forty-three goals out of a total of 81 were scored on opponents' grounds. This figure was inflated due to the generosity of the defenders of Chelsea and Watford, who each conceded eight, and Brentford, whose rearguard yielded five. A week after the Brentford game, Hammers had a taste of their own medicine when visiting Crystal Palace crashed five past big Jim Barrett, deputising in goal following the non-appearance of the regular goalkeeper.

Heading the scorers was George Foreman with 21 London League goals. Three other Hammers – Small, Goulden and Foxall – got into double figures but the best goals per game marksmanship came from Eddie Chapman. He produced six goals in seven appearances including a hat-trick against Aldershot at the garrison town in January. At Reading in November, Harold Cothliff, a pre-war Torquay United half-back 'guesting' at Elm Park, got the ball into the West Ham net inside ten seconds.

One of West Ham's 'guest' players in 1941-42 was Harold Rickett, goalkeeper of Southend United. Rickett had recently been in front of the Football Association's disciplinary committee explaining a misdemeanour. Late the previous season, Rickett was keeping goal for his club in a Regional League match at Crystal Palace. He got himself involved in what he thought was an incorrect decision by the referee. His protest became heated and after a while he walked off the field in disgust. The referee ordered him to return but he declined and play was held up for about ten minutes. The outcome was that Rickett was suspended for one month for improper conduct and leaving the field of play without the referee's permission. Southend United lost the match 7-0.

Progress in the London War Cup was once again blocked by Arsenal. In the group matches the clubs defeated each other and won all their other games (against Clapton Orient and Brighton and Hove) but Arsenal's ten points were backed by a much superior goal-average. Hammers' 4-1 win at White Hart Lane in this competition was watched by 22,000, an indication perhaps, that the authorities were turning a blind eye to earlier restrictions.

As the 1942-43 season neared, a number of West Ham players were approaching or had just passed the century of wartime appearances. George Foreman led the way with 118 in League and Cup, followed by Stan Foxall on 116. On the last day of the previous season, Charlie Bicknell had reached 100 and on the opening day of 1942-43, Goulden reached his century. In the London War Cup-tie against Brighton at Upton Park on 4 April, George Foreman recorded his 100th wartime goal.

A fine 5-4 victory at Portsmouth opened the new campaign and three wins and a draw were to follow. However, three defeats in a row set the club into a pattern of inconsistency that marked the rest of the season. Charlie Paynter used 37 players to get through 28 Regional League South fixtures and they included such names as Sam Bartram (Charlton Athletic), Cyril Trigg (Birmingham) and Peter Kippax, the Burnley and England amateur international who was to gain an FA Cup runners-up medal in 1946-47.

Paynter had experienced great difficulty in raising a side for the first fixture at Portsmouth. He covered countless miles visiting the commanding officers of his various players in an effort to obtain them leave. He told a local reporter that things would get worse now that he had lost the use of his car and was having to do many journeys by bus and on foot.

Two players who would not be helping Paynter in the immediate future were Charlie Bicknell and Eddie Chapman. Bicknell was missing from the opening two matches while recovering from a minor nose operation, and Chapman, who signed professional forms in late September, was now serving as a sapper in the Royal Engineers. One piece of good fortune that came Paynter's way about this time was the signing of Willie Corbett, brother of Norman, already a Hammer of long service.

Top scorer was once again George Foreman with 23 from 28 outings, 11 more than Len Goulden, who missed four matches. Most pleasing was Richard Dunn's 12 goals in 11 games which included two hat-tricks. His first came in the New Year demolition of Clapton Orient, which Hammers won 10-3, and another against Aldershot at the end of the same month. Later in life Dunn became a prison officer at Durham gaol.

In the Football League South Cup Group One, Hammers failed again. But they did maintain an interest right up to the last group match, against Arsenal at Tottenham. Defeated at home by the Gunners and dropping a point at Watford certainly dimmed Hammers' hopes, but Arsenal inexplicably let a point slip at Vicarage Road as well. So Charlie Paynter and his men went to White Hart Lane needing a 2-0 win or better to go through. Yet again the North London club foiled West Ham's endeavours. Three goals, from Denis Compton, Cliff Bastin and Briscoe, against one from Sam Small, put an end to Hammers' dreams. More than 31,000 watched the game.

Watford played an important part in West Ham shortcomings in 1943-44. Two crucial Cup defeats at the hands of the Hertfordshire club, added to the 4-0 setback at Stamford Bridge, left Hammers with too much to do. Even so, they went out with a flourish, beating Chelsea, the qualifying club, 6-1 in the final group match.

In the Regional League South, George Foreman played in very one of the 30 fixtures, the third season in a row he had completed a full house. It was a remarkable performance in the circumstance. In the London *Evening News,*

Charlie Paynter described Foreman, along with Lewis and Small, as 'war workers' which explained their availability being more regular than that of their soldier team-mates.

The season saw 38 players used in the Regional League with a fair sprinkling of 'guests'. Some, like Dai Jones of Leicester City and Harold Hobbis, the Charlton Athletic man, were becoming familiar figures.

For virtually all the war seasons Hammers were blessed with a good supply of capable goalkeepers. Herman Conway was the man between the posts at the outbreak but he was succeeded by Medhurst and Gregory. When these two were unavailable, the breach was filled by George Taylor (Hammers' third-choice goalkeeper) or maybe Sam Bartram (Charlton Athletic), Syd Hobbins (also Charlton), Doug Flack (Fulham) or George Swindin (Arsenal).

Since January 1943, Hammers fans had seen a good deal of Tommy Walker, a 19-year-old right winger from Newcastle United. He filled in when Dunkley of Manchester City couldn't assist, or when Foxall or Jack Wood were unavailable. Young Walker gained FA Cup winners' medals with Newcastle United in 1950-51 and 1951-52.

In February 1944, Paynter gave a first-team chance to a 20-year-old from Worthing named Eric Parsons. He became a great favourite with the Upton Park crowd with his spirited play and his speedy dashes along the touch-line. He probably reminded older fans of Herbert Ashton, another great favourite of pre-World War One days. Eric played in a Football League South Cup Group 'B' match at Southampton and followed this with a home League game against Fulham on 1 April, but then had to wait just under three years before making his next senior appearance.

During the close season of 1950 Parsons would be selected by the FA to go on the England 'B' tour of Scandinavia, where he made a great impression. He impressed the Chelsea management, too, for the West Londoners negotiated his transfer shortly afterwards.

Adolf Hitler's launch of the V1 flying bomb offensive on England in 1944 had a destructive impact on West Ham United when one rocket fell on their ground in August. In order not to give even useless information to the enemy the *Stratford Express* preview of the new season was headlined: 'West Ham FC's Ground Trouble. Away Matches Only at the Start.' The report began: 'West Ham United will commence the season under ground difficulties, and Mr Charles

Paynter, secretary and manager, says that it is probable that all matches for the first two months will be played away. He told a reporter that this does not mean that the club will lose any of its home matches, but that they will be played later in the season. "Clubs have co-operated and met us in our trouble, and the difficulty is being met by reversing fixtures," said Charlie Paynter.'

The missile had landed on the pitch in front of the South Bank on the West Stand side of the ground, removing a good deal of the cover at that end of the stadium.

Despite the massive handicap of playing the first half of the campaign in exile, the season proved to be, in playing terms, a splendid success for the Hammers. Ninety-six goals were pumped into opponents' nets in 30 matches. A sequence of nine consecutive away victories was achieved throughout September, October and November, and late there was a run of ten successive League South wins.

For the League South encounter against Queen's Park Rangers in September, Paynter was lucky to obtain the services of Ephraim (or 'Jock' as he preferred to be called) Dodds. He was a 28-year-old centre forward, currently attached to Blackpool, but had seen a lot of earlier service with Sheffield United. Dodds did not score in the 1-0 win at Loftus Road, but he exploded into action in the next eight games in which he played. In this spell he notched 11 goals including a hat-trick in a pulsating 7-4 triumph at Fulham. Making reappearances for Hammers at Craven Cottage were Sam Small and Benny Fenton, the latter contributing a goal.

During Dodd's reign at centre-forward, Hammers loaned George Foreman to Tottenham Hotspur for a short spell and for the same period had the services of Spurs winger George Ludford. This arrangement appeared timely when Terry Woodgate was tumbled into the pitch surround at Luton and was rendered unconscious for ten minutes. Making a rapid recovery, Woodgate was back in the side at White Hart Lane (against Arsenal) the following week.

On 2 December, Hammers' ended their nomadic existence as they faced Tottenham Hotspur in the first match at the Boleyn since the end of the previous season. Ironically, it was the first and last appearance of Jock Dodds, at Upton Park, in West Ham's colours. The northern goal ace, who had made such a hefty contribution to West Ham's goals for column, would have only this single opportunity to show what he could do in front of home support.

Numerous children were perched in the girders of the roofless stands as 25,000 packed themselves into the still usable areas of Upton Park. But it wasn't a happy homecoming, League leaders Spurs went in front in the 27th-minute, when Harry Gilberg converted a cross from 'Sonny' Walters, and stayed there.

Perhaps looking forward to the days when the war would be over, Charlie Paynter signed 18-year-old Derek Parker from Grays Athletic and recalled Ken Bainbridge from Leyton, where he had been on loan for a couple of seasons.

A few days prior to his club's League South visit to Upton Park in December, a desperate Dave Mangnall, once a Hammer and now manager at Queen's Park Rangers, appealed to Charlie Paynter for the loan of two or three players. The outcome was that Reg Attwell and Ernie Gregory turned out for the visitors and were on the losing side which went down 4-2.

Visiting Brighton and Hove Albion were involved in a dramatic match at the Boleyn in January. The headline of the *Stratford Express'* report read: 'Shocks and Thrills at Upton Park.'

It went on: 'West Ham, without a few of their regulars, experienced some shocks at Upton Park on Saturday before they succeeded in winning this South League match. Brighton showed commendable ball control on a tricky pitch and, aided by a couple of slips by Medhurst in the West Ham goal, took full advantage of their opportunities up to the last half an hour, by which time they led by four goals to one. Little had gone right for the Hammers till then. Passes had gone astray, defenders had blundered and generally the team looked in a bad way and heading for a surprising defeat. Then in a fateful quarter of an hour, the Brighton defence, so resourceful hitherto faltered badly and West Ham scored four goals and snatched a remarkable victory; and to overflow Brighton's cup of bitterness they missed a penalty kick in the closing stages which would have brought them a deserved division of the points.'

Sadly this match, signalled the conclusion of Jim Barrett's splendid career which stretched back to the nearly 1920s. Towering 'Big Jim' is still the best remembered Hammer of the inter-war years and in 1944 the *Stratford Express'* reporter and the crowd still expected him to bust the net with a penalty: 'James Barrett, former West Ham Ham schoolboy player with more than 20 years football service with West Ham, now a sergeant in the Forces, played his first game of the season for his club against Watford at Upton Park on Saturday and scored from a penalty kick. It was West Ham's fifth goal. The crowd at the Boleyn remembered Barrett's penalty kicks and sat up ready to see if the ball would break the netting. They were disappointed. The Watford goalkeeper saved the shot but Barrett trotted forward collected the ball as it came away from the goalkeeper's hands and calmly tapped it into the net.'

More than 20 'guest' players were utilised in this 1944-45 season, which probably reflected the turmoil that was going on within the armed services following the Normandy landings. Leicester City full-back Dai Jones appeared on 17 occasions, making him by far the most familiar of the guests. Isolated single appearances were made by people like Jack Cheetham, Joe Mallett, Bob Thomas and Idris Hopkins, all of Brentford, Bob Ferrier of Oldham Athletic and Les Medley of Tottenham Hotspur. But the vast majority of places in Hammers' teams were still being filled with West Ham registered staff.

Jim Barrett's final game in West Ham colours was not the only loss that cut Hammers' playing strength during and after 1944-45. Hammers' enigmatic winger Stan Foxall, absent following a knee injury sustained at Queen's Park Rangers back in September, did not play again either. Another casualty was George Foreman, who fractured a leg in a League South Cup-tie against Aldershot and failed to make a reappearance until the following August.

Foreman's misfortune, though, did not prevent Hammers winning their group at the expense of Tottenham Hotspur, Queen's Park Rangers and Aldershot, but in the semi-final at White Hart Lane, before 35,000, they came up against Chelsea's solid defence. Guest player Laurie Townsend of Brentford scored Hammers' lone goal but Chelsea replied with two. West Ham subsequently beat Chelsea twice in League games.

Despite the vast number of team changes forced upon him, Charlie Paynter maintained his side's challenge for a top place. Forty-six different individuals wore the club's colours, and more than half of them contributed at least one goal. Brentford's Tom Cheetham went one better and scored twice in the match against Luton Town in May. It was his only outing for Hammers, which made him arguably the club's most prolific scorer. Cheetham accomplished his deed in a match that ended 9-1 in Hammers' favour, but the event was overshadowed by something far more important.

Five days earlier, the Nazi beast was finally

vanquished and peace had been restored to Europe. The nation was intoxicated by the splendid news and it did not wear off for weeks. But there was still fighting in South-East Asia, where at least one Hammer, Charlie Walker, was involved.

By the time the playing staff were convened for the new season, that conflict, too, had been brought to a conclusion. In an effort to be fair to everybody, the Football authorities did not resume from where matters had been left in 1939. Instead they used the 1945-46 season as a sort of acclimatisation period. Large numbers of players were still in the Services, long after hostilities had ceased, particularly in the Far East. The regional system was put into operation for one more season but with a few alterations. First and Second Division clubs which had started the 1939-40 campaign were pooled, then split into a North-South divide at a point somewhere between Stoke and Derby.

The southern group contained only one club that the Hammers had never met in a Football or Southern League encounter – Newport County. The most distant journeys would be as far as Nottingham and Derby in the north and Plymouth and Swansea in the west.

Teams labelled 'Colours' and 'Blues' contested the public trial. Blues, representing the probable reserve team, had numerous strange faces but did contain Derek Parker, who certainly became familiar later on, and Jack Wood, recently recovered from a serious motor-cycle accident. The Colours were the likely first team and this side contained Charlie Walker, who had spent much of the last three years in the Far East. Another member of this side was Dick Walker, who had seen action as a paratrooper since his most recent appearance in a West Ham team back in September 1942.

There was a shock for West Ham fans on the eve of the new season when Len Goulden was transferred to Chelsea for £4,500. His 12 years at Upton Park were clearly his best, for despite sharing the company of players like Joe Payne, Tommy Lawton and later on Tommy Walker at Chelsea, he never quite re-established himself in the post-war period.

It was St Andrew's, Birmingham, where Hammers' season began and a Charlie Bicknell penalty that bagged the season's first points. Most noticeable difference at matches now that peace had returned was the size of the crowds. At Birmingham it numbered 30,000, a figure rarely exceeded since 1939 in games involving the Hammers. A quirk in the fixture arrangements then provided Charlie Paynter's men with four successive home games, which could only be considered a bonus in view of the high interest being shown in football at this time. Soccer at Upton Park during this period was strictly 'alfresco' due to the damage caused by the flying bomb which had left the stadium roofless. Apparently there was no shortage of funds for repairs but there was of labour and materials.

On the first Saturday in October, Len Goulden returned to Upton Park but in the colours of Chelsea. He grabbed two goals as his team took home both points. In front of a large Stamford Bridge assembly seven days hence, he was incapable of breaking down his former club's stout defence. This was partly due to a second-half collision which reduced him to a passenger on the wing.

A five-match unbeaten spell was ended at Derby County when the Rams proved that there was still a gulf between First and Second Division soccer, although it had not been demonstrated for almost six years. Hammers were comprehensively beaten by Derby in both fixtures (5-1 and 3-2) mainly due to the wizardry of Peter Doherty and Dally Duncan. The red-haired Irishman Doherty first played against West Ham in April 1934, but his most recent appearance at Upton Park had been in the Hammers side for a friendly against Portsmouth in the spring of 1943.

A string of six matches in December and January produced 26 goals. Among the victims of this onslaught were Coventry City and Luton Town, but the real pleasure was derived from the six shots that beat Arsenal goalkeeper George Swindin in the FA Cup-tie at the Boleyn on 5 January.

Contrary to the Football League's decision to suspend their peacetime schedule for another season, the Football Association went ahead with their Cup competition. For this one tournament they used the 'two-leg' system.

Hammers' clash with Arsenal at the Boleyn will long be remembered by all who witnessed it. The *Stratford Express*, too, was impressed with the performance of Charlie Paynter's boys and devoted almost 12 column inches of precious space to singing their praises.

Under the headline, 'Blitzkreig at Upton Park' the report read: 'This 'first leg' in the third round tie of the FA Cup between these old rivals at Upton Park was without doubt the sensation of the day. The Arsenal were pulverised by a side that worked like a machine, with speed and accuracy allied with any amount of 'devil'. The Arsenal knew they were beaten at the end of half an hour. During that period the West Ham attack was devastating. Time after time it split the Arsenal defence wide open and scored four goals.

'The defenders had no answer to the Hammers Blitzkrieg and although the home forwards lost some of their effectiveness in the second half, they were still the masters and added two further totals. The score might have reached double figures so overwhelmed was the Arsenal defence, had it not been for the gallant display of Joy at centre-half and Swindin in goal. These two and, in a lesser degree Scot, stood firmer than others in opposition to West Ham's sweeping raids, but their efforts were in vain.

'The teams on this momentous occasion were: **West Ham United:** Medhurst; Bicknell, Cater; Small, Walker, Fenton, Woodgate, Hall, Foreman, Wood, Bainbridge. **Arsenal:** Swindin; Scott, Wade, Nelson, Joy, Collett, O'Flanagan, Henley, Lewis, Drury, Bastin.'

The gates were closed with 35,000 inside but a number of people broke in through bomb-damaged walls and fencing. Club chairman W.J.Cearns appealed to these delinquents to pay up and added that any sum forwarded would be handed to the East Ham Memorial Hospital for which a collection had already been made on the ground. The second leg was a formality. Hammers never touched the heights achieved at the Boleyn but should have won all the same. At White Hart Lane, Arsenal made only a small inroad into Hammers' massive first-leg lead when Horace Cumner scored in the opening minutes.

Drawn to meet Chelsea in the fourth round, again over two legs, Hammers dropped Bainbridge to make room for the return of Archie Macaulay. The attendance of 65,000, was not only the largest of the round but also the biggest gathering to witness a match involving West Ham since the 1923 FA Cup Final.

Goulden, suffering with influenza, was missing from the Chelsea line-up for the Stamford Bridge leg, but he was not needed. The home team dominated proceedings and Hammers had Medhurst, Cater and Bicknell to thank for keeping the deficit down to two. Even so, it could have been one because Dick Spence secured the second goal only in the last moments, from a clever backheel by Lawton. Tommy Lawton was in his best England form but Dick Walker came out level in his aerial battles with Chelsea's recent £11,000 purchase.

The second leg at Upton Park was more of the same but in reverse. Hammers mounting countless assaults at the desperate Chelsea defence. Many would-be spectators were shut out when the gates were closed on another 35,000 full house. The roofless enclosures offered no protection against the severe hailstorm that fell soon after the start, leaving spectators wet and the pitch in a treacherous condition.

Len Goulden, fully recovered from his bout of 'flu, had the great misfortune to break a collarbone and was taken off to hospital. The mishap occurred in the eighth minute and left Chelsea without a midfield link. When Ken Bainbridge put Hall through to make it 2-1 on aggregate just prior to the break, Chelsea's plight became even more critical.

The *Stratford Express* described it thus: ' . . .West Ham started like giant eaters and their 'game' seemed assured when Goulden left the field. They attacked desperately but the Chelsea backs weathered the storm and the perfidious minutes ticked steadily by.'

' . . .Hammers began the second half with tremendous determination. For a long period there was only one team in it. How the Chelsea goal escaped was a little short of miraculous but it was also a tribute to a very gallant defence.'

' . . .In a few minutes that remained Chelsea packed their goal and when the ball was occasionally transferred there was frequently the spectacle of Lawton being entirely on his own. The West Ham defence had an easy time and the attack failed to save the game.'

So, West Ham's first post-war attempt to lift the FA Cup had ended in failure. There was, however, the consolation that the tournament had brought some financial reward, plus the fact that the competition was yet another step toward general normalisation.

Changes though, were on the way. At Plymouth Argyle in February, George Foreman played his final game for West Ham The return fixture at Upton Park a week later would see 21-year-old Don Travis in his place at centre-forward. Manchester-born Travis had spent recent months in the outbacks of Scottish soccer with St Mirren and Cowdenbeath. Now, at Upton Park, he had been induced to sign professional forms on the strength of a four-goal spree against Chelsea Reserves in a Combination match.

Travis made a sensational first-team debut at home to Plymouth Argyle. In scoring four times he equalled the achievement of Billy Grassam, who had done likewise on his first appearance way back in September 1900. Argyle's 7-0 hiding was their heaviest of the season and kept them firmly at the foot of the table.

Amid the euphoria over Travis's performance, another noteworthy record had been equalled. Outside-right Terry Woodgate's hat-trick had been registered in seven minutes, something that had not been done by a Hammer since Syd Puddefoot did so in a Cup-tie against Chesterfield in 1913.

Both men were on the mark again a week later. In the home match against Portsmouth, Hammers trailed 1-0 with half an hour to go, but recovered to win 3-1. The only other goals Travis recorded in 1945-46 came in the home game against Wolverhampton Wanderers in April. Proving something of a lucky charm, Travis was on the losing side only once in 11 first-team outings before moving to Southend. After leaving the Shrimpers, Travis spent the remainder of his Football League career with clubs in the old Third Division North.

Other players on the move in the spring of 1946 were Charlie Walker and Ted Fenton. Accumulating over 100 Football League appearances before the war interrupted his career, Charlie had spent a long spell in the Far East serving with the RAF. Now he was about to take charge of a club of his own, Margate FC on the Kent coast.

Ted Fenton departed Upton Park the same week as Charlie Walker, but he was bound for Colchester United, then in the Southern League. His service to the Hammers was not yet complete, but for the time being he could reflect on a splendid career of 176 first-team matches which saw him line up alongside such famous 'Claret and Blue' heroes as Syd Puddefoot, Vic Watson, Jimmy Ruffell and Tommy Yews. More recently he had rubbed shoulders with equally capable individuals like Len Goulden, Archie Macaulay, Dick Walker, Joe Cockroft and Jack Morton. At Colchester he gained the town national recognition as he inspired his 'oyster-fed' football team to FA Cup fame. In reaching the fifth round in 1947-48, Ted Fenton's club set a new high-water mark for non-League clubs in the modern FA Cup. It has been equalled only twice.

West Ham United ended the last wartime season occupying seventh position in the League South. Only Charlton Athletic of the London clubs finished higher. Hammers had the satisfaction of having beaten the champions, Birmingham, twice and of getting maximum points from ten away fixtures. But the last word on wartime soccer at Upton Park went to Ronnie Rooke, the Fulham centre-forward, who scored a hat-trick in his side's 5-2 victory there on 29 April 1946.

Post-war Days

NOW THAT the war had ended, all League clubs looked forward to resuming their normal duties, although six years of hostilities had brought many changes to the staff. In the Hammers' side at Plymouth for the opening game of season 1946-47 were only three players, Harry Medhurst, Charlie Bicknell and Dick Walker who had played in the last peacetime game in 1939. Soon, however, a fairly settled side began to emerge. Ron Cater, Norman Corbett and Dick Walker, were established in defence, whilst the two wingers, Terry Woodgate and Ken Bainbridge, were playing consistently.

It was goals that were needed and West Ham signed Joe Payne from Chelsea in December. Payne was well-known for having once scored ten goals in a single game for Luton. He managed six goals in ten appearances for West Ham but beset by injuries he later joined Millwall. To replace him Frank Neary was signed from Queen's Park Rangers and did well to score 15 goals in only 14 appearances, which included a hat-trick against West Bromwich Albion. A moderate League placing of 12th was achieved and the season ended with a 5-0 home defeat by Burnley, who themselves were promoted to Division One as well as reaching the FA Cup Final. There was no Cup joy for West Ham, though, as the Hammers went out in the third round when Leicester City won 2-1 at Upton Park.

Goalkeeper Ernie Gregory made his debut in December, the start of a career which would see him make 406 appearances for the club. In 1947 Jack Yeomanson, a full-back, was signed from Margate and fitted in well with his co-defenders, missing only two games that season. In October Ken Tucker made his debut against Chesterfield and the young winger scored a hat-trick. He did not keep his place in the side for long, however.

Indeed, the left-wing position was a problem with six different players tried there during the season, none with much success.

Attendances around the country were remarkable after the sport-starved years of war, and West Ham enjoyed playing before 55,000 at Newcastle and over 40,000 at Birmingham, Cardiff and West Bromwich Albion. Bill Stephens, a centre-forward, was signed from Swindon Town and later in the season he scored a hat-trick at Cardiff. Captain and centre-half Dick Walker was out injured for the two Christmas games against Sheffield Wednesday, and in his absence Wednesday ran riot with Eddie Quigley, their centre-forward, scoring six of the Owls' nine goals in the two games. Once again an early exit from the FA Cup came when Blackburn won 4-2 in a replay at Ewood Park. Eric Parsons ended the season as top goalscorer with 11 goals which helped West Ham finish in a respectable sixth position.

In June 1948, manager Charlie Paynter, mindful of his advancing years, announced that he needed to groom a successor. The club then brought former Hammers star Ted Fenton back to Upton Park as assistant manager. Ted had been enjoying success as manager of Colchester.

A bad blow came in the first home game of 1948 against Lincoln. Bill Stephens fractured his shin bone and after that never played in another first-team game. He made a comeback in an Eastern Counties League match at Bury St Edmunds in April but tragedy struck again when he broke his left leg after only five seconds.

West Ham won only one of their first seven games in season 1948-49 but Republic of Ireland international Tommy Moroney had settled in well at half-back alongside skipper Dick Walker. Inside-forward Eric Parsons was once again ever-present that season.

The game against Grimsby in November was

Spurs goalkeeper Ted Ditchburn collects a high ball as West Ham centre-forward Bill Robinson challenges him at White Hart Lane in February 1949. The other Tottenham defender is Tickridge. The result was a 1-1 draw.

abandoned due to fog. At the time Grimsby were leading 2-1. When the teams met again later in the season West Ham won 1-0. Ken Wright scored twice in both Christmas games which gave West Ham the double over Leeds. In January, Bill Robinson was signed from Charlton to increase the goal tally and scored ten goals in his 17 League appearances which included a hat-trick in a 4-1 win over Leicester.

A League position of seventh was gained but again there was no Cup luck that year as an early exit was made in a 3-1 defeat at Luton. The following season was a poor one and despite a settled side the Hammers slumped to 19th. Bill Robinson scored 23 League goals which helped West Ham remain in Division Two.

In the home game against Barnsley, Ken Bainbridge was adjudged to have scored after only nine seconds of the start. The biggest win of the season came in the FA Cup when Ipswich were beaten 5-1 at Upton Park in the third round. The fourth-round tie, however, brought a 2-1 home defeat by Everton. Reg Pratt was appointed club chairman after the death of W.Cearns.

Match programmes in those days were two old pence for four pages whilst a seat in the stand was five shillings (25p). The visit to Chesterfield in February was marred by a series of mishaps. A freight train collision blocked the line at Leagrave. It was arranged therefore for a convoy of cars to take the team to Leicester to catch another connection to Chesterfield. The team changed into their kit on the train and finally arrived at the ground at 4.25pm. It was snowing by this time and only a sparse crowd of 3,036 were still in attendance. The events had dampened the enthusiasm of the West Ham team and a 1-0 defeat followed.

In July 1950, Charlie Paynter retired and Ted Fenton became manager. 'The Grand Old Man of West Ham' had served the club for 50 years as trainer, secretary and manager. He was granted a testimonial match in September when the Cup holders Arsenal provided the opposition. The game attracted many officials of the Football Association and the League.

The evening was a festive occasion with many old players present, especially those who had played in the 1923 FA Cup Final. An enjoyable game was attended by 18,000 who saw the Hammers win 3-1. Later that month Bill Robinson scored a hat-trick against Sheffield United. Three times West Ham were in the lead but the game ended with Sheffield winning 5-3,

they were also helped by two own-goals from Ernie Devlin.

In November, Republic of Ireland international Frank O'Farrell was signed from Cork United and went straight into the team to replace his fellow countryman Tommy Moroney. The Christmas Day home game against Leeds saw winger Terry Woodgate record a hat-trick in the 3-1 win. In the FA Cup, as in previous years, West Ham struggled. After beating Cardiff City 2-1 at home in round three, they went down 1-0 at Stoke City in the next round. In February, Malcolm Allison was signed from Charlton and he would eventually take over the captaincy from Dick Walker. Bill Robinson had again done well, scoring 26 goals as the Hammers finished the season in 13th place.

The 1951-52 season started with Ernie Gregory gaining an injury at Queen's Park Rangers in the opening League game. He then missed the next 14 League games. George Taylor was an able deputy but he had a difficult day at Sheffield United in September. The home side won 6-1 with Derek Hawkesworth scoring three. Sheffield was not the city to be spoken about around West Ham that year as in December an in-form Wednesday side won 6-0 at Upton Park. Derek Dooley scored three of those goals and went on to score an amazing 46 League goals that season as Sheffield Wednesday became Second Division champions. First Division Blackpool provided the opposition in the FA Cup third round. A thrilling tie enjoyed by over 38,000 saw West Ham triumph by 2-1. It was an excellent win by the Hammers as Blackpool had some household names in their side such as Stanley Matthews, Stan Mortensen and Ernie Taylor.

Later that month revenge was taken out on Sheffield United as three goals by Ken Tucker and two by Gerry Gazzard gave West Ham a 5-1 home win. However, Sheffield had the last laugh when they beat West Ham in an FA Cup replay by 4-2 at Bramall Lane. The full-back pairing at this time was, at right-back George Wright and left-back Harry Kinsell. George was signed from Margate and was selected for an England 'B' trial against an Olympic XI. Kinsell was an experienced defender who had been signed from West Bromwich Albion. Whilst at Albion he played for England in two Victory internationals. The season ended with another mid-table spot. Only three teams had won at Upton Park, but in contrast West Ham had won only twice on their travels.

Season 1952-53 was another campaign which

West Ham manager Ted Fenton talking tactics with his team at their special training headquarters at Letchworth before the FA Cup third-round tie against West Brom in January 1953.

Albert Foan, 'the Alec James of the West Ham team' according to the original caption of this picture, in action at Letchworth during a practise game against the Hammers' reserve team before the West Brom Cup game, which the Throstles won 4-1 at Upton Park.

saw West Ham again finish in a mid-table position. Goalkeeper Ernie Gregory saved them from a heavier defeat on many occasions and was ever-present. The third round FA Cup game with First Division West Brom was won 4-1 by the Midlands side. Top Hammers goalscorer was Irishman Freddie Kearns who netted ten goals which included a hat-trick against Bury in a 3-2 home win. The big event of the season was the first ever floodlit match at Upton Park which took place on 16 April 1953. It was a friendly game against Tottenham, and in a keenly fought match goals by Barrett and Dixon gave West Ham a 2-1 win. The West Ham team played in bright fluorescent shirts.

One match report stated: 'The lights seem to make the game look faster. It was like watching a fantastic ballet in glorious technicolour.' A week later a strong stylish St Mirren side played out an exciting 3-3 draw under the lights.

Season 1953-54 kicked

Hammers centre-forward Fred Kearns beats a Notts County defender to the ball at Upton Park in December 1953. Hammers lost 2-1 on their way to a mid-table finish in Division Two.

Harry Hooper (falling, arm raised) scores West Ham's second goal against Huddersfield Town in the FA Cup third-round game at Upton Park in January 1954. Len Quested and Don McAvoy are the other Huddersfield players.

off with West Ham scoring nine goals in the first two home games, a 5-0 win over Lincoln and a 4-1 win against Leicester. The Hammers were given a jolt, however, as the next match brought a 5-0 defeat at Rotherham. Hammers had signed John Dick and brought him down from Scotland to play at inside-left. No fewer than six players had played in the number-ten shirt the previous season and it was a problem position which needed a solution.

By mid-September, after ten games, West Ham had lost only once and were second in the table. Three players had scored hat-tricks at Upton Park: Fred Kearns against Leicester, Dave Sexton against Rotherham and Tommy Dixon against Swansea.

A huge influence on the side was captain Malcolm Allison who had an insatiable desire for

In the fourth round of the 1953-54 FA Cup, the Hammers met Blackpool and lost 3-1 in a Bloomfield Road replay. Here in the first game at Upton Park, which ended 1-1, Hammers' goalkeeper Ernie Gregory raises the dust as he dives to save.

Albert Foan beats John Charles and goalkeeper Roy Wood to scramble the ball over the Leeds United line at Upton Park in March 1955. West Ham won 2-1.

success. A new generation of players were coming through who were willing to listen to anything that might lead to success. After training the players used to meet at 'Cassatarris', a café near the ground. The talks were not just a break from football, they were more like a football education. There was Malcolm Allison, John Bond, Noel Cantwell, Ken Brown, Frank O'Farrell, Malcolm Musgrove and Dave Sexton. All of these players went on to become managers in the Football League.

By January the team had slumped to 14th place after winning only four times in three months. One of these was a 5-0 home win over Bury with young Johnny Dick netting a hat-trick. On 2 January, West Ham were leading Stoke City 4-1 with only seven minutes remaining. Fog then descended and the game was abandoned. In the re-arranged game later in the season the teams drew 2-2.

The FA Cup brought a 4-0 win over Huddersfield, but in the fourth round Blackpool knocked West Ham out by winning 3-1 at Bloomfield Road in a replay after the 1-1 draw at Upton Park. Ernie Gregory was injured at Blackpool and missed the rest of the season, his place in goal being taken by Peter Chiswick. In a game at Fulham in January the Hammers found themselves losing 3-0, but in a spirited revival they won 4-3 with goals from Sexton, Dixon and two from Dick. Only four more wins were gained until the end of the season. One of these was a surprise 2-1 win at League leaders Everton before a crowd of 40,000.

During the season the floodlit friendlies were proving popular with the fans. There was Scottish opposition from Hearts, who were beaten 7-0, and also St Mirren, who lost 3-1. The continental opponents were Servette from Switzerland who West Ham beat 5-1 and Olaria, from Brazil, who did better in drawing 0-0.

An awful start was made in season 1954-55 with three 5-2 defeats in the first four games two of which were to Blackburn. After conceding 15 goals, goalkeeper Chiswick was replaced by George Taylor. Ernie Gregory had a long-term injury and missed the whole of the season. The team were undefeated throughout September and moved up to ninth place in the table.

There were two more floodlit friendlies in October. VFB Stuttgart were beaten 4-0 whilst the Austrians SR Wacker were also defeated 3-1. At this time Malcolm Allison was injured and missed 16 League games, his place being taken by Ken Brown. There were plenty of goals for the Upton Park patrons in December when home games with Bury and Swansea were both drawn 3-3. On 14 December, a crowd of 35,000 assembled to see the Hammers take on mighty AC Milan. The Italians fielded a side packed with internationals including the giant Swede Gunnar Nordahl and the Argentinian Schiaffino. West Ham were outclassed and lost 6-0.

Another early FA Cup setback took place in January when Port Vale won a third-round tie by 3-1 after a 2-2 draw at Upton Park. Leading the Hammers scorers were Johnny Dick and Dave Sexton. In successive games Johnny Dick scored three at Bristol Rovers whilst Dave Sexton got his hat-trick in the 6-1 win over Plymouth at home in February. An excellent run during March saw West Ham win six successive games and by Good Friday they were third in the table. Malcolm Musgrove had scored in five of those games.

Unfortunately West Ham did not win another game that season and finished in eighth spot. In

West Ham in 1955-56. Back row (left to right): Sexton, Bond, Gregory, Allison, Cantwell, O'Farrell. Front row: Musgrove, Hooper, Dare, Dick, Tucker.

March the friendly with the Dutch side Holland Sports had become the first live televised match at Upton Park. The 0-0 draw, however, was a poor advertisement. The cameras should have been there in February when SC Simmering from Austria were beaten 8-2. Reserve centre-forward Billy Dare scored four of the goals. The attendance of 4,500 for the home League game with Doncaster in February was probably the smallest ever attendance for a League game at Upton Park. It took place on a Thursday afternoon in appalling snowy conditions.

The Hammers' first win of season 1955-56 came on 3 September when Notts County were beaten 6-1 at Upton Park. Billy Dare, who was now the first-choice centre-forward, scored two whilst another two were scored by Harry Hooper who was putting on some dazzling performances on the right wing. The England selectors were aware of this and Hooper was capped twice that season at Under-23 level. October was a good month for the West Ham patrons as 14 goals were scored in three home games. Barnsley were beaten 4-0 with two goals from Billy Dare. Plymouth were also beaten 4-0 and Ken Tucker scored a hat-trick which was almost eight years to

the day since he scored three times on his League debut. Another hat-trick went to Harry Hooper in the 6-1 win over Doncaster Rovers.

Ernie Gregory was now back in goal following his long-term injury. The regular full-back pairing was John Bond and Noel Cantwell and their cool play in the penalty area often brought a rebuke from manager Fenton who wanted them to clear the ball instead of dribbling with it. Another amazing goal feast took place in October when the Irish team Distillery were beaten 7-5 in a friendly match at Upton Park. Billy Dare scored four of the West Ham goals and one of the Distillery goals was scored by Derek Dougan, who later became famous in England. After the win over Doncaster on 22 October the Hammers went another eight games without winning and slumped to 19th in the League table.

A 5-1 win over Swansea Town, however, put the team in good spirits for the forthcoming FA Cup match with First Division Preston North End. The Hammers were 2-1 behind at half-time with one of Preston's goals being a penalty scored by the legendary Tom Finney.

The match report in the Stratford Express read: 'What a magnificent sparkling transformation in

'Special Cup training' seemed to be in vogue in times past. Here, before the fourth-round tie against Cardiff City in January 1956, West Ham boss Ted Fenton gives his boys a pep talk at Hove dog track.

the second half. "Man of the Match" was inside-right Albert Foan who gave the most dazzling performance from an inside-forward seen in years. He gave a demonstration of slide rule passing, quick fire shooting that had the Preston defenders running around in circles." In the second half Albert scored a splendid hat-trick and other goals from Billy Dare gave West Ham a 5-2 win. Sadly Albert could not maintain this fine form and only played in a handful of League games after that. In the next round another First Division side, Cardiff City, provided the opposition. It was goals by Billy Dare and John Dick that gave West Ham a 2-1 win.

Another home tie followed in the fifth round with a visit by Blackburn Rovers. After a hard fought 0-0 draw the teams met again at Ewood Park where two goals by Johnny Dick and one from Harry Hooper gave West Ham a 3-2 win. In the League, West Ham were still struggling but their FA Cup involvement kept the supporters happy. The Hammers had been drawn away to their London neighbours Tottenham, where a

huge crowd of 69,111 turned up to see the sixth-round tie.

The teams were Tottenham Hotspur. Reynolds; Norman, Hopkins, Blanchflower, Clarke, Marchi; Harmer, Brooks, Duquemin, Smith, Robb.

West Ham United: Gregory: Bond, Cantwell, Malcolm, Allison, O'Farrell, Hooper, Dare, Dick, Foan, Tucker.

The match had everything to delight the supporters. The first half was full of incident, Johnny Dick scoring a hat-trick as the Hammers raced into a 3-1 lead before a goal by Harmer pegged them back. The second half was not so furious or fast but was still exciting. It was near to the end when Duquemin flicked in the equaliser. The game finished all square at 3-3 and was remembered by the players and fans for many years. In a dull grim replay at Upton Park, West Ham lost 2-1. Although only five more League games were won that season West Ham still managed to finish in 16th place. In March, to the disappointment of the supporters, Harry Hooper

John Dick scores West Ham's second goal with a back header as they meet Tottenham Hotspur in the sixth round of the FA Cup in March 1956. The sides drew 3-3, Dick netting a hat-trick, before Spurs won the replay at Upton Park.

had been sold for £25,000 to Wolverhampton Wanderers.

On the last day of the season Dave Sexton scored twice in the 3-0 home win over Bristol City. This was his last game for the club before joining Leyton Orient in the summer. Two players had been sent off during the season, Noel Cantwell at Bristol Rovers and Ken Tucker at Fulham.

After three months of the 1956-57 season West Ham had only won one home game a 2-0 win against Barnsley. The away form, however, was much better with four wins and two draws, one win was at Blackburn where Alan Blackburn

Centre-half Malcolm Allison leads out West Ham in March 1956, a season in which the Hammers slumped down the Second Division table.

scored for the Hammers. In November an exchange deal took place with Preston. Centre-forward Eddie Lewis came down to join Hammers whilst Frank O'Farrell travelled north. A narrow 1-0 win over Stoke in November changed the home form as West Ham proceeded to win a further eight successive home games, seven of which had a 2-1 scoreline.

In January, Grimsby Town were beaten 5-3 in a third-round Cup-tie but in the next round at Everton, Hammers lost 2-1. By mid-February, West Ham had reached fifth place in the table but a 6-2 defeat at Huddersfield started a poor run of results. There were only three more wins in the final 12 games which saw West Ham finish the season in eighth place. Eddie Lewis was top scorer with nine goals.

WEST Ham were one of the clubs that were being mentioned as promotion candidates at the start of the 1957-58 season. By the end of September, however, they had won only three games and found themselves in 17th place in the table. Sheffield United had beaten West Ham twice and in the first meeting at Upton Park they won 3-0 with Tommy Hoyland scoring all three. After the return game at Sheffield, Malcolm

Allison was taken ill and within days was in hospital to be told that he had tuberculosis. He was expected to be out of the game for a long time but, sadly, he never played for the club again.

Billy Dare had done well, having scored ten goals which included a hat-trick in the 3-2 win at Bristol Rovers. The first two weeks in October brought a change of fortune. There were local derby wins against Leyton Orient, by 3-2, and a splendid 3-0 win over Second Division leaders Charlton. To add experience to the forward line, Vic Keeble was signed from Newcastle. Whilst he was at St James' Park he scored 67 goals and led their attack in the 1955 FA Cup Final.

During the summer, Dick Walker had retired and on 11 October, West Ham played a testimonial match for him against Sparta Rotterdam. Dick had been a fine servant to the club and had made 211 appearances during a career which spanned 24 years. A near-20,000 crowd witnessed a 5-0 win for West Ham with Johnny Dick claiming a hat-trick and Vic Keeble scoring on his debut.

West Ham were undefeated during November, gaining wins over Huddersfield, by 5-2, and Stoke City, by 5-0, where Vic Keeble scored

In May 1957, the Hammers met a combined Prague team in the Czechoslovakian capital. Here, Macek takes the ball through the Hammers' defence.

Liverpool.

During December, the Hammers had been beaten by Chelsea in the FA Youth Cup. Playing in the match were Bobby Moore, Geoff Hurst and Jimmy Greaves, three players who were going to make a big impact on the international scene with England.

The undefeated League run came to an end on Boxing Day at Ipswich where the home side won 2-1. Two days later, West

three. The Polish team LKS Lódz were another team to visit Upton Park for a floodlit friendly and two goals by Johnny Dick helped the Hammers to a 4-1 win. After beating Lincoln City 6-1 on 21 December, West Ham were third in the table, only two points behind the leaders Ham bounced back with a 6-1 win over Bristol Rovers, a game in which John Smith scored a hat-trick and where Vic Keeble added a further two goals.

The Hammers were now in top form and their FA Cup campaign started with a 5-1 win over

Johnny Dick is beaten by Liverpool goalkeeper Dick Rudham at Upton Park in April 1958. The sides drew 1-1 and a week later, after a 3-1 win at Ayresome Park, West Ham went into the First Division as champions of the Second.

First Division Blackpool. Vic Keeble scored three and Johnny Dick scored the other two. On 18 January, West Ham went to the top of the table as Liverpool lost at home whilst the Hammers crushed Swansea Town 6-2. The fourth round of the Cup brought Third Division Stockport County to Upton Park and in a hard fought match, West Ham ran out winners by 3-2.

The following Saturday West Ham drew 2-2 at Fulham. The attendance of 42,259 was the largest post-war gate for a League game at Craven Cottage.

When the draw for the fifth round of the Cup was made, West Ham were given a home game against Fulham and it was then decided to make this the first- ever all-ticket match at Upton Park. A crowd of 37,500 saw a thrilling match which Fulham won 3-2. The Cottagers went on to reach the semi-finals but their backlog of League fixtures affected their promotion bid.

For the Hammers the strike force of Dick and Keeble was scoring regularly and both netted in the 4-1 win over neighbours Leyton Orient.

It was a particularly good day for West Ham on 8 March, when Johnny Dick scored four as Rotherham were beaten 8-0 to record West Ham's biggest-ever League win. After the match the news came through that Charlton, in second place, and Liverpool, who were third, had both lost 3-1. Both of these teams were still to visit Upton Park. Charlton came at Easter and drew 0-0 whilst Liverpool drew 1-1 a week before the season's end.

On the final day of the season, West Ham, with 55 points, were away to Middlesbrough. Charlton, who also had 55 points in second place, were at home to third-placed Blackburn, who had 54 points. In an amazing match at The Valley, Blackburn beat Charlton 4-3. Up at Middlesbrough, meanwhile, goals by Keeble, Dick and Musgrove gave West Ham a memorable 3-1 win.

The Hammers were champions and were promoted to Division One after a period of 26 years. It had been a wonderful season and the success was due to having a settled side. Ernie Gregory in goal gave confidence to all around him. The full-backs, Bond and Cantwell, were strong and rugged. At wing-half there was Malcolm tough and talented. Ken Brown was the centre-half, strong in the air. The wingers were Grice and Musgrove, both fast and direct. There was Keeble's goalscoring talents and Johnny Dick, the ace marksman in the team.

The Golden Years

EVERYONE at Upton Park looked forward to the First Division with confidence. West Ham were at Portsmouth for the opening game of the 1958-59 season and in front of a 40,000 crowd, which was boosted by 7,000 Londoners, the Hammers won 2-1.

On the following Monday evening, the visitors were Wolves the current League champions. The gates were closed long before kick off with a 37,500 crowd inside.

It was a superb match and goals by Johnny Dick and John Smith gave West Ham a 2-0 victory. The teams were: **West Ham**: Gregory; Bond, Cantwell, Malcolm, Brown, Lansdowne, Grice, Smith, Keeble, Dick, Musgrove. **Wolves**: Finlayson; Stuart, Harris, Slater, Wright, Flowers, Deeley, Broadbent, Henderson, Mason, Horne.

Aston Villa were next to face the onslaught and it was goals all the way as Keeble, Dick and Musgrove all scored twice in a resounding 7-2 win. The return match with Wolves saw a full house of 52,317 at Molineux and they saw a classic game which ended all-square at 1-1. However, the following Saturday at Luton, the Hammers were brought back to earth when they were beaten 4-1.

The next visitors to Upton Park were Manchester United, who were rebuilding their side following the tragic air crash at Munich seven months earlier. The East End crowd witnessed another thriller. West Ham were leading 3-0 when United pulled back two goals, but the Hammers held on to win 3-2. This game marked the first-team debut of Bobby Moore. In the following week's match programme one item read: 'The selection of Bobby Moore at left-half proved justified by a display which foreshadows a grand future for a 17-year-old called upon to make his debut against one of Europe's leading sides'.

The return at Old Trafford a week later drew a huge attendance of 53,057 and they were treated to an exhilarating match where a hat-trick by Albert Scanlon gave Manchester United a 4-1 victory. In early October, Blackburn Rovers were beaten 6-3 at Upton Park. Vic Keeble scored four of the goals and another was scored by the skipper, Noel Cantwell.

He had a good weekend for the following day he scored twice for the Republic of Ireland against Poland. Recognition for two other Hammers came when John Bond and Andy Malcolm played for the Football League against the Scottish League at Ibrox.

The Welsh international inside-forward Phil Woosnam became a costly £30,000 signing from Leyton Orient in November and made his debut in the London derby with Arsenal which was drawn 0-0. Two days later, Malcolm Allison had his testimonial game against an All Star XI which included Stanley Matthews, Tom Finney, Brian Clough and Bobby Charlton. The 21,600 crowd were treated to a goal feast with the final score being 7-6 to West Ham.

By mid-December, the Hammers' League form had suffered and they were 14th in the table. However, after Portsmouth were beaten 6-0 a week before Christmas, West Ham went on to record six victories in their next seven games including a double over Tottenham. The 2-1 win over Spurs was to be the last time that West Ham played on a Christmas Day.

When the draw for the third round of the FA Cup was made it paired West Ham with Spurs. After beating Tottenham twice in the League, the Hammers were confident of progressing to the

Ted Fenton chats to players of newly-promoted West Ham as they arrive at Upton Park for the first day of training in July 1958.

next round with another victory at White Hart Lane. This was not to be, however, and before a crowd of 56,252, Spurs won 2-0.

The combination of Dick and Keeble was still proving lethal in the League and both scored twice in the 5-3 win over Nottingham Forest. On 7 March, West Bromwich were beaten 3-1 and Johnny Dick scored all three, but injuries to goalkeeper Ernie Gregory and inside-right Phil Woosnam forced them to miss the rest of the season.

Noel Dwyer, who had been signed from the Wolves, took over in goal, and young Harry Obeney came into the forward line and scored in both games against Newcastle at Easter. In April, Johnny Dick played for Scotland against England at Wembley to gain his only cap.

In the final home game of the season, West Ham beat Manchester City 5-1, the campaign had been a success with a final League placing of sixth. Five players – Bond, Cantwell, Malcolm, Brown and Grice – played in every match. The first 'Hammer of the Year' award was won by Andy Malcolm.

A promising start was made to the 1959-60 season. Leicester were beaten 3-0 on the opening day and this was followed by victories over Burnley and Preston. The first defeat, in September, came when Leeds won 2-1 at Upton Park in a game which marked the end of Ernie Gregory's playing career with the club. He retired to become the club coach and to work closely with the goalkeepers.

There were 58,909 spectators at the London derby with Tottenham at White Hart Lane which finished 2-2. Ten days later, 54,349 turned up at Stamford Bridge where West Ham beat Chelsea 4-2. The first three games in November were won: Manchester City were beaten 4-1; there was a 3-1 win against Arsenal at Highbury; and finally a hat-trick by Johnny Dick in a 3-2 win over the Wolves at Upton Park.

It was all smiles as West Ham became League leaders and Kenny Brown gained an England cap against Northern Ireland at Wembley. However, disaster struck on 28 November in the away game with Sheffield Wednesday. The Hammers were 4-0 behind at half-time and finally lost 7-0. Two weeks later, a trip to Blackburn Rovers saw a further hatful of goals conceded in a 6-2 defeat.

A step up for West Ham. The first-team squad on the eve of the 1958-59 season. From top to bottom they are: Ernie Gregory, John Bond, Malcolm Pyke, Andy Nelson, Vic Keeble, Noel Cantwell, John Dick, Ken Brown, Bill Lansdowne, Andy Malcolm, Mike Grice, Malcolm Musgrove, John Smith, Bill Dare.

The Hammers' team was losing all confidence and Burnley won 5-2 at Upton Park in early January.

The FA Cup brought further misery. After a 1-1 draw at Huddersfield, the Yorkshire team inspired by a young Denis Law, won 5-1 in the replay. In February, full-back John Bond was moved to centre-forward and he did well in scoring six goals in six games which included a hat-trick in the 4-2 win over Chelsea. After

Newcastle had won 5-3 at Upton Park, goalkeeper Noel Dwyer was dropped and in his place came Brian Rhodes, who played in the remaining 15 games of the season.

In March, an exchange deal with Tottenham brought centre-forward Dave Dunmore to West Ham, whilst Johnny Smith went to White Hart Lane. There was only one win in the last eight games which gave a final League placing of 14th, a disappointing end after being top of the League in November. Malcolm Musgrove was top goalscorer with 15 goals. He missed only one game all season and was named 'Hammer of the Year'.

Arsenal Vic Groves hits the ball across to Jimmy Bloomfield, who scored against West Ham at Highbury in November 1959, as the Hammers tried to establish themselves back in Division One. They did all right in this game against their London rivals, winning 3-1.

There were mixed results in the first two months of the 1960-61 season. At home, the Hammers were winning all their games, but away there had been six defeats: Wolves and Everton both scored four against the Hammers and Manchester United netted six.

In 1960-61 the Football League Cup was born – although many of the top clubs declined to take part – and on 26 September, West Ham played hosts to Charlton and won 3-1. Johnny Dick made history to become the club's first-ever League Cup goalscorer. The teams for this inaugural match were: **West Ham:** Rhodes; Bond, Lyall, Malcolm, Brown, Moore, Woodley, Cartwright, Dunmore, Dick, Musgrove. **Charlton:** Duff; Sewell, Townsend, Hinton, Tocknell, Lucas, Lawrie, Edwards, Leary, Werge, Summers. In the next round, alas, the Hammers were beaten 3-2 at Fourth Division Darlington.

A shock came when skipper Noel Cantwell was sold to Manchester United for £30,000.

Hammers thought this was good business as they had a ready-made replacement in John Lyall.

Ernie Gregory had his testimonial in October and the LD Alajeulence club from Costa Rica were the opponents when the score was 3-2 in the Hammers' favour.

On 22 October, Preston were beaten 5-2 at home with Malcolm Musgrove scoring a hat-trick. This game marked the debut for 17-year-old Ronnie Boyce, who went on to play over 300 games for the club and is still on the staff at Upton Park today.

Noel Dwyer makes a spectacular save from Nottingham Forest's Stewart Imlach at Upton Park in December 1959. The Forest fans thought the ball had crossed the line but the referee said no. West Ham won 4-1.

Ken Brown, West Ham's centre-half, and R.H.Brown, Fulham's amateur international centre-forward clash at Craven Cottage in October 1960. The sides drew 1-1.

Hammers' goalkeeper Brian Rhodes dives at the feet of Arsenal's David Herd at Highbury in March 1961. The result of the match was a goalless draw.

During November, Dave Dunmore scored in seven successive League games which included three in the 6-0 defeat of Arsenal. West Ham also scored five goals on successive Saturdays. There was a remarkable 5-5 draw at Newcastle followed by a 5-0 win over Wolves. Tottenham beat West Ham twice at Christmas and they later went on to win the League and Cup double.

The FA Cup brought no joy as Stoke City won

a third-round replay 1-0. Only a further three games were won that season as the Hammers slumped to 16th place in the table.

In March the board issued a statement that the manager Ted Fenton was on 'sick leave'. Very little publicity was given to the true facts and he later left the club. West Ham were proud of the fact that they had never sacked a manager and it appeared that a compromise had been attempted to preserve that tradition.

On 13 April, Ron Greenwood, who had been assistant manager at Arsenal, was named as the new manager at West Ham. Greenwood had also been a player at Bradford, Brentford, Chelsea and Fulham. It was the start of a remarkable era at Upton Park.

In the summer of 1961 a roof was added to the North Bank and this meant that there was now cover on all four sides of the ground. Lawrie Leslie the Scottish international goalkeeper was purchased for £15,000 from Airdrie and his fearless displays were soon to make him a favourite with the fans. In August, West Ham met Tottenham, the reigning League champions, twice and both games provided superb exciting football. At White Hart Lane the teams drew 2-2 and in the return, goals from Sealey and Scott gave West Ham a fine 2-1 victory.

There were five wins during September and it was Johnny Dick who was scoring regularly. He netted two goals in both 4-1 wins over Sheffield United and Leicester. In the League Cup, Plymouth Argyle were beaten 3-2 but in the next round Aston Villa triumphed 3-1 at Upton Park.

On 4 November, the Hammers were away to Manchester City. At half-time they were losing 3-1 with Peter Dobing having scored all three. But in an inspired second-half display, West Ham scored four times to win the match 5-3. In the last minute Bobby Moore tangled with City's Wagstaffe and was sent-off for the first and only time in his career.

Later that month an exchange deal saw Andy Malcolm join Chelsea and centre-forward Ron Tindall came to West Ham. Tindall scored twice against Arsenal in the 2-2 draw at Highbury in December. He did not gain a regular place in the side, however, and was later sold to Reading.

The Hammers moved into second place when two goals from Bobby Moore helped West Ham beat the Wolves 4-2. In the FA Cup there was a real shock as Second Division Plymouth won the third-round tie 3-0. And the poor form continued in the League with only two wins during January and February.

New West Ham manager Ron Greenwood on the day he took over at Upton Park in April 1961.

On 3 March, West Ham lost 6–0 at Burnley. A few days later Ron Greenwood announced a record signing for the club when he paid £65,000 for centre-forward Johnny Byrne from Crystal Palace. Byrne made his debut in the goalless draw with Sheffield Wednesday at Hillsborough and did not score until six games later, when Cardiff City were beaten 4–1 on Good Friday. This game saw the debut of Martin Peters.

Easter was an eventful time for the West Ham goalkeepers. On the Saturday, Lawrie Leslie

West Ham goalkeeper Lawrie Leslie grabs the ball as Geoff Hurst covers him against Leicester City at Upton Park in September 1961. The Hammers won 4-1.

fractured a finger against Arsenal and John Lyall took over in goal. Leslie later came back on the field and played well as a winger as the teams drew 3–3. Two days later, at Cardiff, Brian Rhodes was the goalkeeper but he, too, suffered a mishap when he dislocated his shoulder. This time it was the turn of Martin Peters to deputise. He did well but Cardiff ran out winners by 3–0.

On the final day of the season Fulham were beaten 4–2 with two goals being scored by Johnny Dick. He finished the season as top scorer with 23 goals which helped West Ham finish in eighth place. Bobby Moore had enjoyed an excellent season and was selected to go with the England team to the World Cup Finals in Chile. On

Leslie makes a despairing attempt to save this header by Fulham's Graham Leggat which gave Fulham their second goal at Craven Cottage in October 1961 when West Ham lost 2-0. The player appearing to support Leslie is John Bond. On the left are Dave Metchick of Fulham and Joe Kirkup of Hammers.

This time Leslie punches clear from Arsenal's Alan Skirton at Highbury in December 1961. Again the nearest defender is John Bond. The game ended 2-2 with both Hammers' goals coming from Tindall.

route to Chile he made his England debut against Peru in Lima. He played well and kept his place for all the World Cup games against Hungary, Argentina, Bulgaria and Brazil.

For the Hammers, though, an awful start was made to the 1962-63 season when they lost their first two home games and conceded ten goals. Visitors Wolves won 4-1 and Tottenham, aided by a John Lyall own-goal, won 6-1.

Johnny Dick, meanwhile, was transferred to Brentford and his goals helped the Bees win the Fourth Division championship that season.

September was a better month for the Hammers. Manchester City were beaten 6-1 at Maine Road and in the League Cup, Plymouth were crushed 6-0 which was ample revenge for the previous year's defeat in the FA Cup. However, the Cup joy was short-lived as Second Division Rotherham won 3-1 at Millmoor in the next round.

In October, winger Peter Brabrook was signed from Chelsea and made his debut in the 1-1 draw with Burnley. Current right winger Tony Scott reverted to outside-left and this move later

resulted in Malcolm Musgrove leaving to join neighbours Leyton Orient. There was more transfer activity in November. Lawrie Leslie had broken his leg against Bolton and to replace him, Jim Standen was signed from Luton Town. Phil Woosnam went to Aston Villa and this enabled young Ronnie Boyce to establish himself in the side at inside-right.

In December there were two away games which brought plenty of goals. There was an exciting 4-4 draw at White Hart Lane when Dave Mackay equalised for Spurs in the last minute, and a week later, two Peter Brabrook goals helped West Ham to win 4-3 at Nottingham Forest. This was to be the last game for six weeks as the icy weather took its toll.

On a snowy pitch in February, the FA Cup trail eventually got under way with a 0-0 draw against Fulham before the replay at Craven Cottage was won 2-1. The Hammers were in a mid-table position and in March there were good wins over Manchester United, by 3-1, and Sheffield Wednesday, 2-0. In the FA Cup, Swansea Town were beaten 1-0 and the next

Young admirers meet Bobby Moore at Chadwell Heath before the start of the 1962 -63 season.

round brought Everton to Upton Park. In a tense struggle a penalty converted by Johnny Byrne gave West Ham a 1-0 victory. Play was held up during this match as the Everton supporters threw bottles in the goalmouth.

The sixth round took West Ham to Anfield to face Liverpool. Before a crowd of 49,036, the Hammers were unlucky not to force a replay and there were only six minutes remaining when Roger Hunt snatched a winner which sent the Reds to the semi-finals.

In April, Nottingham Forest were beaten 4-1 with all the goals coming from Moore, Hurst and Peters. In four years' time these three would be famous throughout the world. Ron Greenwood had moved Geoff Hurst during the season from wing-half to inside-left. This was a good switch as Hurst finished the season as top goalscorer with 13 goals.

The final day of the season saw Manchester City relegated as they suffered a 6-1 defeat at Upton Park. The youngsters had reached the FA

Youth Cup Final and were trailing 3-1 to Liverpool after the first leg. In the home tie, Martin Britt scored four as the Hammers won 6-5 on aggregate. Nine of that side went on to play in West Ham's first team.

During the summer of 1963, West Ham were invited to play in the American Soccer League tournament. Fourteen teams were taking part and were split into two groups. The Hammers were to play their group games in three venues, New York, Chicago and Detroit. Missing from the first two games were Bobby Moore and Johnny Byrne, who were on tour with the England team. Bobby Moore was made captain for the game against Czechoslovakia and Johnny Byrne did well when scoring two goals against Switzerland.

In America, meanwhile, West Ham did not start very well, drawing 3-3 with Kilmarnock and then losing 4-2 to the Italian side, Mantova. Fortunes changed when Moore and Byrne joined the team as Oro (Mexico), Valenciennes

West Ham's Johnny Byrne is beaten to the ball by Arsenal goalkeeper John McClelland at Highbury in October 1962. The result was a 1-1 draw.

(France) and the Germans Preussen Munster were all beaten with Hurst scoring six of the goals.

The final group game was against Recife from Brazil. There was an outrageous incident in this match when Alan Sealey was kicked to the ground and injured. After treatment the referee promptly sent him off. A goal by Johnny Byrne gave West Ham a 1-1 draw and this was sufficient for them to win the group.

The championship play-off was to be played over two legs against the Polish side, Górnik. In

Ken Brown wins a heading duel with Aston Villa's Derek Dougan at Upton Park in December 1962 in another 1-1 draw.

Ron Greenwood chats to his first-team squad at Upton Park in August 1963 as they prepare for the new season. Hopes were high – and at the end of the campaign, the Hammers could look back on a glorious finale.

the first game Johnny Byrne gave West Ham the lead but the Poles equalised and the match finished 1-1. The second match was full of incidents as West Ham took a 1-0 lead through Hurst. Górnik then had two goals disallowed for offside and this upset the Polish fans who invaded the pitch and attacked referee Jim McLean, who was hurt and unable to continue. The game was held up for half an hour while order was resumed. When play continued West Ham held out to win 1-0.

The Hammers had now qualified to meet

Aston Villa's Ron Wylie misses his header against West Ham in the League Cup third-round game at Villa Park in October 1963. West Ham won 2-0.

Dukla Prague in the challenge Cup Final. The first leg was played in Chicago and was an even contest before the Czechs won 1-0. The second leg before a 15,000 crowd was played in New York. Tony Scott put the Hammers in the lead, but a goal from Masopust levelled the scores and the game finished 1-1. Although West Ham had not won the trophy, the tournament had been a great success. The experience gained against teams from other nations was of great benefit.

The Hammers' League form in the first two months of the 1963-64 season was moderate. There had been a double over Blackpool and an excellent win at Liverpool, but by the end of September the Hammers' League placing was 15th. A 2-1 League Cup win was achieved against Leyton Orient and this was the first of an amazing 14 Cup-ties that season.

In mid-October, fortunes changed for West Ham. John Bond came into the side to replace Joe Kirkup and scored one of the goals in the 2-0 League Cup win at Aston Villa. Young Martin

Britt also came in at centre-forward and played very well in successive wins over League champions Everton by 4-2 and away to Manchester United, where Britt scored the only goal of the game.

In November, Swindon Town were beaten 4-1 in the League Cup after a 3-3 draw at Swindon. Johnny Byrne was showing his England form and was scoring regularly. There were two goals from him in the 3-3 draw at Arsenal and two more in the 2-2 home draw with Chelsea.

In the quarter finals of the League Cup it was the turn of Fourth Division Workington to face the Byrne magic. In a 6-0 win at Upton Park, Byrne scored a hat-trick with the other goals coming from Boyce, Hurst and Scott.

On Boxing Day, Blackburn came to Upton Park as League leaders. Johnny Byrne scored twice but Blackburn scored eight to inflict upon the Hammers their record home defeat.

Two days later the teams met again at Blackburn. West Ham had made one change at wing-half, where Eddie Bovington replaced Martin Peters. Again Johnny Byrne scored two goals and this time, to the disappointment of the Ewood Park crowd, West Ham won 3-1.

Charlton Athletic were the visitors to Upton Park for the third-round FA Cup match. Young Johnny Sissons at outside-left was playing in his first Cup-tie and scored one of the goals in a 3-0 win. In the fourth round, West Ham drew 1-1 away to their neighbours Leyton Orient. In the replay two goals from Geoff Hurst saw the Hammers through to the next round by a 3-0 margin. In the week of the Cup replay, John Lyall announced that injuries had forced him to retire from playing and he then joined the office staff at Upton Park.

More Cup action followed and next was the League Cup semi-final against Leicester City. In the first leg at Filbert Street, West Ham were losing 4-1 after 54 minutes, but goals from Hurst and Sealey brought them back into the game. The narrow 4-3 defeat gave them hope for the second leg.

In the League, a brilliant display saw Tottenham beaten 4-0 and this was a good build up to the FA Cup fifth-round tie at Swindon. The attendance of 28,582 set a new Swindon ground record. In an exciting game, the Hammers were encouraged by the vocal support given to them by the 7,000 fans who travelled across from London. Two goals from Geoff Hurst and one from Johnny Byrne gave West Ham a 3-1 win. Centre-forward Byrne was in sparkling form, scoring a hat-trick in the 4-3 League win over Sheffield Wednesday.

The sixth round of the Cup paired West Ham with Burnley in an all-ticket clash at Upton Park. Burnley led 1-0 at half-time but three goals in a 12-minute spell in the second half, two of them from the brilliant Byrne, put West Ham on the road to victory.

Burnley pulled a goal back towards the end but the Hammers held on to win 3-2. In the semi-final they were drawn to meet Manchester United at Hillsborough. West Ham travelled to Sheffield with the Northern Press labelling them as 'no hopers'. In a League fixture a week earlier, Manchester United, fielding five reserves, had won 2-0 at Upton Park.

It had been raining non stop on the morning of the Cup match and the pitch was soon to be turned into a quagmire of mud. United, the Cup holders, had teenage sensation George Best, the menace of Denis Law and the explosive shooting of Bobby Charlton.

West Ham needed to contain the individual brilliance of the United forwards. It was 0-0 at half-time but in the second half West Ham were suddenly dictating the play. Ten minutes went by when Ronnie Boyce looked up to see Gaskell five yards out of his goal and then drove the ball into the top of the net.

Eight minutes later Jack Burkett raced forward and crossed the ball shoulder-high for Boyce to advance it wide of Gaskell's groping fingers. But United came back with a vengeance when Law rose high to nod the ball down past Standen. Two minutes later, Bobby Moore gained possession, went past Charlton and Crerand and put a low accurate pass to Hurst, who took it into his stride and hammered it wide of Gaskell's right hand. The final whistle went with Hammers winning 3-1.

It had been a superb performance from the Hammers team inspired by a world-class display from Bobby Moore. Moore was the complete master in conditions which defied such a performance, Ken Brown had shadowed Denis Law, and Eddie Bovington shackled Bobby Charlton. Ronnie Boyce had been everywhere, cutting out passes, getting in tackles and became the unlikely hero with two great goals. It was a happy journey home for the 20,000 West Ham fans, most of them soaked through by the incessant rain.

They were all looking forward to the FA Cup Final against Second Division Preston North End. But first came another semi-final, this time the second leg of the League Cup-tie with Leicester City. The Hammers, losing 4-3 from the first leg, desperately battled to get back into contention but although having most of the play, a brilliant display from goalkeeper Gordon Banks denied them a goal. Leicester scored two further goals on the night to win on a 6-3 aggregate.

The Monday before the Cup Final West Ham staged a testimonial for John Lyall when an All Star XI including six ex-Hammers were beaten 5-0. On the eve of the Final, Bobby Moore collected his award as Footballer of the Year.

The Hammers were the firm favourites to win the Cup, but Preston had good players with experience in the likes of Lawton, Holden and Dawson. And they went ahead after only ten minutes, through Holden after Dawson's effort was parried.

Ninety seconds later Byrne combined with Sissons to give the youngster the opportunity to equalise. Preston would not lie down, though, and they took the lead again when Dawson

Bobby Moore is tangled up in the net, goalkeeper Jim Standen is falling under an opponent, Ken Brown is watching – and, thankfully, the ball finishes up on top of the Hammers' net in the 1964 FA Cup Final against Preston North End at Wembley.

Geoff Hurst (on knees) watches his header rebound off the Preston crossbar and over the line with goalkeeper Kelly's acrobatic bid in vain.

This time Standen punches the ball away from Preston centre-forward Alec Dawson with Ken Brown helping out and John Bond looking on.

headed home a Wilson corner five minutes before half-time.

Eight minutes into the second half, West Ham equalised again when Hurst headed the ball against the underside of the bar and it bounced down into the net. As the game wore on, it was West Ham who seemed to have the superior stamina and in injury time, Hurst beat two men and sent the ball to Brabrook on the right. A first-time ball from him and there was Boyce, hurtling in to head a dramatic winner. West Ham had won the FA Cup for the first time. They had scored three goals against all their opponents in the Cup run and the same players played in every match.

The teams on the 2 May 1964 were:

West Ham United: Standen; Bond, Burkett, Bovington, Brown, Moore, Brabrook, Boyce, Byrne, Hurst, Sissons.

Preston North End: Kelly; Ross, Smith, Lawton, Singleton, Kendall, Wilson, Ashworth, Dawson, Spavin, Holden.

Immediately after the 1964 FA Cup Final, Bobby Moore and Johnny Byrne joined up with the England party. Byrne scored twice against Uruguay at Wembley and also scored a hat-trick against Portugal in Lisbon. Another Hammer on international duty was Geoff Hurst, who played for the England Under-23 team against Israel and Turkey.

The FA Charity Shield match against League champions Liverpool kicked off the 1964-65

Ronnie Boyce (nearest camera) celebrates his winning goal in the 1964 FA Cup Final. Teammate Johnny Byrne also celebrates.

West Ham players parade the FA Cup on their lap of honour around Wembley after their 3-2 victory over Preston.

West Ham skipper Bobby Moore proudly shows off the FA Cup and the FA Charity Shield before the start of the 1964-65 season.

season. A 38,858 crowd at Anfield were treated to a wonderful match which finished 2-2. Hurst and Byrne were the West Ham goalscorers.

The first home game was a sell-out fixture against Manchester United. It proved a great match with the Hammers winning 3-1.

These were indeed good times at Upton Park, Wolves were beaten 5-0 with Hurst scoring two. Against Tottenham, Johnny Byrne scored a hat-trick in the 3-2 win. Nobody could stop Byrne scoring and he netted in 11 of the first 12 League games.

The first tie in the European Cup-winners' Cup was in Ghent against the Belgian side, La Gantoise. It was a nervous start for the Hammers but they won 1-0 when Boyce headed a corner-kick from Sealey past Seghers in the Belgian goal.

The League Cup took West Ham to Sunderland where they found themselves 4-0 down after 38 minutes. Peter Brabrook pulled a goal back but Sunderland finished worthy winners. The second leg of the Cup-winners' Cup saw the Hammers give a below-par performance. Peters scored an own-goal to give

La Gantoise the lead and Byrne it was who got the equaliser. Thus West Ham went through on a 2-1 aggregate

A groin injury forced Bobby Moore to miss the next three months of the season, but Martin Peters was an able deputy. November was a good month with away victories over Arsenal and Chelsea, both by 3-0, and an excellent 3-1 home win against Leeds.

The Hammers' next opponents in Europe were the Czech side Spartak Sokolovo. It was goalless at half-time in the first leg at Upton Park but ten minutes into the second half John Bond opened the scoring with a terrific 30-yard shot, and eight minutes from the end Alan Sealey added a valuable second goal.

The return leg in Prague proved far tougher, although Johnny Sissons put West Ham ahead after 14 minutes. John Bond conceded a penalty which was brilliantly saved by Jim Standen. In the second half the Czechs scored twice but the Hammers held on to win 3-2 on aggregate. Ronnie Boyce, in the role of sweeper, had been magnificent.

Geoff Hurst in action against Arsenal at Highbury in November 1964.

Jim Standen punches clear during the European Cup-winners' Cup second-round second-leg game against Sparta in Prague in December 1964. The Hammers lost the game but won the tie on aggregate.

In defence of the FA Cup West Ham played hosts to Birmingham City. They were given a shock when Birmingham raced into a 2-0 lead early on. However, they were roared on by a 31,000 crowd and goals from Byrne, Sissons and two from Hurst gave West Ham a 4-2 victory. The fourth-round FA Cup-tie was against London neighbours Chelsea and an all-ticket crowd of 37,000 were packed into Upton Park. In a hard-fought tie an early goal by Tambling for Chelsea proved to be the only one of the match.

The Hammers' League form was on the decline and throughout January and February there were only two wins. Brian Dear, who had been scoring regularly for the Reserves, was brought in at inside-left to boost the attack and promptly scored twice against Sunderland.

Europe beckoned again and Lausanne from Switzerland were the next opponents. In Lausanne, Dear scored first and in the second half Byrne had to run 60 yards before gliding the ball home. Late on, the Swiss reduced the arrears but the Hammers were good value for their 2-1 win. The return leg a week later provided a high level of entertainment as both teams made defensive errors which resulted in a 4-3 win for the Hammers.

West Ham were now in a comfortable mid-table position and were helped by successive wins over Arsenal and Aston Villa which saw Byrne and Hurst score in both matches.

The next European match was going to be a stiff test for West Ham. Their opponents in the semi-final were Real Zaragoza. The Spanish forward line was known as 'Los Cinquos Magnificos', the Magnificent Five. Another packed house at Upton Park were thrilled when Dear and Byrne gave West Ham a 2-0 lead inside 25 minutes. West Ham fell away after that, though, and the game finished with the Hammers taking a slender 2-1 lead to Spain.

It was a good day for Brian Dear on Good Friday. In a morning match against West Bromwich Albion at Upton Park he scored five goals in a 21- minute spell. Martin Peters was the other scorer in the 6-1 win.

West Ham flew to Spain for the second leg of the semi-final without Johnny Byrne, who was injured. In an intimidating atmosphere the Spaniards scored first to level the aggregate scores. Just before half-time, however, Johnny Sissons drove in an equaliser. In a second-half onslaught by the Spaniards both Bobby Moore and goalkeeper Jim Standen were brilliant. There

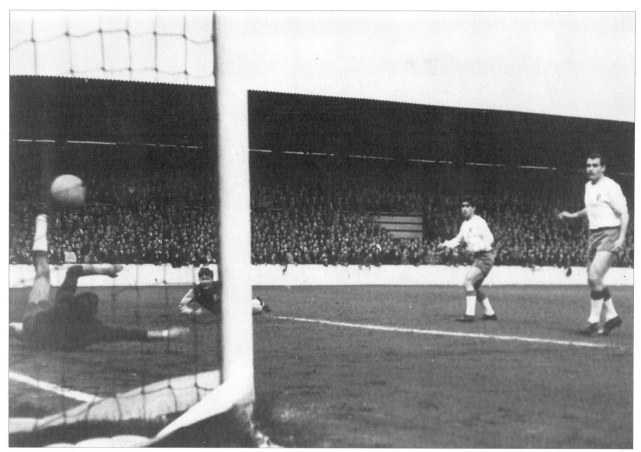

Brian Dear, flat on the ground, watches his effort beat Real Zaragoza goalkeeper Enrique Yarza at Upton Park in April 1965. Hammers won this semi-final first-leg game 2-1.

were no further goals and West Ham were safely through to the Final which would be at Wembley Stadium against TSV Munich.

The League season finished with West Ham in a respectable ninth position with Byrne and Hurst having scored 42 League goals between them.

The date 19 May 1965 will be remembered by everyone who was fortunate enough to be at Wembley on that fine evening. Tickets for the match against Munich had been made available to all the genuine supporters who had stood all year on the terraces. They were all fans who cared about the game. There were 100,000 inside the stadium and 30 million television viewers throughout Europe.

The Hammers team was significantly different from the one which won the FA Cup. Johnny Byrne was recovering from a cartilage operation and in his place was Brian Dear, who was powerful and had a wicked shot. The team was younger on the right flank. Joe Kirkup had taken over from Bond at right- back and Alan Sealey, not Brabrook, was on the right wing. Martin Peters had replaced Bovington and his stealth and intelligence gave a new dimension.

There were chances at both ends in the first half. Sissons and Dear had shots well saved by Radenkovic the giant Yugoslav goalkeeper. West Ham were troubled by the pace of the German centre-forward and captain Brunnenmeier. In the second half Sissons hit an upright before West Ham took the lead on 69 minutes. Boyce put a pass to Sealey, who crashed home a rocket shot from an acute angle. Two minutes later Moore's free-kick found Sealey, who was on hand to stab it home.

As the Hammers fans sang *Bubbles*, Bobby Moore went up to collect the trophy, his second in 12 months. It had been an unforgettable match, football at its best where skill and method flourished together.

Ron Greenwood, talking afterwards, said" "It was the way we won, for me it was fulfilment".

The celebrations that night in the East End went on into the early hours and everyone was proud of their newly crowned 'Kings of Europe'.

The teams on that fine evening were **West Ham United:** Standen; Kirkup, Burkett, Peters, Brown, Moore, Sealey, Boyce, Hurst, Dear, Sissons.

TSV Munich: Radenkovic; Wagner, Kohlars, Bena, Reich, Luttrop, Heiss, Kuppers, Brunnenmeier, Grosser, Rebele.

Alan Sealey is tackled by TSV Munich's Luttrop at Wembley during the 1965 European Cup-winners' Cup Final.

substitute when he replaced the injured Jack Burkett.

By the end of September, the Hammers had only won two League games and had conceded five goals in successive games against Sheffield United, Liverpool, and Leicester. Alan Sealey was missing from the side as he had broken a leg in training.

In the League Cup, Bristol Rovers were narrowly beaten 3-2 at Upton Park after a 3-3 draw at Eastville. Jimmy Bloomfield, the experienced inside-forward, was signed from Brentford and winger Tony Scott was transferred to Aston Villa.

The following season, West Ham found it difficult to adjust to League form after the euphoria of the Wembley win. The Football League were, for the first time this season, allowing a substitute for an injured player. In the game against Leeds United on the 28 August, Peter Bennett became the first West Ham

Although still struggling in the League, the Hammers were doing well in the League Cup. Victories over Mansfield, by 4-0, Rotherham, by 2-1, and Grimsby, by 1-0, saw West Ham progress to the semi-final.

In the European Cup-winners' Cup, West

Hammers players admire the European Cup-winners' Cup at the Chadwell Heath training ground.

Bobby Moore shows of the Cup-winners' Cup at Newham Town Hall, assisted by the Mayor, Alderman Terence C.McMillan.

Ham had a comfortable 4–0 home win over Olympiakos. In the return in Athens, two goals from Martin Peters in the 2–2 draw gave the Hammers a 6–2 aggregate win.

Martin Peters and Dave Bickles in a heading duel with Tottenham's Frank Saul at White Hart Lane in April 1966. The Hammers won 4-1.

In the League Cup semi-final first leg at Upton Park, Cardiff City were easily beaten 5-2, a rare goal by Eddie Bovington being one of the five. In December, West Ham won the BBC TV

Sportsview team award in recognition of their performance in the Cup-winners' Cup Final.

Long-serving defender John Bond joined Torquay United after making 428 appearances for the club. In January, the FA Cup started and Third Division Oldham Athletic were beaten 2-1 at Upton Park after the teams had drawn 2-2 at Boundary Park. In early February, the second leg of the League Cup semi-final took place and the Hammers again scored five against Cardiff. Geoff Hurst scored two of the goals to keep his record of having scored in every round.

The fourth round of the FA Cup brought Blackburn to Upton Park and an exciting 3-3 draw was the outcome but in the return at Ewood Park the Hammers were beaten 4-1. Their form improved in the League as three four-goal victories were gained in succession, against Aston Villa, Blackburn and Sheffield United.

The team were now in good spirits as they faced Magdeburg in the Cup-winners' Cup. It was 1-0 to West Ham at Upton Park and in East Germany a solid performance from the Hammers saw them draw 1-1 to progress to the semi-finals.

At right-back Denis Burnett was turning in some good displays, so it was no surprise when

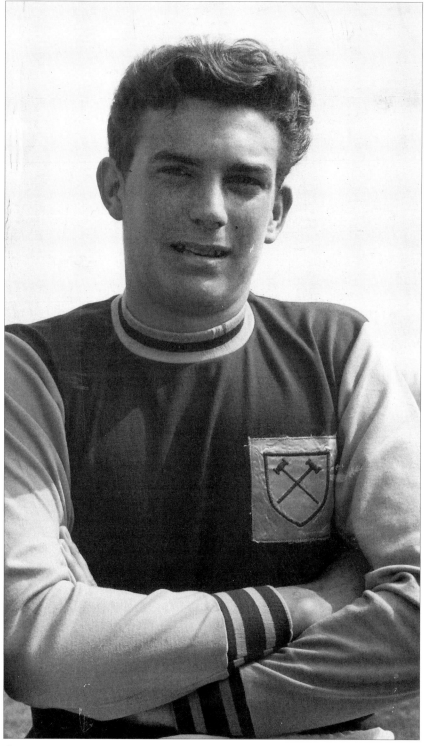

August 1965 and a new apprentice poses proudly in the shirt of West Ham, the club he has supported since he was a small boy. Trevor Brooking was destined to become one of the greatest names in the Hammers' history.

Joe Kirkup moved across London to join Chelsea.

The League Cup Final against West Bromwich Albion was the last to be played over two legs as all subsequent Finals were to be at Wembley. In the home leg, goals from Moore and Byrne gave West Ham a 2-1 lead to take to The Hawthorns. At West Bromwich, an excellent first-half display by the Midlanders gave them a 4-0 half-time lead. Martin Peters pulled a goal back but the Albion were worthy 5-3 aggregate winners.

The next European challenge was the semi-final clash with the formidable West German side, Borussia Dortmund. At Upton Park in the first leg, Martin Peters gave West Ham the lead which was held until the closing minutes then Emmerich scored twice for Borussia. After dominating most of the match this was a huge blow to the Hammers.

In the return in Germany, the shooting power of Emmerich proved lethal again as he scored twice in the first half. Johnny Byrne pulled a goal back just before half-time but Cyliax added another one for the Germans before the end. It had been a brave display by West Ham who were playing in their 20th Cup-tie of the season. Borussia went on to win the trophy after beating Liverpool at Hampden Park.

Final League victories over Arsenal, Spurs and Manchester United helped West Ham to finish in 12th place. Geoff Hurst, named as 'Hammer of the Year', had been in superb form all season and in all competitions had scored 40 goals.

In the summer of 1966, the whole nation was thrilled when England won the World Cup. There were three West Ham players in the team which was a unique honour for the club and made the supporters tremendously proud. There was considerable satisfaction in the performances of Bobby Moore, Geoff Hurst and Martin Peters in the Final against West Germany.

Bobby Moore's captaincy earned him the title of 'Player of the Tournament' from the sportswriters of the world. Geoff Hurst's hat-trick earned him a special award as England's top goalscorer and the goal which put England into a 2-1 lead was scored by Martin Peters, who gave an invaluable all- round display. The headline in

Youngsters meet West Ham's world beaters. The Hammers trio who helped England lift the World Cup in 1966 when Geoff Hurst (left) scored a historic hat-trick against West Germany. Bobby Moore (centre) captained the side and Martin Peters was the other member of the legendary threesome.

the *Stratford Express* said it all: 'West Ham 4 West Germany 2'.

In the opening games of the 1966-67 season, all eyes were on the 'World Cup trio'. Wherever they played they were given a great reception, but despite scoring four goals at Leicester, the Hammers lost the game 5-4. Their first win of the season was not until the sixth game, when

In 1966, Rhodesia was an outcast nation after declaring UDI, so when this football arrived from that country addressed to West Ham United FC, it was impounded by the British Customs. But they relented and allowed the club's World Cup winning trio to autograph it before it was returned to Rhodesia where it was raffled at the premier of the World Cup Final 'Goal', to raise money for the blind.

Manchester City were beaten 4-1 at Maine Road.

In the League Cup, a goal by Geoff Hurst gave West Ham a 1-0 win over Tottenham. In the next round two more goals from Hurst and one from Peters gave West Ham a 3-1 win at Arsenal. In the space of one week in November the Hammers provided great entertainment when they scored 17 goals.

On 5th November Fulham were beaten 6-1 at Upton Park with Geoff Hurst on the score-sheet four times. Two days later, on the Monday evening, a superb performance by West Ham stunned the soccer world. The mighty Leeds United were beaten 7-0. In a League Cup-tie at Upton Park, the Yorkshiremen were crushed by hat-tricks from Geoff Hurst and Johnny Sissons.

The following Saturday at White Hart Lane there were 57,000 to see the Hammers and Spurs turn on a magnificent display of attacking football. West Ham were 3-1 ahead, Spurs drew level at 3-3 and Hurst got the West Ham winner with 13 minutes remaining. The press were full of

Bobby Moore slides into the tackle against Sheffield Wednesday's Gerry Young at Upton Park in January 1967, in a game which the Hammers won 3-0.

praise, The *Evening News* reported: 'The best soccer show seen in London for years'.

In the League both Newcastle and West

Aston Villa goalkeeper Colin Withers dives in vain to stop Martin Peters' second goal at Upton Park in March 1967. West Ham won 2-1.

West Ham's John Charles and Arsenal's Jimmy Robertson go up for a high ball at Highbury in October 1968. The game ended goalless.

Bromwich were beaten 3-0, and in the League Cup Blackpool were beaten 3-1 at Bloomfield Road. The London derby with Chelsea drew 47,000 to Stamford Bridge. It was an amazing match as the goals flowed at both ends. West Ham were leading 5-3, but Chelsea scored two more and the game ended at 5-5.

Over Christmas, Blackpool were beaten twice with the Hammers scoring four times in each match. In the New Year's Honours list, skipper Bobby Moore was awarded the OBE, but January was a bad month for West Ham. In the League Cup semi-final first leg at The Hawthorns, West Bromwich Albion beat the Hammers 4-0, and in the FA Cup, Third Division Swindon Town humbled West Ham, winning 3-1 after a 3-3 draw at Upton Park.

The morale of the team was low and the League form suffered with defeats at Southampton by 6-2 and Everton by 4-0. In the last eight matches of the season there were seven defeats, one of them being a 6-1 home defeat by Manchester United who became League champions. It was a disappointing end to a season which up to Christmas had promised so much. Geoff Hurst went one better this year with 41

goals and was again the 'Hammer of the Year'.

There had been an interesting trip for the team in April when they spent a few days in Texas where they met Real Madrid in the Houston Astrodome. The Spaniards and West Ham became the first teams to play on a full-size pitch completely under cover. In an exciting match before a 33,000 crowd, Real Madrid were 3-2 winners.

Popular centre-half Ken Brown, after making 455 appearances, left to join Torquay United. A testimonial game was played for him against a Select XI and there was no shortage of goals as the Select XI won 9-5.

In February, Johnny Byrne returned to his former club Crystal Palace. He had given West Ham an excellent service, having scored 107 goals in 205 appearances and whilst with West Ham had been capped by England on ten occasions.

During the summer West Ham made three new signings to boost their defence. From Charlton full-back Billy Bonds joined the Hammers for a fee of £50,000. John Cushley, a centre-half, came down from Celtic. And a record fee for a British goalkeeper, of £65,000, was paid to Kilmarnock for the services of Bobby Ferguson. There was one departure when full-back Dennis Burnett joined Millwall.

The new defenders did not settle in quickly and 18 goals were conceded in the first six matches with only one win. In the 3-3 draw with Burnley at Turf Moor, West Ham gave a debut to young centre-forward Trevor Brooking who did well.

The Hammers' League form improved when Geoff Hurst scored twice in the 5-1 win at Sunderland, and four days later Martin Peters scored twice in another 5-1 win, this time in a League Cup-tie at Walsall.

Alan Sealey was transferred to Plymouth and his place at outside-right was taken by Harry Redknapp, whose speed on the wing soon made him a great favourite with the fans.

The League Cup-tie against Bolton was a personal triumph for Geoff Hurst who scored all the goals in a 4-1 win. Alas, in the next round, at Second Division Huddersfield, West Ham lost 2-0, although there was a moment of history when Harry Redknapp replaced Ronnie Boyce to become the club's first-ever League Cup substitute.

On 2 December, Jim Standen deputised in goal for the injured Ferguson against Sheffield United. It was to be his last game for the club before he emigrated to Canada and joined Detroit Cougars.

Brian Dear was brought back into the side during December and scored a Boxing Day hat-trick against Leicester. And four days later in the return, he scored a couple more in the 4-2 win. In the FA Cup, two goals came from Martin Peters in a good 3-1 win at Burnley. And a week later Fulham were crushed 7-2 at Upton Park where Trevor Brooking scored twice.

In the FA Cup fourth round, the Hammers travelled to Stoke City and came away worthy 3-0 winners. It was expected that the Hammers would beat Sheffield United at Upton Park in the fifth round, but the Yorkshiremen triumphed, winning 2-1.

A few days later, Alan Stephenson, the England Under-23 centre-half, was signed from Crystal Palace.

In April, Newcastle were beaten 5-0 at home and Trevor Brooking scored his first hat-trick for the club with Johnny Sissons adding the other two. Frank Lampard was having a good run in the side at left-back but tragedy struck when he broke his leg during the 2-1 win at Sheffield United. The season ended with a 1-1 home draw

with Everton which left the Hammers in 12th place.

There was a sad farewell to the East Terrace, known as the 'Chicken Run', and during the summer it was demolished to make way for the new East Stand.

The Hammers made a good start to the 1968-69 season with only one defeat in the first seven games. Burnley were beaten 5-0 with two goals apiece from Hurst and Brooking, and West Ham moved into third spot with a Martin Peters hat-trick in the 4-0 home win over West Bromwich Albion.

In the League Cup, Bolton Wanderers were beaten 7-2 with three of the goals coming from Hurst, but in the next round Coventry won 3-2 at Highfield Road after a goalless draw at Upton Park.

During October, Harry Redknapp was sent off in the 2-0 defeat at Leeds and Bonds and Sissons were in the England Under-23 team which played Wales at Wrexham.

Sunderland were beaten 8-0 at Upton Park, which equalled the scoreline against Leeds in 1929. It was a personal triumph for Geoff Hurst, who scored six of the goals with the other two coming from Moore and Brooking. On 4 January 1969, the new East Stand was opened for the visit of Bristol City in the FA Cup, when the Hammers celebrated by winning 3-2 with two goals by Martin Peters.

Hurst and Peters were proving an excellent double act and both scored in the next round, a 2-0 win at Huddersfield. There was a shock in store for the Hammers in the fifth round, however, when Third Division Mansfield beat them 3-0 at Field Mill. In the space of two days, Geoff Hurst scored four penalties, two for England against France and two for West Ham in the 5-2 Friday night win against Coventry.

As in earlier seasons, West Ham fell away towards the end of the campaign and none of their last nine games were won. There were four-ever presents during the season – Bonds, Hurst, Peters and Stephenson – whilst Bobby Moore missed only one game.

There were two wins in the opening two League games of 1969-70 which gave hopes for a good season. Hurst and Peters were on the mark in the 2-0 London derby victory over Chelsea. A week later at Stamford Bridge the teams drew 0-0 and West Ham welcomed back Frank Lampard who had been out of action for a year. Making his debut against Arsenal was the young Bermudan Clyde Best, who had played well on the pre-

Geoff Hurst shoots through a crowded Derby County defence at Upton Park in November 1969 and Derby's Roy McFarland takes evasive action watched by Alan Durban, Clyde Best, John McGovern, Dave Mackay and Ron Webster. West Ham beat Brian Clough's newly-promoted Rams 3-0.

season tour of America. The big centre-forward scored his first goal for the club in the 4-2 League Cup win against Halifax Town. The Hammers' League Cup hopes were dashed in the next round, though, where they lost 1-0 at Nottingham Forest.

More goals from Clyde Best followed when he scored three in three days, two against Burnley in the 3-1 win and one in the 3-3 home draw with Stoke City. By Christmas, the Hammers were struggling in 17th place and there was dismay when Trevor Brooking fractured his ankle against Nottingham Forest and despair when West Ham were knocked out of the FA Cup by Middlesbrough, who won 2-1 at Ayresome Park.

On the Monday following the Cup-tie, West Ham paid a club record fee of £90,000 to Sheffield Wednesday for the services of wing-half Peter Eustace. He made his debut against his former club at Hillsborough, where two goals from Martin Peters helped West Ham on their way to a 3-2 victory.

But there was only one win in the next eight games and the question being asked was "How can a team that has three distinguished internationals play so badly?"

In March an exchange deal with Tottenham saw Martin Peters join the North Londoners whilst West Ham gained the services of the great Jimmy Greaves. He made his debut at Manchester City and was soon on the score-sheet, netting after only ten minutes. He added another one later and the Hammers finished 5-1 winners.

The arrival of Greaves sparked a West Ham revival as Liverpool (1-0) and Wolves (3-0) were beaten at home. The final home game brought an exciting 2-2 tussle with Leeds, who finished as runners-up. West Ham, however, had struggled all season and finished 17th.

During the summer of 1970, Geoff Hurst and Bobby Moore were in Mexico with England to defend the World Cup. Unfortunately England lost to West Germany in the quarter-finals.

Back at Upton Park, in early August, John Sissons was transferred to Sheffield Wednesday.

Jimmy Greaves marks his Hammers debut with two goals at Maine Road as West Ham beat Manchester City 5-1. Tony Book and Ron Healy are the City players. Greaves finished the season with four goals in six appearances for the Hammers.

There were many who felt that he had not reached his full potential as his early form had promised so much.

The 1970-71 season opened with a trip to Tottenham where a crowd of 53,640 saw a fine game which ended 2-2. Inevitably Jimmy Greaves scored one of the goals on his return to White Hart Lane.

But there was not a single win for West Ham in the first ten games and the Hammers found themselves third from bottom. The first victory came in the League Cup when Peter Eustace scored the only goal of the match against Hull City. Then Coventry ended Hammers' hopes in the next round by winning 3-1 at Highfield Road.

During September, West Ham played an exhibition match in New York against Santos from Brazil. The game ended in a 2-2 draw with Pelé scoring both Brazilian goals and Clyde Best netting two for West Ham.

Although near the bottom of the First Division, West Ham were still drawing in the crowds. On 17 October the visit of Spurs brought a new record attendance for Upton Park of 42,322 and they saw Tommy Taylor, the

teenage centre-half acquired from Orient, enjoy a marvellous debut in the 2-2 draw.

Blackpool and Burnley, the two teams below West Ham, were both beaten at Upton Park which eased the worries.

In November, West Ham staged a testimonial for Bobby Moore, against Celtic. There were 24,448 present, many of them down from Scotland, and they witnessed an exciting 3-3 draw played in a fearfully competitive spirit. Thus a prestige friendly rose to become a minor spectacle which was a fitting tribute to a model professional.

The trip to Blackpool for a third-round FA Cup-tie in January proved to be a disaster. On a frozen pitch the Hammers played poorly and lost 4-0. It was later found out that four players were at a night club until the early hours on the eve of the match. Two of the group, Moore and Greaves, were suspended by the club. Moore was brought back into the side when he came on as substitute when the Hammers were losing 3-0 to Derby in February. The final scoreline of 4-1 to the Rams made it an unhappy afternoon for the Upton Park faithful.

The depression at the club was lifted when, on

This time Greaves heads his side's goal in their 2-1 defeat at Highbury on the last day of the 1969-70 season. Greaves finished the season with four goals in six appearances for the Hammers.

22 February, Ron Greenwood made a major signing by capturing Bryan Robson from Newcastle United. He was a current England Under-23 international and a regular goalscorer. Two days after signing, he scored in the 2-0 home win over Nottingham Forest, which was the Hammers' first home win since October. Greaves scored twice against Ipswich, Everton were beaten 1-0 at Goodison and goals from Hurst and Robson gave West Ham a 2-1 home win against Manchester United.

Thus, relegation was avoided but it had been a

Clyde Best, the Hammers centre-forward, beats Frank McLintock to head over the Arsenal bar at Highbury in the Hammers, 2-0 defeat against their North London rivals in January 1971.

poor season, one which was best forgotten. Jimmy Greaves announced his retirement from playing to pursue other interests. The great striker had apparently lost interest in football and had personal problems, too.

The Hammers began the 1971–72 season without a goal until the fifth game when Clyde Best scored in the 1–0 win over Everton. This first win of the season prompted a recovery. During September, Best scored two against Coventry in a 4–0 win and two more in the 2–1 defeat of Chelsea. Then Cardiff City were edged out of the League Cup by a 2–1 scoreline, after a 1–1 draw in London.

There were 53,334 at Old Trafford to see Trevor Brooking and Clyde Best score for West Ham. This time, however, it was George Best who stole the honours with a hat-trick for Manchester United in their 4–2 win. After a goalless home draw with Leeds in the League Cup, the Hammers went to Yorkshire and won the replay 1–0. It was Liverpool next in the League Cup and this time, goals from Hurst and

Peter Eustace and Bobby Moore watch as Manchester City's Francis Lee tries a header at Upton Park in February 1971. There were no goals.

Robson gave West Ham a deserved 2–1 win before 40,870 at Upton Park.

After losing 2–1 at home to Sheffield United in

Bryan Robson, Hammers' new signing from Newcastle United, steps out in the company of teammate Geoff Hurst to examine the Upton Park pitch before his debut in February 1971.

the League, the Hammers were drawn to meet them in the League Cup. This time it was different as Pop Robson scored a hat-trick and Clyde Best got two to give West Ham an emphatic 5-0 win to send them to the semi-finals.

In November came a testimonial match for Geoff Hurst. West Ham played a European XI

Geoff Hurst puts in a fierce challenge against Bob Wilson at Upton Park in December 1971. Clyde Best and Bob McNab watch, Peter Simpson only gets in his goalkeeper's way. The Gunners went away with a point from a goalless draw.

and it was Hurst who scored the first goal in the 4-4 draw which delighted the crowd of 29,250.

The Hammers had to travel to Stoke City for the first leg of the League Cup semi-final. Goals from Best and Hurst gave West Ham a 2-1 lead. and in the second leg, John Ritchie scored for Stoke to level the aggregate scores. There was drama in the last minute when West Ham were awarded a penalty. The Hammers were one kick away from Wembley as Geoff Hurst came forward to blast the ball into the top corner, but he was defied by a magnificent save from goalkeeper Gordon Banks.

The New Year started well when League leaders Manchester United were beaten 3-0 at home. And in the FA Cup, Luton Town were beaten 2-1 in a game full of incidents. Geoff Hurst scored after two minutes and later missed a penalty, and Bobby Moore went off on a stretcher after eight minutes.

The League Cup replay against Stoke took place at Hillsborough and with both goalkeepers in good form the tie ended goalless. The second replay was at Old Trafford and the 49,000 fans who saw the game were treated to a marvellous match which had everything in sheer football drama.

After 13 minutes goalkeeper Bobby Ferguson left the field badly dazed and in his place Bobby Moore took over the green jersey. On 25 minutes Stoke were awarded a penalty which Moore saved. But he could not hold the ball and Bernard, following up, slipped the ball into the net.

West Ham had not brought on a substitute and were still playing with ten men. Then, in an inspired nine minutes, goals from Bonds and Brooking gave West Ham the lead. Ferguson returned but was still in a state of shock and could not stop Dobing stealing in for an equaliser just before half-time. Early in the second half, Conroy scored another for Stoke and despite a late rally from West Ham, the Potters held on to win 3-2 and went on to win the League Cup at Wembley.

The teams on that memorable evening were:

West Ham: Ferguson, McDowell, Lampard, Bonds, Taylor, Moore, Redknapp(Eustace), Best, Hurst, Brooking, Robson. **Stoke City:** Banks, Marsh, Pejic, Bernard, Smith, Bloor, Conroy, Greenhoff, Ritchie, Dobing, Eastham.

In the fourth round of the FA Cup, West Ham faced a difficult trip to non- League Hereford United, who had already knocked Newcastle out of the competition. It was a hard struggle and the Hammers were relieved when the final whistle went with the score at 0-0. In the replay there was· a fine attendance of 42,271, but on this occasion there was no Cup shock and a hat-trick from Geoff Hurst gave West Ham a 3-1 win.

Hammers travelled to Huddersfield in the next round where the Yorkshiremen belied their lowly League position to win the tie 4-2. A week later, Huddersfield were the visitors to Upton Park where they lost 3-0 in a League match. A disappointing season ended with a visit from Southampton, who were beaten 1-0.

There was a lot of activity during the summer months with the departure of three players. Alan Stephenson went to Portsmouth whilst Harry Redknapp joined Bournemouth. Also, after 14 years at Upton Park, Geoff Hurst was transferred to Stoke City. He made 499 appearances for the club and scored 248 goals. Hurst will be remembered for his many goals and his World Cup hat-trick earned him a rightful place in Hammers' Hall of Fame.

One player who joined the Upton Park staff was winger Dudley Tyler, who came from Hereford. He had impressed the club with his displays in the two FA Cup-ties.

A 5-2 home win against Leicester gave Tyler his first goal for the club, and Robson was also into the mark with two goals. Pop Robson was again among the goals when he scored twice at Anfield where the Reds won 3-2, and two more in the 2-2 home draw with Manchester United. Bristol City were edged out of the League Cup at Upton Park with Hammers winning 2-1.

In early September there was a good 3-1 win at Chelsea with the half-back line of Bonds, Taylor, and Moore all getting on the score-sheet. Norwich City, newcomers to the First Division, were beaten 4-0 but the Hammers then sunk to a dismal 2-1 defeat by Fourth Division Stockport County in the League Cup.

In November, Manchester United were the opponents in a testimonial match for Ronnie Boyce. The popular Boyce had a pleasant evening with the Hammers winning 5-2.

Peter Eustace, who never properly settled at Upton Park, was transferred back to his old club Sheffield Wednesday, but Bryan Robson was having a good season and scored twice against both Stoke City (West Ham winning 3-2) and Tottenham (2-2). In each of these games, old colleagues Hurst and Peters respectively scored against the Hammers.

After Port Vale were beaten 1-0 in the FA Cup, the Hammers took an early exit when Hull City won their home tie 1-0.

On 14 February, Bobby Moore gained his 100th England cap when he played against Scotland in a game to mark the centenary of the Scottish FA. Moore celebrated his achievement by leading England to a splendid 5-0 win.

At the end of the month centre-forward Ted MacDougall was signed for £170,000 from Manchester United. He scored his first goal for the club in the 2-1 home win over Manchester City.

On eight occasions during the season Bryan Robson had scored two goals in a game and he finally got a hat-trick in the 4-3 win against Southampton in April. One defeat in the last ten games enabled West Ham to finish in a respectable sixth place.

Alas, an awful start was made to the 1973-74 season when the first win did not come until the 12th game of the season, at Coventry. Young full-back Keith Coleman was signed from Sunderland and this allowed John McDowell to move into midfield. MacDougall and Robson scored in the 2-2 draw with Liverpool in the League Cup, but the replay was lost 1-0.

Teenage goalkeeper Mervyn Day came into the side and, despite the poor results, played very well. In November the much-travelled forward Bobby Gould arrived from Bristol City and wing-half Mick McGiven joined the club from Sunderland.

After losing 3-1 at Birmingham in December, West Ham slipped to the bottom of the table.

In an exchange deal with Norwich City, Ted MacDougall went to the Norfolk side whilst midfielder Graham Paddon joined West Ham. Fortunes improved at Christmas when Chelsea were beaten 4-2 and this was followed by a 4-2 win on New Year's Day against Norwich.

The FA Cup started with Hereford United, now a Third Division side, coming to Upton Park. The Hammers struggled in the 1-1 draw and took an early exit when Hereford won 2-1 in the replay.

A revival began after this game with a nine game unbeaten run. Billy Bonds was the

Hammers manager Ron Greenwood speaks to reporters after rumours circulated in September 1973 concerning the future of Bobby Moore, who had been dropped. Moore came back the following week, but this was to prove his last season with West Ham.

Billy Bonds in action against Derby's Roy McFarland in October 1973 at Upton Park.

Hammers goalkeeper Mervyn Day fails to stop a Manchester City shot at Upton Park in December 1973 but the ball rebounded to safety off a post and West Ham went on to win 2-1.

Pat Holland and Orient's Phil Hoadley in action during the Texaco Cup game at Upton Park in August 1974. West Ham won 1-0, but then lost to Luton and Southampton and did not qualify for further progress.

inspiration with a hat-trick against Chelsea and two more goals against Coventry.

Bobby Moore had been injured in the Hereford Cup-tie and had played only a few reserve games since. After playing against Plymouth Reserves on 9 March, he decided to join Fulham. Thus, a wonderful Upton Park career had come to an end. Moore had shown a devotion to his profession which was an example worthy to be followed by any youngster. He

played in 642 games for West Ham, represented England on 108 occasions, and was undoubtedly the greatest defender in the club's history.

In April, Trevor Brooking gained his first England cap in the 0-0 draw with Portugal in Lisbon.

West Ham were now safe from relegation after Leeds (3-1) and Southampton (4-1) were beaten at Upton Park. New skipper Billy Bonds finished the season as top goalscorer and was named as 'Hammer of the Year'. During the close season, Bryan Robson returned to the North-East to join Sunderland.

Again West Ham made a poor start to a season and the 4-0 defeat at Manchester City on the opening day of 1974-75 was not encouraging. Indeed, there was only one win in the opening seven games and the League Cup-tie at Third Division Tranmere was drawn 0-0. Yet by the end of the campaign, Hammers fans would be more than happy.

In September, John Lyall was appointed team manager with Ron Greenwood assuming the role of general manager. A couple of new signings were made when centre-forward Billy Jennings arrived from Watford and Keith Robson came from Newcastle. And then things began to turn around

West Ham suddenly went goal crazy, scoring 20 in four games. Tranmere were crushed 6-0 in the League Cup replay when Bobby Gould scored a hat-trick. Both new signings, Jennings and Robson, scored in each game as Leicester were beaten 6-2, Birmingham 3-0 and Burnley 5-3 in a thriller at Turf Moor. In the League Cup, West Ham went to Fulham where the presence of Bobby Moore added interest. The former Hammer gave his usual immaculate display as Fulham emerged 2-1 winners.

West Ham added another forward to their ranks when 21-year-old Alan Taylor was brought from Rochdale in November.

By the time the FA Cup started, the Hammers were fifth in the First Division. The third-round Cup-tie was at The Dell where, after a hard encounter with Southampton, the Hammers finished 2-1 winners. The next round was a home tie with Swindon which evoked memories of the 1964 and 1967 Cup-ties with them.

The teams drew 1-1 and another giant killing was being talked about. However, goals from Brooking and Holland gave West Ham a 2-1 win in the replay. London neighbours Queen's Park Rangers were the next Cup opponents and before a 39,000 crowd, a thrilling match was won

Leeds United skipper Billy Bremner leaps high for a ball as West Ham's Graham Paddon turns away from Bremner's flying boot at Upton Park in December 1974. West Ham won 2-1.

The semi-final with Ipswich at Villa Park was a poor game. There were very few chances at either end in the goalless stalemate. The replay took place at Stamford Bridge with Ipswich now the favourites. But they complained bitterly when Clive Thomas disallowed two of their goals for offside. Once again Alan Taylor scored twice and an own-goal by Jennings was the only reply from Ipswich.

West Ham were at Wembley where they met Fulham in the Cup Final. The game turned out to be a sportswriters' dream as facing the Hammers was their former skipper, Bobby Moore. The match itself was not a memorable one, however. On the hour Jennings drove in a shot which Mellor could not hold and there was Taylor on hand to squeeze the ball home. Five minutes later another mistake by Mellor gave Alan Taylor the chance to score again and become a Wembley hero.

From an unknown at Rochdale he was now capturing the headlines. West Ham had won the FA Cup and were in Europe again.

The teams at Wembley were **West Ham:** Day,

by the Hammers with Holland and Robson scoring in their 2-1 win.

In the quarter-final West Ham travelled to Highbury, where their secret weapon turned out to be Alan Taylor, who got both goals in the 2-0 win.

Mervyn Day makes a fine save from Arsenal's Brian Kidd in the FA Cup quarter-final match at Highbury in March 1975, which West Ham won 2-0 with goals from Alan Taylor.

All smiles at the Boleyn Ground as West Ham pose for the camera before the 1975 FA Cup Final against Second Division Fulham. Back row (left to right): Robson, Best, Brooking, Bonds, Ferguson, Day, Lock, Holland, McDowell, McGiven. Front row: T.Taylor, Coleman, Gould, Lampard, A.Taylor, Paddon, Jennings.

Mervyn Day and Frank Lampard combine to thwart Les Barrett of Fulham in the 1975 FA Cup Final.

McDowell, Lampard, Bonds, T.Taylor, Lock, Jennings, Paddon, A.Taylor, Brooking, Holland.

Fulham: Mellor, Cutbush, Fraser, Mullery, Lacy, Moore, Mitchell, Conway, Busby, Slough, Barrett.

Mervyn Day had an excellent season and was selected twice for the England Under-23 team. He was also named as 'Young Player of the Year' by the Professional Footballers' Association.

On the Monday evening following the Cup Final there was a testimonial match at Upton Park for Wally St Pier, who had been with the club for 45 years, six of these as a player and the rest as a scout. The Cup-winning side met the 1964 Cup winners and although there were no goals, the 25,000 crowd were still pleased to see their former favourites and the newly won FA Cup paraded around the pitch.

West Ham returned to Wembley in August for the FA Charity Shield match against League champions Derby County. The intensive heat took its toll upon the players and goals from Hector and McFarland gave the Rams a convincing 2-0 win.

The Hammers, though, made a great start to the 1975-76 League season, going nine games without defeat. Alan Taylor was grabbing the headlines again with two goals at Liverpool in the 2-2 draw and two more in the 3-2 home defeat of Burnley.

As well as playing in the Cup-winners' Cup, West Ham were England's representatives in the Anglo-Italian Cup where they would play the Italian Cup winners on a home and away basis. The away leg was in Florence where they met Fiorentina at the Stadio Communale. The 35,000 fans were treated to some good football and the home side scored the only goal of the game.

Opponents in the League Cup were Bristol City and after a dull goalless draw at home, the Hammers made amends at Ashton Gate by winning 3-1. by contrast, there was a feast of football and a remarkable comeback by West Ham in their fixture at Leicester. Trailing 3-0 at half-time, goals from Bonds, Lampard, and a last-minute effort by Holland gave the Hammers a draw.

It was a busy time for the club as they flew to Helsinki for the Cup-winners' Cup-tie against Reipas Lahti and there was a shock after only four minutes when the Finns took the lead. Trevor Brooking equalised before half-time but the Finns went into the lead again which left Billy Bonds to come to the rescue with the equaliser after 76 minutes.

A midair battle between Leighton Phillips of Aston Villa and Keith Robson of West Ham at Upton Park in April 1976. The game ended 2-2.

In the return in London, Reipas held out until the 60th minute, when Robson scored, and further goals from Holland and Jennings in the last five minutes gave the Hammers a respectable 3-0 score line.

In a busy schedule, Darlington were the visitors in the League Cup. The Fourth Division team had not scored in their last six games and were no match for the Hammers, who ran out easy 3-0 winners.

West Ham were without Lock, Jennings and Brooking when they faced a tough task in Russia against Ararat Erevan in the Cup-winners' Cup. However, a great performance and a goal from Alan Taylor gave West Ham a 1-1 draw before a crowd of 66,000.

The Hammers continued to do well in the First Division as leaders Manchester United were beaten 2-1, and then there was a splendid 5-1 win at Birmingham.

The home leg with Ararat brought another victory. The Russians did not care for the atmosphere generated by the close proximity of the crowd at Upton Park and goals from Paddon, Robson and Taylor gave West Ham a 3-1 win.

There were nearly 50,000 spectators at White Hart Lane to see the League Cup clash with Spurs, but the game never lived up to expectations and there were few chances in the goalless draw. The replay had to be fitted into a crowded fixture list, which added to the strain, and that game went into extra-time where Spurs scored two late goals to win 2-0.

Narrow wins over Middlesbrough and Arsenal followed before Fiorentina came to defend their one-goal lead in the Anglo-Italian Cup. The Hammers were hoping for an early goal but this went to the Italians, who held the lead throughout to win the Cup with a 2-0 aggregate.

The Hammers' League form suffered during December with only one win, against Stoke City, a 3-1 victory which brought Billy Jennings his first hat-trick for the club.

In the FA Cup, West Ham were drawn at home to League leaders Liverpool, who had been defeated only once in 17 games. A goal in each half gave the Reds a 2-0 win and West Ham relinquished their hold on the trophy. There was an alarming slump in the Hammers' League form now with defeats by 3-0 at Manchester City, 4-0 at home to Liverpool and 4-0 at Manchester United.

In February, Clyde Best left to join Tampa Bay Rowdies in Florida. He had scored 58 goals during his seven years at the club but many felt that he never reached his full potential. The next opponents in Europe were the Dutch team Den Haag. The first half in the Zuiderpark Stadium was a disaster. Although West Ham did not play well they were hampered by some strange decisions by the East German referee, who gave Den Haag two debatable penalties. Then two further goals from the Dutch game them a 4-0 half-time lead.

A change of tactics in the second half brought two goals from Billy Jennings and the tie ended 4-2, which gave West Ham hope for the second leg. There were nearly 30,000 inside Upton Park for the return game and the Hammers attacked from the start, and by half time were leading 3-0. The Dutch got a goal back in the second half and the tie ended 5-5 on aggregate. By scoring two goals in Holland, the Hammers went through on away goals.

Although doing well in Europe, West Ham's League results were poor. There was not a single victory during February and March and a 6-1 defeat at Arsenal was depressing. Meanwhile, between West Ham and a European Final stood the talented Eintracht Frankfurt.

Trevor Brooking slides the ball past Eintracht goalkeeper Peter Kunter at a rain-soaked Upton Park in April 1976 and West Ham are on their way to another European Cup-winners' Cup Final.

The Hammers, playing away in the first leg, were heartened when Graham Paddon fired in a superb shot to give them the lead. The Germans, however, fought back with two goals and the game ended at 2-1.

The atmosphere in the return was electric. Trevor Brooking was having a brilliant match and scored twice and another goal came from Robson. The Germans came back with a goal but despite several scares West Ham held on to march into the Final.

The glory in reaching the European Final in some way compensated for the poor League results which saw the Hammers finish the season in 18th place.

Now, though, they faced a difficult task in the Cup-winners' Cup Final against Anderlecht as the game was being played in the Heysel Stadium in Brussels, which gave home advantage to the Belgians.

The 10,000 Londoners who had made the trip were ecstatic when Holland put West Ham in front, but tragedy struck just before half-time. Frank Lampard misjudged a pass and Rensenbrink nipped in to equalise. Unfortunately Lampard also tore a muscle and took no further part in the game.

Two minutes before half-time, Van Der Elst put the Belgians into the lead. The Hammers equalised in the second half, when Robson scored from a cross by Brooking. Then Holland robbed Rensenbrink to give away a corner but instead the French referee awarded a penalty which Rensenbrink gleefully put away. West Ham were now chasing the game and were punished with a fourth goal from Van Der Elst.

Although the class of Rensenbrink and Van Der Elst had proved too much for them, West Ham had played their part in a wonderful game of football.

The teams for the 1976 Cup-winners' Cup Final were: **West Ham:** Day, Coleman, Lampard(A.Taylor), Bonds, T.Taylor, McDowell, Holland, Paddon, Jennings, Brooking Robson. **Anderlecht:** Ruiter, Lomme, Broos, Van Binst, Thissen, Doeks, Coeck(Vercauteren), Van Der Elst, Ressel, Haan, Rensenbrink.

Ups and Downs at Upton Park

THE Carlisle United captain and centre-half Bill Green was signed before the start of the 1976-77 season, and he had a difficult debut when Aston Villa won the opening League game 4-0. The Hammers were finding goals hard to come by, although Pat Holland scored twice in the 3-0 League Cup win against Barnsley. In the next round, Alan Taylor's goal was sufficient to beat Charlton 1-0.

There was good news in October when former player Bryan Robson rejoined the club after his spell at Sunderland. Another newcomer was Alan Devonshire, who had been signed from non-League Southall. He played his first game for

Billy Bonds and Frank Lampard close in on Middlesbrough's David Armstrong at Upton Park in December 1976. Hammers had just emerged from victory before a 55,000 crowd at Old Trafford, but 'Boro beat them 1-0.

the club in the League Cup-tie against Queen's Park Rangers, who spoilt his debut by winning 2-0.

A deserved testimonial for Frank Lampard took place on 2 November with Fulham the opponents. Lampard scored the first goal in a 3-1 win, and George Best and Bobby Moore were in the Cottagers' side.

Bryan Robson scored his first goal since rejoining them when Tottenham were beaten 5-3. The win was certainly needed as the Hammers were bottom of the table. Further joy came when Manchester United were beaten 2-0 at Old Trafford, followed by a 2-0 home win over League leaders Liverpool.

Graham Paddon returned to his former club, Norwich, and the Hammers promoted Geoff Pike to take over his midfield role.

Bolton Wanderers were beaten 2-1 in the FA Cup, but hopes were shattered at Aston Villa in the fourth round when the home side won easily 3-0.

Centre-forward John Radford had been signed from Arsenal but he was finding goals hard to

Aston Villa's Andy Gray scores the only goal of the match at Upton Park in January 1977. A week later, Hammers travelled to Villa Park and were knocked out of the FA Cup.

come by. In February there was welcome League points when, on successive Saturdays, there were wins over Stoke, Arsenal and Bristol City. The following week, however, brought a 6-0 defeat at Sunderland who were beneath the Hammers in the table. This was the jolt West Ham needed and

Alan Taylor goes past Arsenal goalkeeper Jimmy Rimmer to score one of his two goals in West Ham's 3-2 win at Highbury in February 1977

Alan Curbishley and Frank McLintock of Arsenal in action at Highbury in October 1977. West Ham lost 3-0 and at the end of the season were relegated.

they lost only two of their remaining 15 games. Relegation was finally avoided when the double was achieved over Manchester United after a 4-2 win at Upton Park.

Fresh from their tour of Norway and Spain, the players reported back for the start of season 1977-78 hoping for a better year. But there were a few injuries and a 3-2 win at Newcastle was the

Mervyn Day can only watch as Ken McNaught opens the scoring for Aston Villa at Upton Park in October 1977. The sides drew 2-2.

Hammers' only victory in the first two months.

Keith Robson was released to Cardiff and West Ham recorded their heaviest League Cup defeat, losing 5-0 at Nottingham Forest.

To boost the forward line, Derek Hales was signed from Derby County. His first goal came in the 2-2 draw with Aston Villa and a week later he scored two more in the 2-0 win against Ipswich at Portman Road.

On 31 October, Trevor Brooking scored the first goal in his testimonial game against an England XI. Hales also added an hat-trick in the Hammers 6-2 win.

A couple of weeks later, Brooking scored his first goal for England in their 2-0 victory over Italy. On the England bench as substitute was Billy Bonds.

There was plenty of activity in early December. After 16 years at Upton Park, Ron Greenwood left to continue his role as England manager, and John Lyall was upgraded from his former title of team manager.

Centre-forward David Cross was signed from West Bromwich Albion. Cross had been a prolific scorer at his previous clubs, Coventry and Norwich.

The first home game of the season was won on 10 December when Manchester United were beaten 2-1 with goals from Brooking and Hales.

After a struggle, Fourth Division Watford were beaten 1-0 at home in the FA Cup. There was disaster in the next round, though, when after a 1-1 draw at Upton Park, Queen's Park Rangers crushed West Ham 6-1 in the replay.

In February John Radford, who had not scored a goal, was transferred to Blackburn.

By mid-March the Hammers were third from bottom but they then staged a recovery. Ipswich were beaten 3-0, with David Cross scoring three

in eight minutes, and during a six-game spell West Ham won five games and the possibility of avoiding relegation improved.

Expectancy grew after 2-1 wins at both Leeds and Middlesbrough and the final game of the season brought a 37,000 crowd to Upton Park to see the game with Liverpool. The Hammers needed a point to stay up, but a 2-0 defeat saw them relegated.

During the summer there were a few departures. Keith Coleman went to KV Mechelen in Belgium, Bill Green joined Peterborough. Derek Hales went to Charlton, and Kevin Lock was transferred to Fulham.

There was a good start to the season when Notts County were beaten 5-2 on the opening day with David Cross getting a hat-trick. A few days later there was a fine 3-0 win at Newcastle, but a shock came when Swindon won 2-1 at Upton Park in the League Cup.

In October, West Ham moved into third place in Division Two after Bryan Robson had scored a hat-trick in the 3-0 home win against local rivals, Millwall.

There was a good attendance of 21,081 for Billy Bonds testimonial match against Tottenham. David Cross scored twice and Bonds netted from a penalty in the 4-2 win.

Cross and Robson were scoring regularly and both found the net in the 4-0 win over Blackburn.

There was a mighty shock in the FA Cup, though, when Fourth Division Newport County gained a 2-1 win at Somerton Park.

In February a record fee of £525,000 was paid to Queen's Park Rangers when John Lyall bought giant goalkeeper Phil Parkes. He was a quality goalkeeper who had gained one full and six Under-23 caps during his spell at Loftus Road.

Although Newcastle were beaten 5-0 during March, the Hammers' promotion rivals Brighton, Stoke and Crystal Palace began to move away at the top. Four draws during April finally ended the promotion hopes and left the Hammers to finish in fifth spot.

A number of changes were needed at Upton Park and six players were allowed to leave before the start of the 1979-80 season. John McDowell and Alan Taylor went to Norwich, whilst Billy Jennings, Mervyn Day and Tommy Taylor joined Orient. Bryan Robson returned to the North-East again when he went back to Sunderland for the second time.

There was one arrival when Stuart Pearson, an experienced international, came from

West Ham's Alvin Martin (not in picture) has just scored against Sunderland at Upton Park in November 1979, in a League Cup fourth-round replay which Hammers won 2-1.

Manchester United. He was soon on the target with a goal when Barnsley were beaten in the first leg of the League Cup. At Oakwell in the return there were goals from David Cross in the 2-0 win. Making his debut at Barnsley was tough tackling full-back Ray Stewart, who had been bought from Dundee United.

For the League Cup-tie against Southend, John Lyall brought in youth-team player Paul Allen, who had a marvellous match and kept his place in the side. After two draws, Southend were finally beaten 5-1 with young Billy Lansdowne scoring three.

By the end of October, however, only five League games had been won, which left the Hammers in 14th place. Another signing took place when the former Spurs winger Jimmy Neighbour joined West Ham from Norwich City.

During November, a trio of Welsh clubs – Cardiff, Swansea and Wrexham – returned home from Upton Park without a goal or points.

Sunderland were knocked out of the League Cup after a replay and the draw paired the Hammers with Brian Clough's Nottingham Forest but after a goalless draw at Upton Park, the

First Division team won 3-0 after extra-time in the replay.

The FA Cup started at West Bromwich where an inspired display from Phil Parkes earned West Ham a 1-1 draw. In the replay, second-half goals from Pike and Brooking gave the Hammers a 2-1 victory. The next round brought a trip to neighbours Orient and, despite a goal from former Hammer Taylor, West Ham won 3-2. Two of their goals had come from Ray Stewart, who was gaining a reputation for scoring penalties.

Swansea City were next in the fifth round and they almost gained a replay until the Hammers scored twice in the last eight minutes.

The three League games during February were all won and this boosted the confidence of the side before Aston Villa were faced at Upton Park in the sixth round. It was a tightly fought contest and with the score still goalless with only a minute remaining, a penalty was awarded to West Ham.

There were many West Ham fans who dared not look as the ice-cool Stewart stepped up to blast the ball home and send the Hammers into the semi-final.

Trevor Brooking and Swansea City's Ian Callaghan in aerial action at Vetch Field in March 1980.

After the euphoria of their Cup win, the Hammers' League form was disappointing and they did not record a single victory during March.

The FA Cup semi-final against Everton took place at Villa Park, and the game was not without incident. Brian Kidd put Everton ahead and was later sent off. Stuart Pearson equalised and Paul Allen thought he had scored a late winner but his effort was disallowed for offside.

The replay at Elland Road was a tremendous tussle and at full-time the teams were still level at 0-0. In extra-time, Alan Devonshire, who had been brilliant throughout, put West Ham ahead, only for Latchford to equalise. But towards the end, Frank Lampard popped up in the Everton penalty area and gleefully headed the winner. The joyous scene that followed, of Lampard dancing around the corner-flag, will never be forgotten. West Ham were at Wembley again where they would meet Arsenal in an all-London Cup Final There also was still an outside chance of promotion, but this disappeared when Birmingham won 2-1 at Upton Park in April. It was a tense affair which saw both Billy Bonds and Colin Todd sent off for fighting.

Arsenal were the favourites to win the Cup

Frank Lampard and Arsenal's Liam Brady take a tumble in the 1980 FA Cup Final at Wembley.

The goal that won the FA Cup. Trevor Brooking's low header which proved the only goal of the 1980 Final.

with their striking duo of Stapleton and Sunderland and the midfield wizardry of Liam Brady, so John Lyall decided to use Stuart Pearson in a deeper role with David Cross alone up front.

West Ham thus encouraged Arsenal to attack and hoped for a goal on the break. On 13 minutes, a Devonshire centre found Cross, who hit a shot which rebounded to Pearson. Pearson hit the rebound and there was Trevor Brooking, stooping low to head West Ham into the lead.

After this the Hammers defended stoutly with Bonds and Martin superb at the heart of their defence. In the second half Rix and Brady tested Parkes but the Gunners did not have the imagination to prise open West Ham's iron grip.

Towards the end the Hammers were looking much the stronger side. Seventeen-year-old Paul Allen was having a brilliant match and only a cynical foul by Willie Young at the end stopped him from adding West Ham's second goal.

The Cup was won and as the ecstatic fans sang *Bubbles,* their thoughts turned to the following season's European trips and an assault on the Second Division championship.

The teams on that glorious Wembley day in May 1980 were: **West Ham:** Parkes, Stewart, Lampard, Bonds, Martin, Devonshire, Allen, Pearson, Cross, Brooking, Pike. **Arsenal:** Jennings, Rice, Devine(Nelson), Talbot, O'Leary, Young, Brady, Sunderland, Stapleton, Price, Rix.

West Ham returned to Wembley again in August where they met League champions Liverpool in the Charity Shield. McDermott scored for Liverpool after 18 minutes and this goal turned out to be the only one of the game with both defences on top throughout.

A few days later a major signing was made when the Hammers invested £800,000 for Paul Goddard, a proven goalscorer from Queen's Park Rangers. Goddard got his first goals for the club when scoring twice in the 4-0 home win against Notts County. In the League Cup, Third Division Burnley were beaten 6-0 on aggregate over two legs. Cross and Goddard were forming a good partnership for the Hammers and were scoring regularly.

The first trip in the Cup-winners' Cup began with West Ham travelling to Spain to face Castilla in the Bernabeu Stadium. David Cross gave West Ham the lead, but there was a disappointing second half with three goals conceded. There was also disappointment off the pitch when a minority of English fans caused trouble in the

Happy Hammers players parade the FA Cup around Wembley after the Second Division club's memorable win over Arsenal.

stadium. The UEFA ruling that followed was that the home leg should be played behind 'closed doors' at Upton Park. Thus that game was played in a strange, eerie atmosphere in front of officials and the media totalling 262. West Ham set about the task very well, though, and David Cross scored three in a 5-1 win.

There were narrow League Cup wins over Charlton and Barnsley before the Hammers faced Politehnica Timisoara from Romania in their next European tie. At Upton Park it was a good night when the Hammers rocked the Romanians with three goals in a six-minute spell in the first half. Cross added a fourth late in the game and the 4-0 result made the second leg almost a formality. In the return the Italian referee needed to be on top form as the Romanians resorted to some rough play. The Hammers held out but conceded the only goal of the game to lose 1-0.

Terry McDermott celebrates his winning goal against Hammers in the 1980 FA Charity Shield game at Wembley.

Sunderland's Kevin Arnott scores the first of his side's two goals against West Ham at Roker Park in May 1980. The goals secured Sunderland's promotion to Division One. West Ham, of course, were still basking in the glory of winning the FA Cup.

This was the first European tie where West Ham had not scored, and as this was their 28th game in Europe it was a record of which to be proud.

In the League there was an unbeaten run of 15 games which put the Hammers top of the table and made them promotion favourites.

True, during November there was a couple of setbacks with away defeats at Luton and Derby, but there was joy when West Ham marched into the League Cup semi-finals after Cross scored in the 1–0 victory against Tottenham. Excellent wins over Sheffield Wednesday and Derby during December kept the side at the top, although there was a shock on Boxing Day in a 3–0 defeat at Queen's Park Rangers.

In the FA Cup there was a mammoth saga with Wrexham before, after 334 minutes of football, the Welsh club won 1–0 in a second replay at the Racecourse Ground. A good 3–1 win at second-placed Swansea and a 5–0 thrashing of Preston followed. The team were playing with confidence and seemed certainties for promotion but a disappointment occurred in the League Cup semi-final first leg at Coventry.

West Ham were leading 2–0 when Coventry scored three times in a 12-minute spell to finish

Trevor Brooking takes on the Liverpool defence in the 1981 League Cup Final.

Sammy Lee (8) is happy after Kennedy scores for Liverpool in the 1981 League Cup Final.

3-2 winners. In the return at Upton Park, Paul Goddard reduced the deficit and, with only a minute remaining, extra-time loomed and there were joyous scenes when Jimmy Neighbour came through to score the goal which put the Hammers into the Final.

Against Chelsea in February, Billy Bonds made his 500th League appearance for the club. It was

Trevor Brooking weaves through the Everton defence at Upton Park in October 1981. The game was a 1-1 draw as West Ham settled back in the top flight.

a sparkling team performance with two brilliant goals from Brooking in the 4-0 victory. A week later, before another packed home crowd, the Hammers scored four against Cambridge and the 4-2 win gave them a nine-point lead at the top of the Second Division.

The quarter-finals of the Cup-winners' Cup brought Dynamo Tbilisi to Upton Park. The Russians proved to be one of the best European sides that had ever been seen at West Ham. They left with a 4-1 win and a standing ovation.

Then it was back to Wembley for the League Cup Final against Liverpool. At full-time there was still no score and all the incidents were to come in extra time. First there was controversy when Kennedy scored for Liverpool but the linesman acknowledged that Lee was in an offside position. Referee Clive Thomas, however, amidst uproar, gave the goal.

There was also drama in the last minute when McDermott fisted a Martin header over the bar with Clemence beaten. The responsibility for taking the resultant penalty went to Ray Stewart and, as usual, he proved equal to the occasion and scored to end the game at 1-1.

A few days later the Hammers travelled to Tbilisi for the return leg with the Russians. It was a nightmare journey and, with interrupted schedules, they finally arrived a day late. It was hardly the best preparation for a game but the players wanted to salvage some pride after the 4-1 home defeat. There were 80,000 inside the Lenin Stadium, who were shocked when Stuart Pearson scored to give West Ham a 1-0 victory, which was some consolation against a quality side.

The League Cup Final replay took place at Villa Park. Paul Goddard scored with a header to put West Ham in front, but two goals in three minutes from Dalglish and Hansen gave Liverpool a deserved victory.

On 11 April, West Ham became champions after David Cross had scored four goals in a 5-1 win at Grimsby. It had been a marvellous season with 11 club records broken including being undefeated in 18 successive League games and gaining a record 66 points. Also that season there was success for the Youth team when they won both the FA Youth Cup and the South-East Counties League Cup. John Lyall was named as Second Division Manager of the Year and individual honours followed when Alvin Martin made his England debut against Brazil and Ray Stewart was awarded his first cap for Scotland against Wales. In June, Trevor Brooking was awarded the MBE and celebrated by scoring twice for England in their 3-1 win in Hungary.

Before the 1981-82 season started there were a

couple of goalkeeping changes. Bobby Ferguson emigrated to Australia and in his place Tom McAllister joined Hammers on a free transfer from Swindon. The opening day of the season saw visitors Brighton gain a 1-1 draw both goals being penalties.

On the following Monday evening there was a terrific result at Tottenham with David Cross scoring all the goals in a 4-0 win, and by the end of September, West Ham were League leaders and undefeated. Derby County were beaten home and away in the League Cup before the first defeat took place when League champions Aston Villa pipped West Ham 3-2 at Villa Park.

Alvin Martin scored twice against Coventry in a 5-2 win, and a week later, it was Trevor Brooking's turn to score twice when the Hammers drew 3-3 at Leeds after being 3-1 down. After two drawn games, West Bromwich Albion knocked West Ham out of the League Cup, winning 1-0 in the replay where Paul Allen got his marching orders.

Due to the frost and snow there was only one game in December, but an event which caused some excitement was the signing of Francois Van Der Elst, the Belgian international who had played brilliantly against West Ham in the 1976 Cup-winners' Cup Final.

The FA Cup-tie with Everton beat the weather and West Ham won 2-1 in a game where Phil Parkes saved a late penalty. Another new signing was made when Neil Orr, the Scottish Under-21 international, was purchased from Morton. January was a poor month with an FA Cup defeat at Watford followed by three League defeats. By March, Van Der Elst had settled in and showed his goalscoring ability by netting in four games.

On 7 April, West Ham hosted the England Under-21 international against Poland and an attendance of 6,680 saw the 2-2 draw.

Paul Goddard was now a regular scorer and bagged two goals in each of victories against Middlesbrough (3-2) and Wolves (3-1). In the thrilling 4-3 home win over Leeds, Trevor Brooking also scored twice, which meant that he had scored four times against Leeds that season. The campaign came to an end with draws against Spurs and Manchester United which left a final League placing of ninth.

A free transfer was given to Stuart Pearson and during the summer, David Cross, who had netted 97 goals for the club, joined Manchester City. Coming into the side as the 1982-83 season got under way was Sandy Clark, the Hammers' new

Phil Parkes looks on in despair as Alan Sunderland's shot defeats him at Highbury in May 1982. The Gunners won 2-0 but West Ham eventually ended the season in a creditable ninth place.

centre-forward bought from Airdrie for £200,000.

The game with Ipswich in September set a new appearance record when Billy Bonds played in his 545th League game for West Ham to beat Bobby Moore's record.

New boy Sandy Clark was soon getting goals, scoring in four games, in a run of five successive victories. There were two big games in October when Liverpool and Manchester United were the visitors. Over 30,000 watched each game and both were won 3-1 by West Ham. After the Hammers drew 1-1 at Stoke in the League Cup, the home tie went 2-1 in the Hammers favour.

The League game at Stoke, however, was different as the home side won 5-2. Then Lincoln City were beaten 2-1 in the League Cup after the teams had drawn 1-1 at Lincoln.

There were a few injuries at the club. Bonds had fractured a bone in his foot, whilst Brooking had been missing all season with pelvic trouble. Added to the depression was a 3-0 home defeat by Coventry. An exciting League Cup match took place at Meadow Lane when Notts County took a 2-0 lead in the second half. A hat-trick from Van Der Elst put West Ham in front, only for County to equalise in the dying minutes. Van Der Elst was in good form and a week later he scored twice for Belgium against Scotland.

The League Cup replay against Notts County was convincingly won 3-0 to give the Hammers a tough trip to Liverpool. Two youngsters from the Youth team were given their first-team debuts and both scored. Alan Dickens netted his goal in the 2-1 win at Notts County, whilst Tony Cottee got the first goal when Tottenham were beaten 3-0 on New Year's Day. An early exit from the FA Cup was made when goals from Coppell and

Seventeen-year-old Tony Cottee and Spurs' Gary O'Reilly battle for the ball at Upton Park on New Year's Day 1983, when Cottee marked his League debut with a goal.

Stapleton gave Manchester United a 2-0 win at Old Trafford.

Ten days later there was another defeat, this time in a League Cup match at Anfield. Amidst hail and snow, West Ham and Liverpool were drawing 1-1 with four minutes remaining when Souness scored the Reds' winner.

A friendly match was arranged with Dundee United in February, following the exit of both clubs from their respective Cup competitions. A crowd of 6,425 at Upton Park saw an interesting 2-2 draw.

During March, Sandy Clark, who had not properly settled into English football was sold to Glasgow Rangers. In his place John Lyall signed Dave Swindlehurst from Derby County. The arrival of a big target man helped Goddard and Van Der Elst and there was a four-match unbeaten run. Included in this was a splendid 5-1 away win at Swansea, where Dickens and Pike both scored twice. The season ended with Tony Cottee coming on as substitute at Coventry and scoring two goals in the 4-2 win.

The usual transfer activity took place before

the start of the 1983-84 season. West Ham welcomed Steve Walford – a defender from Norwich and Steve Whitton – a forward from Coventry. Departures included Pat Holland and Jimmy Neighbour, who both went into coaching, and Francois Van Der Elst, who went home to Belgium to join Lokeren.

There was a good start to the season with five consecutive victories which ensured a place at the top of the table. On the opening day, Birmingham were crushed 5-0 with two goals coming from Cottee. Steve Walford got his first goal for the club in the 1-0 win at Everton and the other new boy, Steve Whitton, scored in the 2-0 win against Spurs.

There was an exciting scoring burst in the home game against Coventry. After 15 minutes West Ham were losing 2-0 and had missed a penalty. Then, in a amazing four minutes, West Ham scored three goals to leave Coventry shattered. The Hammers added two more in the second half to win 5-2. Dave Swindlehurst collected his first match ball as a Hammer when he scored a hat-trick.

In October, West Ham announced that they would be involved in shirt sponsorship for the first time and that the sponsors would be Avco Trust Ltd. There was a narrow 2-1 win at Bury in the League Cup and the return leg at Upton Park attracted only 10,896. Those who were there were treated to some superb football which resulted in a West Ham record victory of 10-0. Teenage Tony Cottee led the massacre with four goals, with two apiece from Brooking and Devonshire.

Dave Swindlehurst did not score in the goal spree but he was on target five times in the next four League games with both goals in the 2-1 win over Ipswich.

Brighton were the opponents in the next round of the League Cup and they proved much more difficult than Bury before a goal by Swindlehurst ten minutes from time proved to be the winner. The tie was West Ham's 100th game in the competition. In the next round, after a 2-2 draw in London, Everton won 2-0 in the replay after extra-time.

At Christmas there was a sparkling performance against Tottenham. A Ray Stewart thunderbolt was the pick of the goals in the 4-1 win.

There was a tough FA Cup-tie when Third Division Wigan Athletic came to Upton Park. The Hammers were without Martin and Whitton, who had both been injured in a car accident, and there was a further disaster after 15 minutes when Alan Devonshire was carried off on a stretcher with torn ligaments. The injury proved to be long term and he was out of the game for over a year. The Hammers progressed into the next round when Ray Stewart converted a penalty in the 1-0 win.

It was London neighbours Crystal Palace who were the next Cup opponents and after a 1-1 draw at Selhurst Park, West Ham won the replay 2-0. It was a black day in the next round, however, as Birmingham City easily won their home tie by 3-0 in a game spoilt by pitch invasions from a hooligan minority.

The tall Bury defender Paul Hilton joined the club and no doubt was happier to be playing for West Ham than against them as he did in the 10-0 thrashing earlier in the season. By mid-March, the Hammers were in fifth spot, but then came two poor away defeats, by 4-1 at Leicester and 6-0 at Liverpool. The Hammers never recovered from these defeats and won only one more game that season.

On the final home game of the season there was a sad farewell to a great footballer. After 635 games for the club, Trevor Brooking was retiring. Brooking had been a credit to his profession and West Ham would suffer without his elegant artistry. Although he would be remembered for his midfield skills, it should be noted that he also scored 102 goals for the club.

The season came to an end when Pat Holland, now coach at Orient, was given a testimonial against Tottenham which West Ham won 4-1. Holland was an all-action, competitive player who did not always get the appreciation he deserved.

Prior to the start of the 1984-85 season, West Ham signed defender Tony Gale from Fulham for £150,000. Gale was an experienced player who had already played in over 300 games for the West Londoners. A knee injury to Phil Parkes ruled him out of contention for the start of the new season but Tom McAllister was able to step in as replacement.

A drab goalless opening game against Ipswich did not give encouragement. The mood soon changed, though, after three consecutive wins. Paul Goddard scored twice at Southampton in a 3-2 victory and Ray Stewart also scored two, both from penalties in a 3-1 home win over Coventry.

The League Cup-tie at Bristol City was drawn 2-2 with the Hammers having better luck in the replay winning 6-1. A nightmare game at Old Trafford saw Manchester United win 5-1 before West Ham bounced back winning 4-2 at Stoke and 3-1 against Arsenal at home. Back in Manchester again, the League Cup-tie against City ended 0-0. A disappointing display in the replay however saw City go through winning 2-1.

The Hammers' League form up to Christmas was poor but there was a good 2-2 draw at Tottenham on Boxing Day, followed by a 2-1 win at Coventry where Tony Cottee scored twice.

The FA Cup began with a 4-1 defeat of Port Vale, where Paul Goddard scored a hat-trick. Snow and ice put paid to the League programme and it was not until February that Norwich were the visitors for a fourth-round Cup match. Now managed by former Hammer Ken Brown, they took a one-goal lead, but two goals in two minutes from the Hammers saw them through to round five.

Paul Allen was having a marvellous season and gained applause from all quarters. And the team was given a terrific boost when Alan Devonshire returned to face Wimbledon in the FA Cup. The first game at Plough Lane ended 1-1 and in the replay, a Tony Cottee hat-trick ended the Dons' hopes in a 5-1 win.

A few days later, despite a spirited display, West Ham went out of the Cup, beaten 4-2 by Manchester United at Old Trafford. After 16 years without a West Ham goal at the City Ground, home of Nottingham Forest, Tony Cottee finally broke the hoodoo and Paul Goddard added another in the 2-1 victory. The joy was short-lived, however, as two days later West Ham lost 5-0 at Watford.

At Queen's Park Rangers, goalkeeper Tom McAllister took a blow in the ribs from Rangers' Steve Wicks. It was a bad injury which resulted in broken ribs and a punctured lung. Ray Stewart replaced him but then conceded two goals as Rangers went on to win 4-2.

In April, Paul Allen skippered the England Under-21 side in Romania. Also in the team was clubmate Tony Cottee.

There were only 8,000 fans at The Hawthorns for the game against West Bromwich Albion. The missing home fans wished they had turned up as the Hammers were beaten 5-1. Now just above the bottom three, it was vital to win the home game against Stoke City. Once again Billy Bonds boosted the side and scored two goals. Further goals by Pike, Stewart and Hilton helped to crush Stoke 5-1. And for the final game of the season, Frank Lampard was brought in for his last appearance in a West Ham shirt. The Reds, runners-up to Everton in the League, finished strongly, winning 3-0.

Best-ever – Then More Ups and Downs

WEST Ham welcomed two new signings for their opening games of the 1985-86 season. Mark Ward, a winger from Oldham, was bought to replace Paul Allen who had left to join Tottenham. Also in the side was Frank McAvennie, the blond striker from St Mirren. McAvennie was soon on the mark with two goals in the 3-1 win against Queen's Park Rangers.

At the end of August, he scored two more in a 2-2 draw with Liverpool and was beginning to form a lethal partnership with Cottee. Both scored in the 3-0 League Cup win against Swansea, and in the return in Wales there were two penalties converted by Ray Stewart in a 3-2 win. The team began to play with great confidence and there was an unbeaten run of 18 League games which included nine consecutive wins.

There was some good victories over the Midland clubs. Leicester were beaten 3-0, Aston Villa 4-1 and West Bromwich 4-0. Gale and Martin were superb at the heart of the defence and Devonshire was back to his best, although there was one disappointment when Manchester United won the League Cup-tie 1-0 at Old Trafford.

Frank McAvennie gained his first Scottish cap in the 2-0 World Cup victory against Australia. The in-form striker scored the second goal and observers likened him to Denis Law, the former Scottish hero.

The unbeaten League run came to an end on Boxing Day when a goal five minutes from time by Perryman gave Spurs a 1-0 home victory. A late goal by Tony Cottee gave West Ham a 1-0 FA Cup win against Charlton and the next round brought a clash with Ipswich Town. Following two drawn games, West Ham won 1-0, courtesy of a Cottee goal at Portman Road. The weather played havoc during February and the only game played was a Sunday fixture against Manchester United at Upton Park. The match, shown live on television, ended 2-1 with goals from Cottee and Ward. Manchester United were soon back at Upton Park, this time for a fifth-round FA Cup-tie which ended 1-1. In the replay, a rare headed goal from Pike and a Stewart penalty gave the Hammers a great 2-0 victory.

A few days later came a trip to Hillsborough for the quarter-final Cup-tie against Sheffield Wednesday. Despite a late rally and a Cottee goal, West Ham went down losing 2-1. Cottee was having a good season where he had scored 19 goals. At the annual PFA dinner he was named as 'Young Player of the Year'.

A brilliant performance against Chelsea at Stamford Bridge saw West Ham win 4-0. Devonshire, Cottee (two), and McAvennie were the scorers. It proved to be a good Easter as, two days later, there was a 2-1 home win against Tottenham. By mid-April West Ham were fifth and faced a tough schedule of four home games in ten days. Newcastle were their first opponents and what a night that turned out to be. The Geordies were crushed 8-1 with skipper Alvin Martin scoring a unique hat-trick against three different goalkeepers. First he scored a tap-in past Thomas, then a header which beat Hedworth and finally a penalty was scored against Beardsley.

Coventry and then Manchester City were both beaten 1-0 in tense affairs. A crowd of 31,000 packed Upton Park for the final home game of the season. With the score at 1-1 and only three minutes remaining there was drama when West Ham were awarded a penalty. Again it was that man Stewart who scored to give Hammers a 2-1 win.

Alan Devonshire evades a tackle by Glen Roeder in the Hammers' magnificent 8-1 victory over Newcastle United in April 1986, as West Ham strode on towards their best-ever finishing place in Division One.

Now third in the League they needed to win at West Bromwich whilst hoping that Chelsea would beat Liverpool. It was a struggle but, to the delight of the large contingent of travelling fans, West Ham emerged 3-2 winners. There was disappointment later, however, when it was learnt that Liverpool had won to clinch the championship.

Nevertheless, it had been an excellent season, for third in the First Division was the highest final placing in West Ham's history. It was a shame that the ban on English club playing in Europe precluded West Ham from playing the following season in the UEFA Cup.

After winning the Groningen tournament in Holland the Hammers looked forward to a good 1986-87 season. A Tony Gale free-kick which curled into the top corner proved to be the winner on the opening day against Coventry, and after McAvennie had scored twice in a 3-2 victory at Manchester United, hopes were high.

Within a fortnight, however, there were two home defeats, one of these being a 5-2 reverse to Liverpool. Fortunes changed when Cottee scored a hat-trick in the 3-2 win at Queen's Park Rangers and another three in the League Cup against Preston.

Indeed, Cottee's success earned him a call up to the England squad where he made his debut in Stockholm against Sweden.

There was an exciting game against Chelsea where the Blues were twice in the lead before two penalties from Stewart and another two goals from Cottee gave West Ham a 5-3 win. Narrow wins were recorded in the League Cup against Watford and Oxford.

In November, Paul Goddard left to join Newcastle, who paid a club record fee of £415,000. Goddard was a great favourite at Upton Park but could not get a regular place in the side. A few weeks later he played against the Hammers when Newcastle won their home game by 4-0. It was an eventful day for Goddard as he collided with George Parris and ended up in hospital.

Nineteen-year-old Paul Ince scored on his home debut against Southampton and gained good newspaper reports as being 'one for the future'. Christmas saw two London derby defeats by Wimbledon and Spurs before the FA Cup started with a visit to Orient. A penalty in the last minute earned Orient a 1-1 draw but the replay saw them beaten 4-1.

A major signing was made when John Lyall captured Stewart Robson from Arsenal in a £650,000 deal. Robson was a natural competitor

Ex-West Ham colleagues and now rival First Division managers, John Lyall and Norwich's Ken Brown.

with skill and authority in midfield. He made his debut at Coventry where Tony Cottee scored his third hat-trick of the season.

The League Cup quarter-final paired West Ham with Tottenham. After a 1-1 draw at home there was a sad defeat at Spurs with the Hammers losing 5-0 in the replay. Robson scored his first goal for the club in the 4-0 FA Cup win over Sheffield United. Another Sheffield team, the Wednesday, were the next Cup opponents and they ended Hammers hopes by winning 2-0 in London.

The team now needed a lift after the FA Cup defeat and this came when John Lyall signed two new players. There was excitement when Liam Brady came from Ascoli. Although past his best, Brady still had delicate control and touch. The other capture was 25-year-old Gary Strodder from Lincoln City. He would fill the centre-half spot now vacant due to the injuries of Martin and Hilton.

In early April there was a good 3-1 win against Arsenal. Robson and Brady were playing against their old club and it was Brady who drove the ball into the far corner for Hammers' third.

Injuries to Stewart, Devonshire and Orr forced John Lyall to buy again when he signed the Aberdeen full-back Tommy McQueen. Bad away defeats at Everton and Aston Villa, both by 4-0, followed before Cottee and McAvennie scored in the 2-1 home win over Spurs. After Manchester

City were beaten 2-0 on the final day they were relegated, leaving West Ham to finish 15th.

It had been a disappointing season with the side being beset by injuries throughout. During the summer Geoff Pike moved on to Notts County. Pike was a great club man who did not always get the praise he deserved.

An opening day shock was in store when the Hammers kicked-off in their home game at the start of the 1987-88 season. Trailing 3-0 to Queen's Park Rangers at half-time they never recovered and lost by that score. Tony Cottee began scoring and was twice on target in the defeat of Norwich and he netted further goals in the drawn games with Liverpool and Wimbledon. Neil Orr, who was struggling to gain a regular place, went back to Scotland and joined Hibernian.

There was disaster in the League Cup-tie against Barnsley. West Ham were leading 2-0 and then collapsed conceding five goals. The fans were unhappy and depressed further when Frank McAvennie returned home and signed for Celtic in a £750,000 deal.

Away wins over Oxford and Watford followed by an exciting 3-2 win over Nottingham Forest helped to dispel the gloom. At Christmas there were local derby defeats against both Wimbledon and Spurs and the New Year's Day meeting at Norwich ended in a 4-1 defeat. Despite the promise of Ince and Keen in midfield, and the determination of Bonds, the Hammers were finding it tough, especially Cottee who was now the lone striker.

Liam Brady and Cottee scored the goals in the 2-0 FA Cup win against Charlton. Queen's Park Rangers were beaten 1-0 in the League but a week later on the same ground they knocked West Ham out of the Cup winning 3-1.

It was a proud day for Billy Bonds on 9 February when he went to Buckingham Palace to receive the MBE from the Queen. He followed in the footsteps of Moore and Brooking who had also been honoured.

Despite a creditable draw at leaders Liverpool, the Hammers still struggled and by mid-March were 15th. To partner Cottee, Leroy Rosenior was bought from Fulham and he scored in his first three games. One of the best young full-backs in the game was acquired in April when Julian Dicks was purchased from Birmingham City for £300,000.

It was not known at the time but the 2-1 defeat at Southampton proved to be Billy Bonds' last appearance for the club.

If West Ham were to avoid the Play-offs they needed to beat Chelsea at Upton Park. Fortunately they played their best football of the season in winning 4-1. Two goals were scored by Rosenior, who was later sent off after a clash with Clarke.

The season came to its end when Geoff Pike, who was enjoying success at Notts County, returned for his testimonial match against Dynamo Zagreb. The Yugoslavs had too much class on the night and won 4-1.

During July, and after much transfer speculation, Tony Cottee joined Everton for a British record fee of £2.5 million. West Ham then spent some of the money on two international players. Allen McKnight, the Northern Ireland goalkeeper, was signed for £250,000 from Celtic, and David Kelly, the Republic of Ireland forward, joined from Walsall for a fee of £600,000.

Billy Bonds announced his retirement from playing and everyone was pleased to hear he would be staying on as Youth-team manager. Bonds was a legend at Upton Park and his enthusiasm for the game would be good for the youngsters.

After returning from their tour of Finland, the final pre-season game was for Alvin Martin's testimonial and goals from Gale and Hilton gave West Ham a 2-0 victory against Tottenham.

After avoiding relegation the previous term, the

West Ham were looking to a good start when the 1988-89 campaign got under way. It turned out to be a bad day as the Hammers crashed 4-0 at Southampton. David Kelly scored twice at Sunderland in a League Cup-tie and scored another in the second leg to see West Ham through on a 5-1 aggregate.

Nineteen-year-old Stuart Slater came into the side and his pace made a big impression, but the League results were disappointing. The team were saving their best form for the League Cup as Alvin Martin scored two in the 5-0 win over Derby County, but after a 3-3 thriller with Nottingham Forest, the Hammers crashed 4-1 at Luton. Goalkeeper Alan McKnight was finding it difficult in the First Division.

Another night of League Cup glory took place when Liverpool were beaten 4-1. It was a great performance with two superb goals by Paul Ince which brought him much acclaim. Ince scored again the following Saturday to dent Millwall's unbeaten home record. The 1-0 win made history as this was West Ham's 1,000th Football League win.

Arsenal were the visitors in the FA Cup and they came back to draw level after being 2-0 down. The replay at Highbury caused a shock when Rosenior scored the only goal to give Hammers a boost and their Cup form continued when West Ham reached the League Cup semi-final after overcoming Aston Villa by 2-1.

Swindon Town were next in the FA Cup and after a 0-0 draw at the County Ground, a lone Rosenior goal was enough to see West Ham through.

The League Cup semi-final against Luton was a huge disappointment. A below par team performance and two goalkeeping errors helped the Hatters on their way to a 3-0 victory.

Phil Parkes was immediately recalled to the side and he played well in the 1-0 FA Cup win at Charlton. Paul Ince, celebrating his call up to the England Under-21 squad, scored against Coventry and got the winner against Aston Villa. In the FA Cup there was a tough 0-0 home draw with Norwich City before Hammers bowed out losing 3-1 at Carrow Road in the replay.

The big news on the day was that Frank McAvennie had rejoined the club from Celtic, but there was depression when both Middlesbrough and Southampton won at Upton Park, although spirits lifted when Millwall were beaten 3-0.

After this there were five victories in six games including away wins at Newcastle, Sheffield

Wednesday and Nottingham Forest. To stay in the First Division, Hammers had to win their final game at Liverpool. The teams were level at half-time but Liverpool scored four in the second half to win 5-1.

West Ham's seven-year spell in the First Division had come to an end.

There was a big shock on 5 June when the club announced that they would not be renewing John Lyall's contract. Lyall had been a loyal servant to the club where he had spent 32 years, as both player and manager. On 6 July 1989, Lou Macari was named as the Hammers' new manager. Macari had enjoyed a distinguished playing career with both Celtic and Manchester United and had been successful as manager of Swindon Town.

New sponsors were appointed in July when BAC, the window company, took over from Avco Trust. During the summer Manchester United made it known they were interested in signing Paul Ince and there was a lot of media speculation. Unfortunately, to the anger of the supporters, Ince's photograph appeared in a national newspaper with him wearing a Manchester United shirt whilst still a West Ham player.

A point was gained at Stoke on the opening day of the 1989-90 season but there was bad news when, following a tackle by Kamara, Frank McAvennie broke his leg.

Against Plymouth West Ham paraded their new £660,000 signing Martin Allen, who had come from Queen's Park Rangers. He scored one of the goals on his debut in the 3-1 win. The Paul Ince saga finally came to an end in September when he joined Manchester United. Part of the fee went to finance the purchase of centre-half Colin Foster, who came from Nottingham Forest for £750,000.

Julian Dicks, now club captain, was proving a big inspiration and his blistering shooting power resulted in goals which knocked both Birmingham and Aston Villa out of the League Cup. Mark Ward scored twice at Sheffield United in a 2-0 win and young Eamonn Dolan took great delight when scoring a couple in the 5-0 demolition of Sunderland.

A great volleyed goal from Martin Allen was enough to beat a tough Wimbledon side in the League Cup, although there was a black mark when Julian Dicks was sent off. A few days later there was a remarkable game at Blackburn. The Rovers swept into a 5-1 lead but West Ham fought back to 5-4 and were unlucky not to

equalise as they attacked to the end. At the end of December there was an exchange deal when the unsettled Mark Ward moved to Manchester City whilst City players Ian Bishop and Trevor Morley joined West Ham.

A few days later Lou Macari was busy again when he signed Jimmy Quinn, the Northern Ireland international from Leicester. All three new players made their debut against Barnsley when Kevin Keen scored twice in the 4-2 win. It was a big blow when Fourth Division Torquay United won the FA Cup match at Plainmoor with a lone goal near the end of the game, but there was a better display in the League Cup. After two drawn games with Derby County, they were finally beaten 2-1 in the second replay at Upton Park.

The evening of 14 February 1990 will long be remembered by those 6,000 fans who travelled to Oldham for the first leg of the League Cup semi final. Although Oldham played well on their artificial pitch, the Hammers let down their fans by giving a miserable performance in losing 6-0. A few days later, the Czechoslovakian goalkeeper Ludek Miklosko was signed from Baník Ostrava. He went straight into the side at Swindon where Jimmy Quinn scored twice in the 2-2 draw.

In the Press there was a lot of speculation concerning illegal payments to Swindon players during Lou Macari's reign and due to the pressure this caused, Macari resigned as manager. The board acted quickly and immediately appointed Billy Bonds, the supporters' choice.

Some of West Ham's pride was restored when Oldham were beaten 3-0 in the second leg of the League Cup semi-final, and against Sheffield United, Stuart Slater was brilliant and set up goals for Jimmy Quinn, who scored a hat-trick in the 5-0 victory. David Kelly, though, could not gain a regular place and was transferred to Leicester City for £300,000.

West Ham under Bonds were now buzzing and after away wins at West Bromwich and Oxford, a 4-1 home victory over Bournemouth put them in seventh place. A Play-off place was missed, however, following away defeats at Oldham and Newcastle. The final home game saw a great team display when Wolves were beaten 4-0. Liam Brady was retiring and it was a marvellous moment when a minute from time he scored the fourth goal.

The Phil Parkes testimonial match against Ipswich was the opening game the following season. Old boys Brooking, Lampard and Pike were some of the names who played in the 1-1

Ian Bishop scores from a penalty at Boundary Park in March 1991. The Hammers were on their way back to the top flight.

draw. Parkes was now on the Ipswich staff, having joined up with former manager John Lyall.

The Hammers were hoping that this 1990-91 season would see them return to the First Division. An early season departure to West Bromwich Albion was Gary Strodder, who was always in the shadow of Gale and Martin. Victories over Watford, Leicester and Ipswich came in an eight-match unbeaten run. Stoke City were beaten 5-1 on aggregate in the League Cup but a late goal by Oxford knocked West Ham out of the competition at the Manor Ground.

Hull City were demolished 7-1 at home in October when Dicks and Quinn scored two each. Morley and Quinn were the regular strikers and McAvennie was proving to be a 'super sub' when he came on and scored vital goals at Bristol City and Swindon. Billy Bonds made his first signing when he paid Luton Town £600,000 for full-back Tim Breacker. The local derby against Millwall at The Den was drawn and, following victories over Brighton and Plymouth, West Ham were now in second spot behind Oldham. Julian Dicks was out injured with a knee injury and as cover Billy Bonds turned to the services of the Spurs and Republic of Ireland international, Chris Hughton.

In November, Bonds played in his second testimonial match and scored in the 4-3 win over Spurs. Bonds' incredible appearance record of 795 games will surely stand for all time.

The unbeaten League run came to an end in December when Barnsley won 1-0 at Oakwell and in the FA Cup, Trevor Morley was the man in form. He scored twice against Aldershot in the 6-1 win and two more in the 5-0 defeat of Luton. During February heavy snow disrupted the fixtures but West Ham managed to beat Millwall 3-1 and Third Division Crewe 1-0 in the FA Cup.

The Hammers struggled a bit during March with defeats by Oxford and Sheffield Wednesday. Everton came to Upton Park for the FA Cup sixth-round tie which was shown live on television. It was a great performance from the Hammers with Stuart Slater the man of the match. Despite a late goal from Everton, West Ham held on to win 2-1 with goals from Foster and Slater.

Stewart Robson, who had been plagued with injuries whilst at Upton Park, left on a free transfer to Coventry. To boost the final push for promotion Iain Dowie, the Northern Ireland striker, was signed from Luton for £480,000, and scored on his home debut in the 3-2 defeat of Barnsley.

The FA Cup semi-final with Nottingham

Tony Gale fouls Nottingham Forest's Gary Crosby in the 1991 FA Cup semi-final at Villa Park and seconds later is harshly sent off.

Forest took place at Villa Park and the occasion was spoilt by a controversial refereeing decision in the 26th minute. Tony Gale was chasing a loose ball when he tangled with Crosby. He expected a free-kick to be given against him but was stunned when shown the red card by referee Hackett. The television media and newspaper coverage later condemned the decision and it was a sad blow for Gale to be sent off for the only time in his career.

Parris and Slater hit the post and the ten men did well with the score 0-0 at half-time. In the second half, the absence of a player took its toll and Forest took control to score four times without reply. Although their side had lost 4-0, the tremendous West Ham supporters never stopped singing and they were a credit to the club.

There were victories against Ipswich and Swindon which guaranteed promotion, but it was the championship West Ham wanted. This they would win if Notts County were beaten, and provided that Oldham did not beat Sheffield Wednesday. It was Notts County who took a two-goal lead but this did not matter so much as news came that Oldham were also losing 2-0. West Ham pulled a goal back but finished up losing 2-1. It was understood that Oldham had drawn, which left thousands on the pitch celebrating the title. Then came the stunning news which shocked everyone to silence. It was now known that Oldham had scored from a penalty in injury time which gave them the championship.

Ludek Miklosko was named 'Hammer of the

Year' after a brilliant season. Ray Stewart had made a brief comeback after being out injured for a year and was given a free transfer where he joined St Johnstone. He had enjoyed a good career at Upton Park and his 84 goals as a full-back was remarkable.

There was plenty of transfer activity as the Hammers prepared for season 1991-92 back in the First Division. Jimmy Quinn went to Bournemouth and within a week of the new season, Ian Dowie was sold to Southampton for £500,000. The new acquisitions were Mitchell Thomas, a £500,000 signing from Spurs, and Mike Small, a striker from Brighton bought for £400,000. Full-back Kenny Brown was taken on loan from Plymouth and was later given a contract. Young Kenny was the son of Ken Brown, the former Hammers' favourite of the 1960s.

Although without a few players, the signs were not encouraging when in a pre-season tournament at Highbury, the Italians, Sampdoria, outclassed West Ham in their 6-1 win. The 3-1 home win against Aston Villa was the only win during August. During September, Mike Small was scoring regularly and netted twice in both games against Crystal Palace and Nottingham Forest, and Bradford City were beaten 5-1 on aggregate over two legs in the League Cup.

At the end of October there were three good wins within a week. London rivals, Arsenal, were beaten 1-0 at Highbury, Sheffield United were knocked out of the League Cup by a 2-0 margin at Bramall Lane and, to end the week, Spurs were

Steve Potts and Arsenal's Ian Wright in action at Highbury in November 1991. The Hammers won 1–0.

3-0 victory. On transfer deadline day, Clive Allen was transferred from Chelsea for £250,000 and scored on his debut against his old club, but Hammers lost 2-1.

Young Matthew Rush was brought into the side against Norwich City and his two headed goals helped West Ham on to a good 4-0 win. Their joy was short lived, however, as further home defeats by Southampton and Crystal Palace ended any hopes of staying up.

The Hammers, now relegated, saved their best displays of the season for their last two home games. Manchester United, on course for the title, were rocked by a Kenny Brown goal which gave Hammers a 1-0 victory to delight the supporters. On the final day of the season, Frank McAvennie, who had been given a free transfer, said goodbye to his fans by scoring a hat-trick in the 3-0 victory over Nottingham Forest.

West Ham, back from their Scottish tour, were looking forward to the new season in the hope that they could win promotion to the Premier League at the first attempt. During the summer, old favourite Harry Redknapp joined the club as assistant manager. Redknapp had done a good job as manager of Bournemouth and his knowledge of the lower Leagues would be invaluable when recruiting new players.

A new sponsorship deal was announced in August when local company Dagenham Motors were named as club sponsors. The big transfer news was the sale of Stuart Slater to Celtic for £1.5 million. Joining West Ham were winger Mark Robson, from Tottenham, midfielder Peter Butler, from Southend, and Matty Holmes who came from Bournemouth.

A lone Clive Allen goal at Barnsley in a 1-0 win got West Ham off to a good start to the 1992-93 season. There was disappointment to follow, though, with a home defeat by Charlton and a 2-0 defeat at Newcastle, where Julian Dicks was sent off.

September saw a big improvement with three good away wins at Peterborough (3-1) Bristol City (5-1) and Portsmouth (1-0). Both wingers, Keen and Robson, were playing well, creating chances for Allen and Morley.

This season the club were playing in the Anglo-Italian Cup and they qualified for the

beaten 2-1 at home. After the televised game against Liverpool which ended 0-0, the Hammers' League form slumped. A 4-0 away defeat at Everton was followed by further reverses at Aston Villa and Notts County.

In between these was a League Cup defeat at Norwich, where the Hammers were beaten by a disputed last-minute penalty. Non-League Farnborough were the opponents in the FA Cup. West Ham found them difficult to beat and the non-League side were good value for their 1-1 draw. The replay was also tight and it took a last-minute goal from Trevor Morley to deny gallant Farnborough.

There was sad news when it was known that Jack Helliar, the Hammers' historian aged 75, had passed away after a short illness. He had been a part of West Ham life for over 60 years and his firm had printed the club programme for most of his life.

Welsh club Wrexham were next in the FA Cup and they took all the glory when drawing 2-2 in London. They had already beaten Arsenal in the previous round and no doubt were expecting to win the reply at the Racecourse Ground. It was indeed another tough match, but Colin Foster came to West Ham's rescue when he headed home the winner in the second half.

February was a nightmare month for both players and supporters. On the pitch there were injuries, a loss of confidence and a depressing home FA Cup defeat by Sunderland. Off the pitch the supporters directed their anger and frustration at the board over the much-criticised Bond Scheme. The atmosphere generated against the Bond Scheme affected the players, and pitch demonstrations during defeats by Arsenal and Everton added to the depression.

Away to League leaders Leeds, the Hammers came away with a good draw but days later were sunk by a Gary Lineker hat-trick in Tottenham's

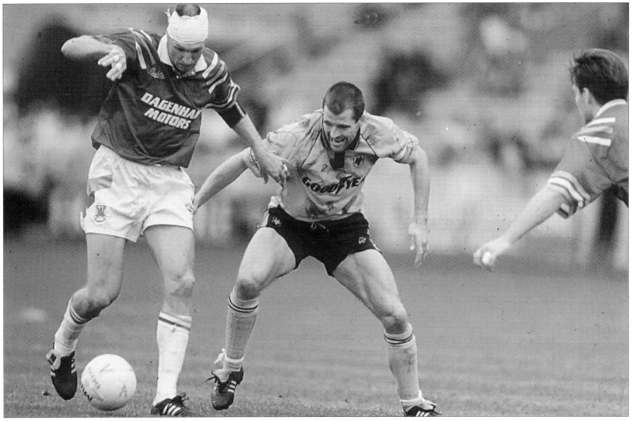

Alvin Martin takes the ball of Wolves' Steve Bull at Molineux in October 1992.

international stage after winning their group which included Bristol Rovers and Southend United.

Third Division Crewe caused a shock in the League Cup by winning their home tie 2-0 after the teams had drawn 0-0 at Upton Park. The Hammers bounced back from this reverse, however, with an excellent 6-0 home win against Sunderland, followed by a 4-0 win at Bristol Rovers. November was a busy month, the Anglo-Italian Cup-tie in Cremonese was lost 2-0 but Hammers gained their first points in this stage of the competition after beating Reggiana.

Martin Allen and Julian Dicks missed the local derby at Millwall and, despite a super goal from Mark Robson, the Hammers lost 2-1. West Ham and Oxford served up a 5-3 thriller at Upton Park where top man was Julian Dicks, who scored two great goals. Joining the club at this time was young striker Steve Jones, who was a prolific goalscorer with Billericay Town.

There was a setback at Tranmere where Hammers were drawing 2-2, but they conceded late goals to lose 5-2. Steve Jones made his debut in the 1-0 victory at Cosenza in the Anglo-Italian Cup, but the Hammers were eliminated from the competition after drawing 0-0 at home to Pisa.

Clive Allen and Mark Robson were the two scorers in the 2-0 FA Cup win at West Bromwich, but Hammers' Cup hopes were shattered in a poor display at Barnsley with the home side winning 4-1.

At Derby County there was a very good 2-0 win with the Hammers playing with ten men for most of the match. All the newspaper headlines were centred on Julian Dicks, who had been sent off for the third time that season. Dicks was an excellent player but his disciplinary problems would often let him down. While Clive Allen was out injured with calf trouble, Steve Jones did well, scoring in successive games against Barnsley and Peterborough.

The whole nation was stunned on 24 February when it was announced that Bobby Moore had died, aged 51. The former West Ham and England captain passed away after a courageous two year fight against cancer. There has never been a player more respected and dearly loved throughout the football world. In the week leading up to the game against Wolves, hundreds of floral tributes, messages and assorted memorabilia was laid at the club's main gates and forecourt.

On the Saturday there were nearly 25,000 inside the ground to pay their last respects. Before the kick-off, Geoff Hurst and Martin Peters,

Trevor Morley scores West Ham's second goal at Derby in January 1993.

accompanied by Ron Greenwood, carried to the centre-spot a giant number six shirt composed of claret and blue flowers. The teams came out, heads bowed, for a meticulously observed minute's silence. As a tribute to Moore, the West Ham team lined up numbered 1 to 12, missing on the day was the number-six shirt.

The game itself was not a spectacle but it was fitting that West Ham won 3-1. Unlike the bubbles in West Ham's song, the memory of Bobby Moore will never fade and die.

Julian Dicks was proving an inspirational captain as he scored twice against Grimsby and got two more in the 2-0 win against Tranmere. Long-serving defender George Parris joined Birmingham City and West Ham, aware of Clive Allen's injury problems, signed the experienced David Speedie on loan from Southampton.

The away form was causing concern but at home it was a different story. Speedie scored twice in a 3-0 victory against Leicester, and Brentford were well beaten 4-0. To gain automatic promotion the final two games needed to be won. At Swindon, there was a great performance where both substitutes, Kenny Brown and Clive Allen, scored in the 3-1 win. The biggest home crowd of the season turned up for the game against Cambridge United. The

tension was unbearable as news came through of other promotion rivals. A few minutes into the second half, David Speedie volleyed home to ease the tension. Two minutes from the end, Julian Dicks came through on the left and his pass gave Clive Allen a simple tap-in. The goal sparked a pitch invasion but order was quickly restored. The final whistle went which was the signal for thousands to swarm on the pitch to begin their celebrations. West Ham were now proud members of the Premier League.

The pre-season transfer activity started when Kevin Keen was sold to Wolves. In his place came Dale Gordon, a winger from Glasgow Rangers. In his Norwich days, Gordon was always a thorn in West Ham's side. Other new signings were the Bournemouth pair Paul Mitchell and Keith Rowland. Simon Webster had also been bought from Charlton and it was a huge blow when he broke his leg in training. The South Stand had been demolished during the summer and work was now under way for the building of the Bobby Moore Stand which was due to be completed by January.

After two poor home defeats by Wimbledon and Queen's Park Rangers, West Ham were already being tipped as relegation candidates. Two goals from Clive Allen came in the 2-0 win

David Speedie receives his teammates congratulations after putting West Ham ahead against Cambridge. Clive Allen later put the Hammers further in front and promotion to the new Premier Division had been achieved with just two minutes of the game remaining.

Champagne-time as West Ham are promoted

Ludek Miklosko saves from Leeds United's Brian Deane at the start of the 1993-94 season.

over Sheffield Wednesday and Dale Gordon scored his first goal for the club in the 1-1 draw at Coventry. After a 0-0 home draw with Swindon, drastic measures were called for and on 17 September there was some busy transfer dealing. The fans favourite, Julian Dicks, went to Liverpool in exchange for David Burrows and Mike Marsh.

Billy Bonds, who was celebrating his 47th birthday, also purchased the experienced Lee Chapman from Portsmouth. All three played the following day at Blackburn, where Chapman scored in a good 2-0 win.

Chesterfield were no match for the new-look Hammers and they were beaten 7-1 on aggregate in the League Cup. The next round at Nottingham Forest was tougher and, despite the return of Alvin Martin, the Hammers bowed out losing 2-1.

A sparkling 3-1 win against Manchester City was seen live on television and brought praise to the team. Arsenal were outplayed at Upton Park and just when it seemed Morley would break the deadlock and score, he was brought down by Seaman, who was promptly sent off. Successive away wins at Southampton and Wimbledon lifted the Hammers to tenth spot. The next away game, however, was a disaster. A brilliant display by

Waddle prompted his teammates to turn on a super show in beating West Ham 5-0. Mike Marsh scored his first goal for the club when Hammers overcome Watford in the FA Cup, and it was Lee Chapman who headed a late winner in the next round against Notts County.

For the fifth-round tie, West Ham faced a tricky tie away to Conference club Kidderminster Harriers. The non-League side played very well to contain West Ham and again Chapman came to the rescue with a header to clinch a 1-0 victory.

The impressive Bobby Moore Stand was full for the visit of League leaders Manchester United. The atmosphere was electric throughout and when West Ham took a 2-1 lead in the second half, it seemed United's unbeaten run had come to an end. Alas it was not to be, as former Hammer Ince equalised in the last minute. Ince had been booed all through the match as the supporters had not forgiven him for the circumstances of his departure from Upton Park.

In March there was a good attendance of 20,311 for the Bobby Moore memorial match. The new stand was officially opened by members of the 1964 FA Cup winning side and in an interesting match, West Ham beat an FA Premier League XI 2-1.

Billy Bonds, West Ham manager, shouts instructions to his team. On the eve of the 1994-95 season Bonds was to shock Hammers fans by announcing his resignation.

Billy Bonds congratulates Mike Marsh after his debut against Blackburn Rovers in September 1993.

Keith Curle, Michel Vonk, Lee Chapman and Clive Allen in action in the match at Maine Road in February 1994.

After the Cup defeat, the Hammers' confidence was low and there were depressing defeats at Chelsea and Sheffield United. On transfer deadline day, West Ham released Colin Foster to Watford, Clive Allen to Millwall, and Mitchell Thomas to Luton.

Billy Bonds recalled Matthew Rush to the team for the Easter game with Ipswich and the youngster responded with a great goal which helped West Ham on to a 2-1 victory. More joy came at Tottenham when, to the huge delight of the travelling fans, Spurs were well beaten 4-1.

The sixth-round FA Cup-tie brought Luton to Upton Park and a nervous display from West Ham saw the tie finish goalless. In the replay, a hat-trick by Oakes gave Luton a semi-final place.

Steve Jones and Ian Bishop celebrate against Tottenham Hotspur in April 1994.

games when he scored at Highbury in a splendid 2-0 win against Arsenal.

The final home game of the season, against Southampton, saw a farewell to the terraces as Upton Park prepared to be an all-seater stadium. In an exciting 3-3 draw, West Ham equalised with a last-minute goal which sparked a pitch invasion and ended the game. It was Tony Gale's 300th League appearance and on the following day he played in his testimonial game when West Ham beat the Republic of Ireland International team 4-2.

But another long-serving Hammers stalwart was soon to part company with the club. On 10 August, only a few days before the start of the new season, Billy Bonds stunned supporters by announcing his resignation. It seemed that Bonds had simply tired of the daily grind of professional football and Harry Redknapp took over.

It was a shock but as West Ham move into 1995 in their impressive all-seater stadium, those early Thames Ironworks players who started it all 100 years ago would have been proud of the progress their club has made.

Liverpool scored a last-minute winner at Upton Park, but the day belonged to Julian Dicks, who was given a tremendous reception on his return. Martin Allen scored his fourth goal in as many